WITHDRAWN

THE REVOLUTION THAT BIT ITS OWN TAIL

The revolution that bit its own tail

How economic history changed our ideas on economic growth

J.W. Drukker

aksant

Amsterdam
2006

Translated from the Dutch by the Caribbean Development Institute (director: Dr. Gregory Rusland) at Paramaribo (Surinam).

This publication has been made possible with the financial support of the Unger-Van Brerofonds.

ISBN 90 5260 198 4

Lay-out and cover design: Bert Heesen Produkties, Utrecht

Aksant Academic Publishers, Cruquiusweg 31, 1019 AT Amsterdam, The Netherlands, www.aksant.nl

Contents

Foreword

When I decided to write an introduction into modern economic history for readers with no knowledge whatsoever of mathematical economics and econometrics (two specialized fields whose language have deeply influenced economic historical writing during the last fifty years), three things were clear from the outset: The book would have a theoretical and thematic angle, because it was first of all intended to deepen the knowledge of economic history that students of history were offered during their foundation course. Such knowledge is usually ordered in a chronological manner, which indeed is at the expense of theoretical depth. Secondly, the book had to deal with recent historiography and the current state of affairs in the field. And finally, it had to be as short as possible, in order to be of good use for pre-graduate students in history and economics, as economic history is generally competing with other subjects in these curricula. Whether I have met the first two conditions is left to the discretion of the reader. The third condition I have in any case violated and merits an explanation.

The fact is, that halfway through the book, it began 'to write itself'. Initially I planned a text which — later on — finished up in the first four or five chapters: The gradual victory of the new economic history over traditional economic history. While writing chapter 4, it dawned on me that the book would already be dated on its first publication, if I was to leave it at that. By the end of the seventies of the past century (following the flush of victory of the new economic history) the first outlines in economic history of a development that indicated the constraints of the new economic history had become visible and in the nineties this development joined in with two movements that deviated from the mainstream in pure economics: Evolutionary economics and the so-called new institutional economics. I am convinced that this development shall have a far-reaching impact on the field these next few years, for which reason I ultimately added the second half of chapter 5 and the chapters 6 and 7, despite the fact that this made the book twice as big as originally intended.

In working on this book, the advice and substantial help of a large number of friendly colleagues has been indispensable: In the first place my friends Henk-Jan Brinkman and Brigitte Slot, whose suggestions contributed to the final contents; my colleagues from the Department of Economic and Social History in Groningen, who made essential comments on an earlier version of the text, and my colleagues from Delft, Timo de Rijk, Yeo Jin Jo, Marco Jansen and Corrie van der Lely, who provided indispensable moral and logistical support. I am especially grateful for the (sometimes exceptionally exhaustive) answers I was privileged to receive over the course of time to questions I had raised to Frank Ankersmit (Groningen), Bart van Ark (Groningen), Jörg Baten (Tübingen), Sebastian Coll-Martin (Cantabria), Stanley Engerman (Rochester), John Komlos (München), Angus Maddison (Groningen), Joel Mokyr (Chicago), Peer Vries (Leiden), and Jan Luiten van Zanden (Utrecht, Amsterdam). In conclusion, I owe many thanks to Aksant Academic Publishers which, in the person of Marti Huetink, made a quick and flawless publication of this book possible when the ink of the English manuscript had barely dried.

Originally this book was written with Dutch students in mind. Consequently, some (but not all) of the examples I offer to illustrate some theoretical issues have been taken from Dutch economic history. However, all these illustrations are of such a general nature, that almost every modern western economy could have served the same purpose. For this reason, some international reviewers suggested that the book would also be of interest for non-Dutch readers, despite the apparently national character of some of its examples. Of course, its author (and, I'm lucky to add: Also its publisher) heartily agreed.

In recent historiography of economic history, the term "path dependence" is central: The idea that an economic development process is also determined by its own history. While writing, I have only too often been aware of the fact of how much my own thinking is "path dependent", in the sense that it is deeply influenced by my own teachers. In college, I was lucky enough to have two teachers (Joop de Kimpe and Sjoerd de Vries) for precisely the two subjects that would later be so decisive for my own studies - mathematics and history. They really knew how to teach their classes in such an inspiring manner, that after pre-university school I had a rather exceptional ideal for an adolescent: To become a teacher myself. I now realize that at university Han Baudet, Angus Maddison and Simon Kuipers had an immeasurable impact on me. This book would have been dedicated to them, were it not for two other people who had formed (*nolens volens*) a more intimate bond with the inception of this book than they: My wife Joke and my son Lars. This book is dedicated to the two of them.

Stuifzand, Januari 2006.

Introduction

In 1905, the German sociologist, economist and historian Max Weber published *Die protestantische Ethik und der Geist des Kapitalismus*. In spite of the fact that, compared to the size of his other studies, it involved a modest monograph and moreover — but that was not unusual for German scholarly works of that era — the notes and glosses by far exceeded the size of the body text, this has become the book par excellence Weber is still associated with: The central thesis he defends in *Die protestantische Ethik* to the present day is known in economic and social history as 'Weber's thesis'. For no small part this may be attributed to the fact that this central thesis at first glance strikes even the most unprejudiced of readers as rather eccentric. Weber's thesis argues brief and to the point that the dominant economic organizational system in the modern Western world, capitalism, is rooted in Protestantism in its most puritan varieties.

The reason for Weber's idea that there apparently existed a relation between Calvinism and capitalism, was his conclusion that wherever in the Western world for the first time a social organization had come into existence which was showing clear capitalist features, religious life was dominated by some version of strict Calvinism. This had been the case in the Dutch Republic in the first half of the seventeenth century; the country that in economic history is generally regarded the first modern capitalist society in the Western world and that, moreover, precisely in that period, as to its standard of living left all other countries of the world far behind. It had become again noticeable in those regions of England where, more than a century later, the first signs began to show of what later was to be called the Industrial Revolution. And the same phenomenon had, later still, also occurred in the United States: The American industrialization is rooted in the textile industries of Massachusetts and it was there of all places that social life in that era was dominated by the Puritans.

Weber's explanation for the correlation between Calvinism and capitalism is founded on the doctrine of predestination, which was exactly the breaking point between doctrinal and liberal variants of Protestantism.

The predestination theory poses that in God's plan of creation every-thing, but every single thing, from the beginning until the end, to say so, has been fixed in advance, and that for that reason humans cannot change anything whatsoever. The central implication of this is that it is inher-ent in God's plan of creation who is chosen by Him and who rejected. The inevitable consequence is that the believer is his whole life through, tormented by a dreadful doubt: Chosen or rejected? Weber's reasoning is that the unshakable dogma of the predestination theory (rejecting it equals, according to the view of the strict Calvinist, doubting God's om-niscience) produces an intolerable religious situation — for: Continuously tormented by an existential death fear — which in practice demands one solution or other. That solution is found within strict Calvinism by that which is magisterially described by Weber as *innerweltliche Askese*. The idea behind this, is that an ascetic way of life, after the example of Jesus, which within the Roman Catholic church was traditionally practiced by the monks (and which there, within the walls of the monastery, hence re-mains *ausserweltlich*), was elevated in Calvinism to the compulsory code of conduct for *all* believers and thus is made *innerwelthlich*.

In the practice of everyday life, the *innerwelthliche Askese* would have resulted in as great a labour effort as possible in one's profession (in We-ber's terms: *Rastlose Berufsarbeit*), combined with a minimization of con-sumption (*asketischer Sparzwang*) and accompanied by a systematic and rational self-analysis of such conduct and its results.

Calvinist religious practice taught that (apart from the unshakeability of faith as most important condition) success in the performance of one's profession could be interpreted as a 'possible' sign of election, which to a certain degree mitigated the intolerable implications of the predestina-tion theory in everyday life.

This combination of rules of conduct, linked to the thus religiously le-gitimized pursuit of profit would, in Weber's view, from a social point of view, inevitably lead to strict rationality as crucial guideline for ac-tion and to maximal creation of capital. In that manner, strict Calvinism would have formed an optimal breeding ground for the development of a 'capitalist mentality'.

In the sixties of the previous century, Weber's thesis faded into the back-ground. Sure, it was still mentioned briefly in prevailing university intro-ductions to sociology and economics, but chiefly as an intellectual curios-ity from the history of dogmas of the discipline concerned: There were, by then, but a few sociologists and economists who really believed Weber's thesis. This was in part the result of the fact that numerous critics, following Weber's original publication from 1905, had pointed out that Weber's supposed connection between Calvinist ethics and capitalist mentality had been much less unequivocal than Weber had argued.

Perhaps even more important was the point that the fundamental idea on which Weber's thesis was founded was rapidly losing its popularity, namely, that social mentality, prevailing standards and values in a society, in short, the whole culture, would form decisive factors as to whether or not an economic modernization process would set in. The 1960s were the era par excellence in which the idea of a 'makable society' was conceived: Every nation, irrespective of its specific cultural traits, could in principle attain a high level of prosperity, provided that a sensible economic policy which was aimed at attaining that objective as soon as possible, would be followed consistently. Within economics something developed which followed naturally from that type of ideas and which I, with a disrespectful reference to the famous book of Dijksterhuis, would entitle "the mechanization of the world view of economists".

The key to a high level of prosperity, so it was generally thought, was to be found in steady economic growth over a long period. By carrying out comparative quantitative-empirical research into the successful economic development of rich countries in the Western world, it should be possible to discover the main reasons for such economic success in the long term. By subsequently applying this 'success formula' to countries which until that moment had not succeeded in launching a steady process of economic development, in the long run, in principle all countries in the world would reach prosperity. Such an optimistic world view held no room for the idea that some countries did indeed and others did not attain economic development precisely because of their specific, cultural nature. Modern economic growth, every right-mined economist reasoned in those days, was especially the result of technological progress that was embodied by capital intensification. That was, to everyone who wanted to see, noticeable in the steadily growing quantity of ever-more advanced capital goods which accompanied production in the Western countries. That was everywhere and always the crucial source of the incredible increase in productivity of Western countries and whether the worker who operated all those machines was Roman Catholic, or Hindu, Islamic or a nonbeliever made no difference for his productivity.

Under the influence of that mechanistic view on economic growth, and exactly in the same period, a methodological revolution took place in economic history which in less than ten years changed the discipline beyond all recognition. The literary descriptive method which had characterized economic history ever since it came into existence, was now replaced by a rigorous quantitative analytic approach, with the result that a large number of previously generally accepted ideas within the field of economic history became unsettled. This so-called cliometric revolution was given relatively little attention beyond the circle of professional economic historians, despite the fact that it had drastic consequences for our ideas about economic development. The main reason for this, was the very nature of the revolution itself: Suddenly, articles on economic history in specialist journals had become barely accessible to the interested layman because they were written in a language that was derived directly from highly specialized disciplines such as neoclassical economic theory and econometrics.

The overwhelming success of cliometrics or new economic history, as this revolution became known, led to yet another change in the 1990s: Gradually the awareness grew that although new economic history *could* explain the historically unprecedented successful economic development process in the Western world, it could not answer the question why a similar development never did emerge elsewhere or why, when it did emerge, it would, after a promising start, become suffocated by stagnation and dissolution. The new economic history had to acknowledge that for a satisfactory explanation of that last issue, a decisive role was reserved for institutional and cultural factors, and these were pre-eminently the matters which had played a prominent role in traditional economic history and had been systematically disregarded by cliometrics.

With this the cliometric revolution as it were bit its own tail. Traditional economic history, which it had at one time rejected as 'unscientific', appeared to be of vital importance for that which cliometrics itself regarded its central problem definition, that is: The explanation for the phenomenon of modern economic growth. The ensuing conciliation between economic history, evolutionary economics and neo-institutionalism implies that economic history in the year 2005 is once again on the threshold of a radical process of change. This most certainly does not mean that the method of quantitative analysis within the discipline shall be considered superseded: The approach has been invaluable to our knowledge of economic development processes and will undoubtedly continue to be so in the coming years. It probably does mean an expansion of the theoretical perspective whereby a greater space will have to be devoted to non-economic (technological, but especially also social and cultural) factors.

From this, it can be inferred that it is to be expected that the barriers which over the course of time have been erected between economic history, social history, history of technique and cultural history, and to which cliometrics has undoubtedly contributed some of the necessary building blocks, will for the most part be broken down in the future.

To my opinion, this can mean nothing else than that the body of ideas of the Historical School, of which Max Weber was a prominent exponent, is ready for rehabilitation. In all probability this would not mean that all of a sudden the numerous critical opinions on the relation between Calvinism and capitalism will end up in the wastepaper basket and that everyone will again embrace the original Weber's thesis as the supreme truth about economic modernization. It probably does mean, however, that in the future more space will be devoted to the fundamental idea of the Historical School that the specific, own history of every society to a not unimportant extent is contributory to the future economic development of that very same society.

It is true that this will put the optimistic ideas from the 1960s about the 'makability' of society largely into perspective. Without doubt the economic future from a global point of view was brighter then, than it is now, but then again, the unrealistic expectations from those years have given way to a greater degree of realism.

17

1 The cliometric revolution

1.1 The 'American Revolution' in economic history

This book is about the revolutionary change in the field of economic history in — roughly — the second half of the twentieth century. The term 'roughly' in the previous sentence is there with a reason: Political revolutions — albeit with some difficulty at times — can be assigned a date: 1776, 1789, 1917. With revolutions in science this is a lot more difficult and there is an incontestable reason for this: Scientific revolutions occur at a much slower pace.[1] Only after *Die Grundlagen der allgemeinen Relativitätstheorie* was published in 1916, the full extent of the significance of the three articles Einstein had published in the *Annalen der Physik* already in 1905 — subsequently[2] — became clear. If in exact sciences, such as physics, and in the 'more or less' exact disciplines, such as economics, one can still in all decency speak about revolutionary changes (the theory of relativity in physics and the 'Keynesian revolution' in economics, for instance), the 'softer' a field of science is, so it seems, the more gradual the character of its changes.

In the literary-oriented sciences changes usually occur so gradually that the word 'revolution' seems to be totally out of context. A typical example is history. Indeed, anyone opening any nineteenth century manual about history and comparing it to a recent reprint of *A History of the Modern World* by Palmer and Colton (2002), will notice huge differences, but — different than with physics or economics — it often is difficult to find out how and why those changes have occurred over the course of time.

Here as well, there are exceptions which prove the rule. The character of economic history has changed so much these past fifty years that it is not an exaggeration to speak of a revolution. The causes be clearly discerned. Without exaggeration, we can speak of the 'American

Revolution'. Since the mid-fifties of the twentieth century, a group of young Americans advocated a drastically different approach to economic history. That they were aware of the fact that they wanted to effect a clean break with the manner in which their field of study was practiced until that moment, is clear from the fact that they expressly distanced themselves from their predecessors by giving their movement a different name.

A different name? That is putting it euphemistically: With the self-assuredness — some might prefer 'conceit' — that characterizes the true revolutionary spirit, they proclaimed the new theory under a shockingly great number of different names. The simple *new economic history* was one of the first flags under which the modernists went to war, but already soon, confusingly, many different banners made their appearance on the scene of battle: *Quantitative analytic history, econometric history, retrospective econometrics, cliometrics* (an exotic fusion of the name 'Clio', the Muse of history, and the field of econometrics), and even *scientific history*.[3] Especially the last name did not fail from raising the opponents — and there was no shortage of those, especially in the initial phase of the battle - to a state of purple indignation, because it impertinently assumed that *all* approaches in economic history, of course with the exception of those which the militant *new economic historians* themselves professed, had one thing in common, namely: Being unscientific.

Whatever the other merits of the new approach of economic history might have been, one thing is very clear: The economic history discipline has undergone a complete change under the influence of the new economic history.

If the debate before that time was characterized by detachment (not to say lethargy), as soon as the youthful rebels showed themselves at one of the many American congresses and seminars, the adrenaline content in the blood of the participants increased by leaps, so much so even, that at various occasions the congress president had to prevent the learned debaters from literally assailing one another, whereby the tendency to underscore the reprehensibility of the opponent's arguments with a firm box about the ears seemed strong among the followers of the old, traditional approach rather than among the revolutionary modernists.[4]

Such a situation was quite new in this respectable field of study and hence the question arises what the new economic historians had asserted for that matter to trigger such strong reactions in their older colleagues.

1.2 What was new about the NEH?

The answer to that question becomes clear by comparing any page from a famous traditional economic history handbook on the economic history of the United States to the same page from a comparable work written according to the canon of the new economic history (see illustrations 1.1 and 1.2).

The first illustration from *Industrial History of the United States* (Bolles, 1881) will be recognized by one and all as a 'normal' page from a 'normal' — albeit meanwhile apparently dated — handbook on economic history. The text deals with the manner in which around 1800 the quality of the American livestock was upgraded by bringing some specimens of improved breeds from Europe to America and the writer illustrates this by adding to his text a fine picture of the animals concerned.[5]

Figure 1.2 seems, with its utterly inhospitably looking mathematical formula and curves, a treatise from the field of mathematical economics rather than a page from an introduction on American economic history. Nevertheless, this is a page from *The Reinterpretation of American Economic History* (Fogel & Engerman (Eds.), 1971), one of the first economic history handbooks written strictly by the canon of new economic history and edited by two youthful revolutionaries of the first hour, Robert William Fogel and Stanley Engerman.

21

Indeed, while economic historians in former days availed themselves of the narrative method which was also used elsewhere in history and whereby they distinguished themselves, besides choice of subject, at the most by using often somewhat more statistical data in support of their arguments,[6] a number of young American economic historians had radically renounced that method. Virtually without exception, in the years following the Second World War, they were trained as economists and so armed with quite an arsenal of economic concepts and theories which were formulated precisely at that time in increasingly mathematical terms. Moreover, without exception they were also thoroughly schooled in the principles of the then still young econo-

Fig. 1.1 Page 152 from *Industrial History of the United States* (1881)

Fig. 1.2 Page 152 from *The Reinterpretation of American Economic History* (1971)

metrics; the science that endeavors to test economic theories cast in mathematical moulds against statistical data to prove their empirical value. Econometrics had been developed with, at the back of one's mind, the idea that it could prove to be a very powerful instrument to assess the effects of various economic and political government measures by which devastating economic crises, such as that of the 1930s, could at best be prevented and at least somewhat curbed. There was not a living soul who had ever thought that econometric methods and techniques would also be useful for the study of economic developments in the remote past. The young new economic historians came to the surprising discovery (surprising, because study in that direction had started more or less as a joke) that the ultramodern analytical instruments of mathematical economics and statistical testing of econometrics could be successfully applied to economic history issues. The equally ultramodern computer — then still cumbersome and pricey gigantic machines that needed to be operated in a tiresome labor-intensive manner with punch cards — appeared to offer unparalleled possibilities in analyzing large volumes of quantitative data.

The amazing result was that a great number of facts and explanations which were for many years regarded by traditional economic history as more or less unquestionable, suddenly took on a totally different aspect or, even worse, became completely unsettled. In itself this would already be enough to ferment serious trouble in the traditional economic history camp.
In addition, mathematical economics and econometric jargon used by new economic historians was frequently not understood at all by their traditional colleagues who often had studied history and not economics. And if the mostly older, traditional economic historians did indeed have an economic training — because there were those too — even then they usually were not acquainted with recent developments in mathematical economics and econometrics; simply because those subject matters had been introduced only recently into the curricula of American faculties of economics.

Imagine: A somewhat older, respectable and highly erudite professor of economic history with an excellent reputation, is suddenly confronted at an economic history congress with a brat in his late twenties who has only just graduated. This young man has submitted a 'paper', written in unintelligible 'thieves' slang', interspersed with weird formulas and completed with lengthy statistical appendices, in which he states without batting an eyelid in the conclusion — the only intelligible part — that the professor concerned, however erudite and respectable he may be, has been absolutely mistaken in the highly specialized field in which he had been a great name for years and years. Such was the situation with which traditional economic historians were confronted time and again in the America of the sixties. No wonder that feelings were running high.

1.3 The NEH enthusiastically received by economists

The result naturally was that the new economic history initially had very little success with its attack on the traditional economic history bulwark. The fact that internally authoritative scientific journals of economic history, such as the *Journal of Economic History* and the *Economic History Review* in the early years of new economic history systematically refused articles written according to the new canon[7], speaks volumes as far as that is concerned. And since the young revolutionaries — not without self-confidence verging on arrogance — hardly even bothered to 'translate' the new approach into terms which would be comprehensible to readers not trained in mathematics and econometrics, it would not have been unthinkable for the new economic history to have died a gentle death soon after a tumultuous start.[8]

It worked out differently. In spite of serious conflicts with the academic economic history establishment, the new economic historians managed to gain ground, initially only in the United States, later on — as from the mid-seventies approximately — elsewhere as well. It is significant that two new economic historians from the very beginning, Robert William Fogel and Douglass Cecil North, in 1993 saw their work rewarded with a Nobel Prize in economics.
This is also the key to the ultimate victory of new economic history: While the history-oriented, traditional economic history had turned away from the new approach in disgust, the new economic history from the very start was received enthusiastically in faculties of economics.
Economic history — originally arisen in the second half of the nineteenth century as an alternative to neoclassical economics — in the course of the twentieth century had gradually become estranged from

mainstream economics, precisely because of the formalization of economic theory in a mathematical sense.[9]

These diverging opinions came to an end with the new economic history. Economic history issues could successfully be analyzed with the help of mathematical economic models, and explanations for economic development processes from the past could be tested excellently with the help of econometric testing methods. Moreover, when it became clear that the results often produced conclusions that were of importance to pure economics and economic policy, new economic history ensured a revaluation of economic history in the eyes of economists. It was not without a reason that Robert William Fogel in 1965 published a general article on the first results of the new economic history under the title of 'The Reunification of Economic History with Economic Theory'. And it was no coincidence either, that this essay did not appear in an economic history journal, but in one of the leading journals in the field of pure economics, the *American Economic Review* (Fogel, 1965).

That the new economic history from the very beginning was enthusiastically received in economic faculties has a simple explanation. First of all, the 'language problem' did not play a significant role. Other than in historical institutions established within the faculties of arts, economists had no trouble understanding the terms, theoretical concepts and testing methods used by the new economic historians.

Second, they could contribute significantly to an issue that played a central role in the sixties in academic economic research: The issue of economic growth. In the wake of the economic crisis of the thirties, research in the forties and fifties was especially aimed at explaining the cyclical fluctuations, that is: An analysis of short-term fluctuations in the economic process. After the Second World War, pure economics again displayed a greater interest in the analysis of long-term problems, in particular the explanation of the phenomenon of economic growth.

The problem of the rebuilding of Europe and the fact that at that time, the economic development of a great number of former European colonies that had only recently become politically independent was high on the international political agenda, were at the basis of this.[10]

1.4 NEH in the faculties of arts: Originally a divisive element

The swift acceptance of the new economic history within faculties of economics resulted in the quick closing of the gap between pure economics and economic history after 1960. The rejection of the new method within the faculties of arts, however, had as a consequence that a new divisive element announced itself, this time within economic history itself. In education and research between the faculties of arts on the one hand, and the faculties of economics on the other, the same thing threatened to happen as that which had earlier occurred between pure economics and economic history! The widening divergence between the traditional economic history and the new economic history could be observed all around until the second half of the seventies. The last quarter of the twentieth century was characterized by a rapprochement and the initiative for such rapprochement, surprisingly enough, came from the side of the former revolutionaries, the new economic historians.

1.5 After 1975: Attempts at reconciliation, at the initiative of the NEH

The reason for the rapprochement was that a quarter of a century of econometric and historical research for the explanation of economic growth, suggested that the institutional structure — the social and cultural environment created by man in the course of time in which the economic process is taking place — was essential to the manifestation of economic growth, stagnation or decline. And it was exactly the description of that institutional structure which had been the object of exhaustive studies in traditional economic history and which the new economic history, leaning heavily on the paradigm of neoclassical economic theory, had completely scratched out of its vocabulary.

Yet, however desirable that synthesis, there was still the "language barrier" between the two schools. The new economic historians were still speaking and writing a lingo that was not understood by the great majority of economic historians who were trained in history. There was a danger that the for scientific reasons so urgently desired synthesis, for practical reasons threatened to get an utterly half-hearted character: The new economic history was making fierce attempts to integrate the results of traditional economic history into its explanation of the phenomenon of economic growth, but at the same time traditional economic historians because of their "language deficiency" remained deprived of the results of the new economic history, or at least, the manner in which those results had been attained.

To solve this problem, in the English-speaking regions, just in the period in which the new economic history was seeking to approach traditional economic history, a number of cliometrists was trying to "translate" the results of their approach and the discussions that preceded the results into understandable language[11] for readers who had no economic background. This book should be placed in that same framework.[12]

1.6 Two questions: Economic history and economic growth

Two — closely correlated — questions are central. The first question is of a methodological and historiographic nature and runs: What have been the most important changes in the discipline of economic history during the latter half of the last century? The second question is: Why does economic growth occur, and — by implication — what are the causes of economic stagnation and decline?

The second question has in fact always been a central issue of economic history, even when new economic history did not yet exist: At the time when economic history came up as an independent scientific discipline (the second half of the nineteenth century) the then Western world (say, the United States and North-Western Europe) distinguished itself by a historically unique and unprecedented social phenomenon. Never before in the history of humankind did material circumstances in which the majority of the people were living — very gradually but still — structurally change without such change being undone within a shorter or longer period.

1.7 Economic growth into the background in the 1930s and 1940s

Was it in the nineteenth century especially the historically astounding phenomenon of economic growth itself that had placed the response to the question as to the why high on the agenda of pure economics, in the twentieth century — when economic growth, that is in the West at least, was gradually being experienced as 'normal' — the interest in the explanation of economic growth faded into the background. This had to do with the economic crisis of the thirties. As a result of the fierceness and the persistency of the depression that spread across the Western world after 1929, the question to what extent the crisis had worsened by the economic policies followed in the different countries and if so, whether, and to what extent, another fiscal and monetary policy would have resulted in a less disastrous economic development were put in center stage. John Maynard Keynes's magnum opus, which was published in 1936, *A General Theory of Employment, Interest and Money*, for a few decades dominated the discussion in economic theory, as a result of which (Keynes' theory was typically a short-term analysis) long-term problems, such as the explanation of economic growth, faded into the background.

1.8 Renewed interest in growth after the Second World War

After the Second World War the tide turned. Initially the renewed interest in the phenomenon of economic growth, from a social point of view, was nourished by the acute problem of economic reconstruction of Europe and the issue of the economic development in the former colonies of the Western countries, but during the final quarter of the twentieth century the social backgrounds of that issue shifted. Four factors played an important role in this.

1.9 Four social developments as explanation

First, the Western countries at the beginning of the seventies were confronted with an economic development which could hardly be reconciled with the then dominant Keynesian theory: An economic recession (stagnating production and increasing unemployment) combined with high — and during the recession still growing — inflation rates.[13] It became clear that in the sixties the approved incentives policy of Keynesianism could only have the opposite effect in this instance. Did this mean the end of the 'makable' society? Would Western economies, just as it was for the last time in the thirties, again become the victims of uncontrollable cyclical fluctuations resulting in the material progress that was made during a number of years of boom, long being cancelled out again? And if that would happen, would it not also be the end of the unparalleled rapid economic growth that had characterized the economic development of most Western countries during the glorious 1960s? In other words, would substantial and sustained economic growth also be possible without the government pursuing an active policy of economic incentives in a Keynesian sense?

Secondly, at the beginning of the seventies Western concern emerged about the negative side effects of economic growth. By order of an informal but nonetheless influential, international party of politicians, scientists, representatives of international organizations and business-people, 'the Club of Rome', Dennis Meadows, professor at the prestigious *Massachusetts Institute of Technology (MIT)*, in 1972, published a report entitled: *The Limits to Growth* (Meadows et. al., 1972). On the basis of a simulation model of the world economy he had developed together with his MIT colleague Jay Forrester (1971), they concluded that an unmodified continuation of the rapid economic growth, which had begun after the Second World War, within some generations would lead to a global disaster of heretofore unknown dimensions; among other things characterized by damage to the ecological balance as a result of industrial pollution, scarcity of food as a result of overpopulation and global exhaustion of a number of raw materials and additives that were considered indispensable. It was, the report implied, not unthinkable that the worldwide crisis, which would give rise to one thing and another, would result worldwide in an acute — probable nuclear —threat of war.

The report of the Club of Rome came as a real bombshell. This had not so much to do with the precision of the predictions.[14] The impact the report made was especially the result of the background of those who had commissioned the report and those who wrote it: The Club of Rome was not listed as a collection of notorious anti-capitalist hippies and if there was only one university institution in the world where the blessings of technological development were highly regarded, it would be the MIT. If even the Club of Rome and the MIT already contended that the world would collapse because of economic growth, then something was very wrong indeed, was the general response to *The Limits to Growth*.

The result was that a discussion started on the desirability of economic growth in general (certainly as it concerned the 'rich' West) and that people started to wonder whether it would also be possible

29

to create economic growth devoid of the harmful side effects on the long run which Forrester and Meadows had pointed out; the issue of so-called 'sustainable growth'.

Thirdly, in the 1970s gradually a completely incongruous development in the non-Western world became noticeable: The awareness grew that in the decade before, expectations about the anticipated effect of Western development aid had been much too optimistic. At that time the idea had reigned that large-scale financial aid to developing countries coupled to actual support in the field of education, medical care and technological development, would bring about economic development in the non-Western world as well, so that this would gradually close the gap between rich and poor countries. In the course of the seventies it became apparent that the global poverty issue was much more difficult to solve than had been assumed in the previous years. In a number of countries, in particular in South America and Africa, the economic development — frequently precisely in those countries that in the decades before had been the recipients of enormous amounts of development aid — began to show persistent stagnation symptoms or, worse even, an unstoppable process of economic deterioration began to set in, which within a few years smothered the seeds of economic development that had been sown in the years before, into total social desintegration.[15]

At the same time, however, a number of Asian countries which had not ever received any form of Western development aid at all, started to show growth rates from the early seventies onwards — thus precisely in the period when economic growth in Western Europe and the United States was leveling off — which if possible were even higher than the economic growth which that preceding decade had been realized on average by Western countries.[16]

Fourthly, by the beginning of the 1990s the world was confronted with the unexpected and, from a historical perspective, extremely rapid disintegration of the communist power bloc in Eastern Europe. The subsequent transition from a centrally planned economy to a market economy for some countries in the long run seemed to give a favorable impulse to their economic development (Hungary and Poland, for instance), whereas in other countries (the former Soviet Union in the lead, naturally) the transition caused a serious disruption of their economic and social system.[17]

All the same, the issue of economic growth retained its high social priority, also in the last quarter of the twentieth century, even if the backgrounds totally differed now from those which in the years following the Second World War had played such an important role.

1.10 Current relevance of the growth issue: Rich and poor countries

The explanation of the phenomenon of economic growth — and hence, by implication, also the explanation of economic stagnation and decline — today as well, is in a social context, one of the most urgent problems in economics. The urgency ensues form the four developments mentioned above which may be summarized in the conclusion that the prophets of the 'makable society' from the 1960s have been much too optimistic: Economic growth in their eyes was a phenomenon that — even in poor counties — would in the long run occur 'automatically', at least if through international efforts in the field of development aid, those countries would be given the opportunity to import modern Western technology (medical technology included) and along the same road of international assistance, the population of those countries would get the opportunity to become educated. In that way, it should be possible, they thought, to reduce the gap between rich and poor countries and perchance it would totally disappear in the long run.

History does not seem to put in the right the followers of the so-called convergence theory[18] since the nineties of the previous century. The market economies of the West do not seem to evolve towards the centrally planned system; one sooner gets the impression that the government is increasingly withdrawing from the economic process. Also the collapse of the communist economies in Eastern Europe and their intermittent transition to market allocation, which in some cases looks suspiciously like a brigand economy, are difficult to fit in the theory of convergence.[19]
However, the most important aspect in which the theory of convergence has failed, is in the field of the global distribution of wealth. Since the last quarter of the century there have not been any signs that the income differential between rich and poor countries is diminishing; and even if there is convergence, then it applies to the rich countries themselves.[20]

The latter determines the social urgency of the issue of economic growth today. The optimism from the sixties that the gap between rich and poor countries could be reduced in a not too distant future by international development aid, has given way to skepticism arising from the fact that the effectiveness of development aid, as an instrument to reduce global income inequality seems to become ever more dubious. At the same time, the idea that further increasing income inequality would some day be an international political and social time bomb still rules: Don't we already today see the first omens of mass migration from the poor south and east to the rich west?

In addition, in the same period in which the fiasco of 'traditional' development aid from the sixties (essentially characterized by capital movements and technology transfers) gradually became obvious, the ideas as to how economic growth came about changed drastically. That drastic change had all to do with the intense cooperation between economists and economic historians that originated from the bloom of new economic history. One can persist, without exaggerating, that a large part of the new insights which this day are becoming widely accepted in economic sciences on the causes of economic growth, stagnation and decline, are a direct result of that which Robert William Fogel called the *reunification of economic history with economic theory*. This book deals with the manner in which those new insights have been attained.

Notes

1   The classical work that illustrates this point is of course The *Structure of Scientific Revolutions* by Thomas Kuhn (Kuhn, 1962). The funny thing is that this book, which offers an in-depth analysis of the manner in which structural changes occur in sciences, in turn was itself the reason for a methodological upheaval in philosophy of science.

2   Of course, Einstein's articles from 1905 immediately upon their publication came as a real bombshell in the restricted circle of theoretical physicists. This does not alter the fact that it took years before it became more widely known that the concept of relativity turned the entire theoretical physics upside down: It took until 1922 before Einstein was awarded the Nobel Prize for physics.

3   Further on, I shall use for the 'American Revolution' in economic history, which is referred to here, exclusively the two concepts which ultimately

took root: *New Economic History* or the in American literature generally used abbreviation NEH, and cliometrics.

4 That this is not exaggerated, is shown by the description given by Fogel and Engerman of the discussion about the economic aspects of American slavery which was held at the annual congress of the *Economic History Association* in Philadelphia in September of the year 1967 where during the discussion about the renowned study by Alfred Conrad and John Meyer — which by then was already ten years old (!) — new economics historians, neo-Marxists and economic historians from the traditional school came to blows with one another to such degree that the chairman had the great difficulty to prevent an actual fight (Conrad & Meyer, 1958; Fogel and Engeman, 1974, Vol. 2, pp. 12-19).

5 That things did not always go very smoothly, is illustrated by the sequence on p. 153, where Bolles describes how at the beginning of the nineteenth century two merino sheep and a ram survived the crossing from Europe to the VS only through the supreme efforts of a Spanish shepherd who had traveled with them. Unfortunately, the large landowner who was made a gift of the expensive small stock by the importer, apparently was unaware of the intention. When the generous giver after some time informed after the welfare of the animals, it appeared that their owner had eaten them with relish.

6 A certain differentiation is in order here. Also in the years when there was no new approach in economic history at all, some economic history publications did appear, which were completely quantitative by nature, for instance in the field of the history of prices; the first professor of economic history in the Netherlands, N.W. Posthumus, owes his — deserved — fame especially to his great merits in the field of price history. The reason for not reckoning such publications to the new economic history lies *in the purpose* that was served by such publications: Quantitative illustrations to support economic development processes which were described in other economic history studies. The historically statistical material published in those writings, was not used in traditional economic history to test econometric models for their usefulness and that was what essentially distinguished the new economic history from the traditional approach.

7 Here as well there are of course exceptions which prove the rule. An example is the article 'Aspects of Quantitative Research in Economic History' by Lance Davis, Jonathan Hughes and Stanley Reiter from 1960 which was published in *The Journal of Economic History* (Davis, Hughes & Reiter, 1960). And even though this article did indeed deal with the new approach in the discipline, the writers in their terminology meticulously avoided emphasizing this. Quite the contrary: By avoiding the term new

economic history and emphasizing the long tradition of quantitative historic research in traditional economic history (see footnote 6 to this chapter, above) they in fact tried — in this instance apparently with success — to make the new economic history, without so much as calling it by its name, *salonfähig* in the eyes of their traditional colleagues. Only in the second half of the sixties, the new economic historians started to publish regularly in economic history journals.

8   There is a good reason for this supposition. In the same years in which the new economic history made a name for itself, Marx's economic theory in the Western world was rapidly gaining popularity. The student revolts, at the end of the sixties, created an intellectual climate in which leftist radical ideals suddenly became much *en vogue*. Within the university, especially social scientists appeared sensitive to this political and cultural change in course and also economics could not avoid this influence, albeit that the influence of neo-Marxism here was less than in sociology. Many economic faculties introduced chairs in Marxist economic theory in the 1970s. The ensuing loss of the Soviet Russian bloc in Eastern Europe also meant the end of the popularity of neo-Marxism. These days there is hardly any chair in Marxist economic theory among the faculties of economics in Europe and in the United States.

9   This 'alienation process' between economic theory and economic history which occurred in the first half of the twentieth century is discussed in great detail in Chapter 2.

10 It goes without saying that these two issues in the field of international economic policy are essentially of a long-term nature. A Keynesian analysis (which had become a formidable competitor of the neoclassical tradition during the 1950s) is to no avail here. For a more comprehensive argumentation of this subject, see chapter 2.

11 The first manual that attempted to summarize the results of the new economic history is, to my knowledge, *American Economic Growth: An Economist's History of the United States* (Davis, Easterlin, Parker *et. al.*, 1972). As the title already indicates, this book was in first instance oriented towards colleagues and not to the interested layman. A first step to make the results of the 'new economic history' accessible also to a wider public was taken by Fogel and Engerman who put their famous study into the economic aspects of American slavery, *Time on the Cross*, in two volumes. The first part contained the conclusions of the research in terms that were understandable for laymen as well. The second part dealt with the manner in which they had arrived at those results and was aimed at their seasoned fellow new economic historians who were well versed in economic jargon (Fogel & Engerman, 1974). *The Quantitative Approach to*

Economic History (Lee, 1977) goes too far from a technical economic point of view to be useful as an introduction to readers who are not trained in economics and econometrics. The first new economic history manual, that exclusively focused on a broad public, was *A New Economic View of American History* (Previant Lee & Passell, 1979). A later attempt (at a more modest scale) was *Econometric History* (McCloskey, 1987). In *Explaining Long-term Economic Change* (Anderson, 1991) a rather wonderful attempt is made to briefly summarize the rapprochement between the 'new economic history' and the traditional economic history which had started in the second half of the seventies. This brief summary does have as a result however, that the book is not as easily digested by others than economists as it would seem at first glance. The fact that it contains no formula or table is deceptive in this respect!

12 Given the fact that the revolution of the new economic history originated in the United States and has developed itself in that country in the first decades in a relatively isolated manner compared to the manner in which elsewhere in the world the economic history was practiced, the American research stands central. Where this was obvious, I have quoted also non-American research. Finally, where possible, I have taken some illustrative examples from Dutch economic history.

13 This recession (in fact there were a number of subsequent recessions) is known in history books as 'the first oil crisis'. That designation is not incorrect (one of the main reasons for the recession was the fact that through the major oil-exporting countries, united in the OPEC cartel, the world oil price sharply increased in a short period of time, resulting in sudden substantial huge cost increases in the industrialized countries in the West) yet incomplete. The increased oil price combined with large deficits of the American government owing to the Vietnam War, the large-scale social rehabilitation programs which had started under Kennedy and were continued under Johnson, the arms race and the American space program, resulted in a gigantic deficit on the American balance of payment, which caused a devaluation of the American dollar in the early 1970s. The latter meant the end of the postwar international monetary system of Bretton Woods. In the wake of the American economic recession, many European economies also ran into difficulties. The increased oil prices in combination with the often substantial budget deficits (among other things the result of many years of an incentive policy à la Keynes) played a part in this as well.

14 Later studies showed that the predictions set forth in the model applied in *The Limits to Growth* were highly sensitive to minimal changes in the mathematical properties of the model applied, and in econometrics the

rule of thumb is: The more sensitive the model predictions are to changes in the model parameters, usually the more unreliable the predictions of the model.

15 Between 1950 and 1973 the average annual growth in the real gross domestic product (RGDP) per head of the population both in Latin America and in Africa is more than 2 per cent in its entirety. This, however, was a bit less than in the Western world for that same period, where the annual per capita growth was slightly more than 3.5 per cent, but that does not alter the fact that in those years in South America and Africa there still was a substantial improvement in the long run. Between 1973 and 1995 the growth rate for Latin America declined to a meagre 0.6 per cent, while in Africa the development turned into an economic decline in absolute sense: In this period the RGDP per capita declined on average by more than 0.3 per cent per year (see: Maddison, 1999).

16 Naturally Japan is the most obvious example, but here a process of a remarkably rapid economic growth had manifested itself earlier already. Since the seventies, especially the so-called *New Industrializing Countries*, thanks to spectacular growth rates, achieved great prosperity within a few years, as if it came out of the blue: Taiwan, Singapore, South Korea and Hong Kong are most appealing examples. In the nineties the growth in most of these countries (likewise in Japan) began to show manifest signs of wear, but now it was suddenly China that attracted attention by a remarkable acceleration in economic growth.

17 According to Maddison (1999) the per capita RGDP in Eastern Europe decreased by an average of 0.75 per cent per year in the period of 1973 until 1995. This rate is heavily dominated by the former Soviet Union. All the same, the economic decline in Eastern Europe in the relevant period took place even more rapidly than in that same period in Africa!

18 The Dutch economist Jan Tinbergen, together with the Norwegian Ragnar Frisch winner of the first Nobel Prize for Economics (1969), was an outspoken adherent of the theory of convergence. In the time when Tinbergen was writing, the term 'theory of convergence' actually had a double meaning: It concerned both the prediction that on the long run the different systems of economic organization (communism versus capitalism) would converge towards one mixed economic order, and the expectation that internationally coordinated development aid in the broadest — and large-hearted — sense of the word could diminish the gap between rich and poor countries and, in the very long run, probably even fully close that divide. The latter expectation did not only rest on the naive belief in progress of the sixties. For, the neo-classical growth theory also predicted that under 'normal circumstances' economies with a low income level would

show the tendency to grow harder than economies which were characterized by a high income. (see for instance: (Barro, 1996, p.4). Following the collapse of the communist bloc, at the beginning of the nineties, the emphasis was placed especially on the second meaning: Convergence of welfare differences.

19 In defense of the theory of convergence at the most one could argue that, today, indeed a limited number of countries can be found where a process of convergence, within the meaning of the theory, is noticeable: In the first place China, of course, but also Hungary and Poland, for example, could be placed in that category to a certain extent.

20 Statistically this is an extremely tricky matter: Dependent on the countries one would wish to involve in the comparison and the period the comparison is to cover, different, in themselves sound and respectable studies arrive at contradictory conclusions. A recent and in-depth research with an empiric underpinning by Van Ark, Barrington and McGuckin (2000) draws the conclusion that the difference in real income per head of the population between rich and poor countries on average from 1973 to 1997 increased in absolute terms, yet in relative terms it did not. In 1973 the average per capita income in real terms (thus: Corrected for price changes) in the 25% richest countries in the world was US$ 14 682 and that of the 25% poorest countries US$ 1 017. So the difference between the two averages in 1973 amounted to US$ 13 665. In 1997 the same figures were US$ 18 320 and US$ 1681 respectively, which means that the difference had increased to US$ 16 639. From the same figures one could also conclude that, on average, the 25% richest countries in 1973 were 14.2 times as rich as the 25% poorest countries whereas in 1997 they were 'only' still 12.2 times as rich.

2 The origin of traditional economic history

2.1 Economic history determined by the phrasing of the question

Despite the fact that there is a range of profound and scholarly definitions of the concept of history, we can hardly go wrong on the conclusion that historians in fact do one thing only: Answer questions about the past of the human race by describing certain aspects of that past — namely those which the historian deems of importance in the light of the phrasing of the question — and one way or the other place it in a coherent perspective. In distinguishing between that which we for the sake of convenience call 'general' history and economic history, it is a matter of choice for that perspective.

In answering questions about the history of the human race, from the very start, the historian will perforce select certain aspects and for that reason one can easily insist that the economic aspect always played a certain role in historiography already. Also the earliest historians (for instance, Herodotus and Tacitus) have written about the way in which peoples, whose lives and times they described, tried to support themselves.

How is it possible, then, that it is standard academic practice to officially recognize economic history only by the end of the nineteenth century as an independent scholarly field of study? The explanation is that only in the second half of the nineteenth century a new type of historiography emerged in which, unlike before, the economic perspective is not *one of the many* from which questions about the history of the human race may be answered, but *the only one*. Without overdoing it too much, one could insist that an economic historian has voluntarily provided himself with blinkers: Any questions about the history of the human race are answered from an economic perspective in economic history.

Was this voluntarily elected methodological myopia the consequence of a process of specialization within general history in the nineteenth century? That conclusion seems obvious, yet it is wrong. This is so, because economic history is no specialist splinter of general history; it is rooted in economics. To understand this, we should pause for a short while at the emancipation of the life and social sciences in the nineteenth century.

2.2. Life and social sciences in the nineteenth century: Positivism prevails

The development of the natural sciences, that first became noticeable during the Renaissance and which boomed since the years of the Enlightenment, was followed by an overtaking maneuver of the life and social sciences. In first instance, economics, sociology, psychology and history gradually evolved into independent scientific disciplines. During that emancipation process most of those life and social sciences, in terms of method, borrowed from their meanwhile successful predecessors such as physics, chemistry and astronomy. In doing so, they gradually let go of their initially mostly empirically-oriented, literary descriptive method and chose a formally-oriented approach in which an important role was reserved for the philosophy of 'positivism'. For, positivism implied that the methodology of the life and social sciences was wholly derived from the natural sciences.[1]

Knowledge, so positivism dictated, should be based on empirical facts and be free from metaphysical speculation. The empirical facts in turn served as the building blocks of a strictly logical hypothetical theory: A description of the manner in which the phenomena observed, were supposed to be causally connected. Verification of predictions derived from that theory would then have to prove ultimately whether the causal relations postulated by the theory were correct.

Some of those new scientific fields went much further in this respect than others (in economics for instance this tendency was more strongly present than in sociology), but in all life and social sciences this development could be detected to a lesser or greater extent, except... in history.

2.3 History in the nineteenth century and the role of historicism

Among historians, the body of thought of historicism began to dominate in historiography and the fundament of historicism is the exact opposite of that of positivism.[2] The rationale was the idea that individual and social life in all its facets forms a unique process that unfolds in the course of time and that, for this very reason withdraws from fixed patterns. Because according to historicism, also all cultural phenomena - including the ways in which people view their world - form part of that historical evolution process, it follows that it is in effect impossible for the researcher to take a stand that is unrelated to the historical process of which he himself forms part. To think that there are fixed historical patterns is an illusion in this realm of thought. The essential difference between the natural and the life and social sciences, according to historicists, lies precisely in the *nomothetic* nature of the natural sciences and the *ideographic* character of the life and social sciences, of which history is pre-eminently a part.
'Nomothetic' means that science has the duty to discover laws that describe how natural phenomena are linked together. In the eyes of historicists, this would not be possible for history. The only thing a historian can do, is to try to reconstruct in his own mind on the basis of critical study of the sources, the unique processes that have unfolded in the past and to describe it as faithfully as possible, and that is precisely the essence of the concept of ideography. In the words of a distinguished — late — historicist, Collingwood: '... The history of thought, and therefore all history, is the re-enactment of past thought in the historian's own mind...'(Collingwood, 1946: pp.214-215) The result will never be a law or a theory, but the description of a unique process that shall never repeat itself in that manner.

2.4 Positivism and historicism are methodologically incompatible

It does not require much fantasy to realize that positivism and historicism as fundamental principles are at right angles. The increasing popularity of historicism among historians in the nineteenth century and the positivist principles of the other life and social sciences caused history on the one hand and sociology, economics and psychology on the other to grow ever more apart in terms of methodology.

2.5 Economics and sociology do not facilitate laboratory experiments

The problem of a number of those nomothetic life and social sciences — especially sociology and economics are faced with it; psychology has the least difficulties with it — is that they have not been able to borrow the methodology of the natural sciences in one crucial respect, namely where the controlled experiment is concerned to test hypotheses derived from theory for their empirical tenability. The only option these disciplines have left is to conduct comparative historical research, that is, to examine whether the relations assumed in theory and which according to that same theory should lead to certain outcomes, agree with experiences from the past.

In this way, the analysis of historical processes in economics and sociology became the empirical substitute for the laboratory experiment of the natural sciences; all this of course to the horror of sincere historicists who were convinced that the past of humankind and society by definition were not fit for this role.

2.6 The *Methodenstreit*: 'Neoclassical' versus 'Historical School'

This methodological conflict, which naturally pushed to the fore as the nomothetic life and social sciences increasingly squeezed themselves in the straightjacket of models derived from the natural sciences, finally came to erupt in the second half of the nineteenth century, first in Germany and Austria, and is registered since as the *Methodenstreit*; and it was this *Methodenstreit* that heralded the birth of economic history as an independent scholarly field.[3]

In its diligence to equal the successful natural sciences, especially theoretical economics had in the course of the nineteenth century rigorously withdrawn from the empirical, descriptive method applied by the so-called 'Classical School' which emerged in the second half of the eighteenth century and to which are linked the names of the patriarchs of economics, such as Adam Smith, David Ricardo and Jean Baptiste Say.

In its place, particularly in the second half of the nineteenth century, a formal, deductive-oriented and, as regards the body of concepts, especially mechanics-related analysis of economic phenomena began to unfold. This was the main characteristic of the Neoclassical School which was dominated by writers such as Alfred Marshall, William Stanley Jevons and LéonWalras.[4]

This formalization initiated a new specialty, mathematical economics, and drastically changed the nature of economics. The reformulation of the theory, which mostly in the verbal-descriptive form was well-known (because... adopted from the Classical School!), in the form of a mathematical model, opened the possibility to scrutinize the theory for its logical consistency. If the fundamental principles had been defined exactly and the assumptions on which the theory was based were not contrary to empirical evidence, and finally the theory itself was not self-contradictory, then the theory, according to the line of reasoning of neoclassical authors, was 'true'; in the same sense as 'laws', stemming from natural science are 'true' and hence, universally valid.

The pretension of universality would probably have given hardly any cause for discussion if the subject of the study of economics would have been the behavior of gasses or of celestial bodies. However, the point is that economics studies the behavior of human beings and this implies that it is particularly troublesome to pass judgment on the extent to which the theory pronounces upon how a system *is actually composed*, or on how the system (in the opinion of the writer) *should ideally be* composed. In other words: In the life and social sciences the risk is greater than in natural science that all types of normative statements, which in fact are nothing more than subjective value judgments of the person developing the theory, unintentionally become part of the theoretical construct. And if this happens, then the claim of universality which is founded on the example of the natural sciences expires, simply because the theory no longer describes 'how it is', but — at least in part — 'how it could or should be', and that is definitely something else. It can hardly be denied that within the neoclassical paradigm it was difficult — and to this day, it is — to separate the subjective and normative elements in the theory from the objective.

The evolution of the Classical into the Neoclassical School implied that the thinking of English economists in the second half of the nineteenth century as well was to an important extent determined by the ideas of Adam Smith and David Ricardo. The *wealth of nations*, such was the general belief, could be promoted by international specialization and division of labor, and that process would only be able to optimally emerge within the framework of an unhindered performance of national and international markets. For this purpose, the guarantee of a stable, generally accepted, international means of exchange was seen as a precondition. Under such 'ideal' circumstances, competition would ensure that all goods and services would be offered to the customers everywhere and at any time at the lowest possible price for which they could be produced. Op-

43

timal allocation (and consequently the greatest possible prosperity for all peoples), would occur 'automatically' in a completely unhindered operation of markets, provided that free access to these markets was guaranteed and that there were no monopolies, via the working of the price mechanism, the famous *invisible hand* of Adam Smith.

2.7 Economic-political backgrounds of the *Methodenstreit*

When one considers that it were especially the Anglo-Saxon and French economists who dominated the Neoclassical School and one also recognizes that in the second half of the nineteenth century more than half of the industrial world production originated in England and the United States, it is hardly surprising that the neoclassical paradigm aroused highly negative responses in countries which at that time were much less strongly industrialized, such as present-day Austria, which at least partly were inspired by motives of an economic-political nature. Germany and Austria, were after all, in this period endeavoring to cultivate an own industry behind protective tariff walls to try to get out from under the overwhelming industrial supremacy of England. The high initial costs, which are involved in a major social transformation process such as industrialization, and which England had known in the previous century (but then without any international competition worthy of mention), necessitated countries that wanted to try such an overtaking maneuver with success, to protect their own emerging industries during the first phase of industrialization with import tariffs against foreign industrial products, according to the German economists who stood at the cradle of the *Zollverein*.

Needless to say that this so-called *infant industry protection argument* in the eyes of their English colleagues was unacceptable, because it was at odds with the doctrine on the optimal allocation of scarce means, which, according to neoclassical theory, was precisely the consequence of an *unhindered* operation of markets. In the eyes of genuine neoclassicists, import tariffs, whichever way one looked at it, infringed on the principle of free market operation and for that reason were unacceptable.

Because neoclassical theory claimed universality and moreover, was thus doctored by subsequent generations of economists that it had gradually come to show a rather unassailable logical consistency, it was exceptionally difficult for the German economists to attack their English colleagues on that latter point.

A roundabout route brought the solution: The German attack was not concentrated on the theory itself, but on the manner in which it had come about. For this, surprisingly enough, they sought the support of the historians who, in the framework of historicism, had renounced the no-mothetic nature of the humanist sciences. For that reason, the German-Anglo-Saxon debate, originally inspired by economic-political motives, crystallized out as a methodological dispute: The *Methodenstreit*.

2.8 The essence of the *Methodenstreit*: Induction versus deduction

The attack was launched close to home. Also in the German-speaking territory, more in particular in Vienna, there existed a group of scholars at that time who were well-disposed towards positivism. Among them was the economist Carl Menger who — in the lion's den, so to speak — was a strong advocate of neoclassical thought, and, even more than that, who had with his own work and with that of his students Friedrich von Wieser and Eugen von Böhm-Bawerk introduced such important theoretical refinements in the neoclassical paradigm, that their joint contribution in the history of economic thought is known to this date as the Austrian School. Menger's *Untersuchungen über die Methode der Sozialwissenschaften und der Politischen Ökonomie insbesondere* from 1883, in which he wipes the floor with historicism as the basis for the social sciences, got him severe criticism from his more historically *angehauchte* colleagues, such as Gustav von Schmoller and Karl Bücher. The 'English theory' (as the latter two mockingly dubbed neoclassical thought) derived her method from the natural sciences, and precisely that made her unfit to study an economic system. Every economic theory, they argued, is historically bound (there you have the influence of historicism) and can therefore only have validity for the specific historical circumstances of the period for which the theory had been formulated.

The consequence of all that is, according to the adherents of the Historical School, that economics should avail itself of a method other than that of the natural sciences. If it is possible in the natural sciences to arrive at universal theories through the method of deduction - the logical and consistent construction on the basis of some hypotheses that do not conflict with empirical evidence - for economics this is not possible. The economist, given the fact that the way in which society is organized, is always the result of a historic development process which in itself is unique, will have to resort to the inductive method, the — in principle, perpetual — collection of empirical data about the genesis of that society to only arrive at a certain degree of generalization; the formulation of a 'theory', which in view of the method applied, will rather have the nature

Fig. 2.1 Carl Menger (1840 - 1921)   Fig. 2.2 Gustav von Schmoller (1838 —1917)

of a historic description of the way in which the economic organization of the society examined developed.

2.9 From Historical School to traditional economic history

The *Methodenstreit* heralded a serious schism in economics. Theoretical economics opted, for the time being any way, in principle for deduction. The inductive-oriented Historical School of Von Schmoller *cum suis*, however, over the years indeed won the necessary followers also beyond Germany and Austria, but its contribution to economic theory remained limited, simply because it was too stuck in a pre-theoretical stage: The collecting — as said: In principle, perpetual — of empirical (that is: Historical) data.

The contribution of the Historical School to economic theory remained limited to — often alarmingly broad — historical descriptions of the development of economies, which were always cast in the form of a so-called *Stufen-theorie* (in English: Theory of phases). Typical of such theories of phases was, that the entire development process of an economic system was squeezed into the straitjacket of the phased development of some element, regarded as fundamental.[5] Thus Bücher (1893) in his *Entstehung der Volkswirtschaft* made a classification according to the household he considered to be dominant for the relevant historical development phase: The *Stammwirtschaft* in certain conditions would evolve into a *Stadtwirtschaft*, which in turn would merge into a *Volkswirtschaft*. The economic analysis restricted itself at best to a specification of the conditions in which one phase would change into the other, whereby historical research was regarded as the method of choice to track down those conditions.

With the principal choice of the Historical School for empirical-historical research as the basis of the development of economic theories, it denied itself an important set of analytical tools, namely the strictly logical analysis of economic systems in the form of a mathematical model, while this approach became increasingly important in economic theory throughout the twentieth century. Thus the Historical School isolated itself from the mainstream in theoretical economics. Moreover, the pattern of the theories of phases began gradually to act as a true Procrustean bed, in which the unruly historical reality would often only fit when one was prepared to seriously mutilate it.

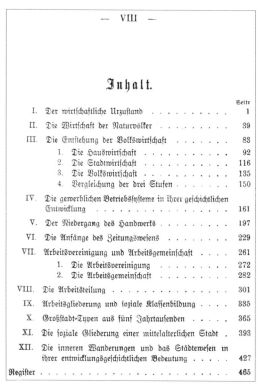

Fig. 2.3 Page of content from Karl Bücher's *Die Entstehung der Volkswirtschaft* (1893)

In the long run, even in circles of the Historical School this was also experienced as such: In the course of the twentieth century the phase pattern was abandoned gradually, as a result of the fact that empirical-historical research itself suggested that there was probably no such thing as one general, 'universal' economic development theory. It was this expansion of perspective that marks the gradual transfer from the Historical School to traditional economic history. For, although the Historical School in the end had lost the battle for the 'true' methodological basic principles for theoretical economics, the fact that it had gained quite a following in the course of its existence, did not remain without effect.

The fact is that in the course of time, several faculties of economics established chairs with names such as 'chair in economics according to the historical method'. These chairs were in fact the first academic centers for economic history. The first time this happened (outside of the German-speaking regions, where it was of course often considered superfluous during the hey-day of the Historical School to add that specification to a chair in economics) was with the appointment of Ashley to the University of Harvard, and this example was followed by various other institutions, in the Netherlands by the appointment of N.W. Posthumus to the then 'Economische Hoogeschool' in Rotterdam (the precursor of the Erasmus University), at the same time as its establishment on 8 November 1913. To this day, the term 'historical economics' is an accepted name for the field of economic history, and this still clearly reflects the above-outlined background.

2.10 The importance of traditional economic history

The earlier remark that the contribution of the Historical School to the development of economic theory has been limited, is correct in itself, but who then draws the conclusion that the importance of the Historical School and its successor, traditional economic history, for economics in a broad sense, is also virtually negligible, is wide off the mark. The contribution of traditional economic history was indeed not in the theoretical field, but rather in the area of our knowledge of the manner in which economic systems have evolved in the course of time.[6] The numerous, often highly detailed studies about the economic ins and outs of human societies in the past, have tremendously enriched our historical knowledge of that area.

A reproach is sometimes hurled at the economic history from a neoclassical perspective, namely that economic history is not concerned with the *analysis and the explanation of the economic process*, but fully focussed on the *description of the social environment* in which that process occurred and the manner in which that environment changed in the course of time, does therefore does not cut ice: One cannot reproach the butcher for not baking bread. Traditional economic history simply considered it her main *duty* to map out as clearly as possible the manner in which economic life was organized in the past and the manner in which that organization changed over time, and with respect to the scientific relevance of that duty it was able to table a very strong argument: That same duty was systematically neglected by the neoclassical model builders.

A second point of criticism often heard in those years from theoretical economics about economic history was, that economic historians did hardly or not at all make use of concepts and insights originating from economic theory, and that, as they sporadically already did, theory was applied in a manner that could not possibly stand the test of criticism: '...*Analysis in economic history is more often than not haunted by either a total lack of economic theory, or, even worse, by bad theory...*', as the phrase went. And even if one finds as an excuse that many economic historians originally had been trained in history and not in economics, this reproach in many cases was just. It would, however, take until the Second World War for this to improve.

49

The emergence, and initially, quite slow development of economic history as a new specialized field of general economics, however, did not mean that historical research began to play an important role in the development of general economics. On the contrary, the rapid ascent of mathematical economics, rather strengthened the deductive nature of economic theory development.

In the first decades of the twentieth century (especially the period between the two world wars) gradually a completely new specialization developed within economics that was strongly empirically-oriented indeed: Econometrics. Econometrics is a form of economic research in which hypotheses deducted from economic theory cast in mathematical form, are tested for their empirical tenability against quantitative data with the help of statistical methods and techniques.

On the basis of the empirical nature of econometrics, it would in itself not have been inconceivable that this occasioned a certain rapprochement between economic history and the rest of economics, but ... nothing of the sort (not yet, anyway): The highly-specialized methods which econometrics availed itself of and which were rooted in the theory of probability, differed so much from traditional historical methods of which economic history availed itself, that their shared empirical nature was insufficient grounds for a process of rapprochement.

In plain words: Economic historians usually did not at all grasp the impenetrable formulas with which econometrists tackled the empirical world, and econometricians in turn considered the publications from the camp of the traditional economic history at best as erudite writings, which however, hardly could contribute to the advance of theoretical economics. Neither party could at that time apparently look over the wall erected in the nineteenth century between positivism and historicism.

Consequently theoretical economics (in the meantime equipped with quite an arsenal of ever more refined empirical testing procedures) and economic history were developing isolated from each other, for the simple reason that their practitioners did not understand one another's language. This separated development persisted into the mid-fifties of the past century, when a number of events in the United States heralded the beginning of a methodological revolution in economic history that would change the nature of the discipline beyond recognition. That was the birth of the *new economic history*.

The essence of the new economic history was that economic history suddenly started to use methods and techniques that originated in mathematical economics and econometrics, with the result that diverging opinions arose within economic history itself, namely between economic historians with their roots in economics and their colleagues who were trained in history.[7]

The success of the new economic history however was of a paradoxical nature, which may at best be described with the title of a collection of poems by Dutch poet Rutger Kopland: "*Wie iets vindt, heeft slecht gezocht*", that is: He, who thinks that he has found something, did not look carefully enough. Namely, as the new economic history further developed, it became clear little by little that with the methods and techniques it used, it was indeed able to explain how economic growth in the course of time in itself had become a self-sustaining process in the Western world, but that those same methods and techniques failed in answering the question why in other circumstances the growth process had never set off or, after a promising start, after a shorter or longer while, was smothered in stagnation or decline. New economic history offered, in other words, indeed a satisfactory answer to the question why some countries had become rich, but at the same time failed to provide the answer to the question why other countries had remained poor.

During the 1970s it became clear in which direction the solution to that paradox had to be sought and that was specifically owing to one of the new economic historians of the first hours, Douglass North, who for this reason in particular, saw his work rewarded in 1993 with the Nobel Prize for Economics.

New economic historians in their analyses of economic development processes, invariably started from insights borrowed from neoclassical economic theory and that is which was, as North argued, both the strength and the weakness of the cliometric approach: Modern economic growth in the West was caused by technological progress in a world that was characterized by competition within a system of ever further developing, freely operating markets. That a market economy seemed to promote technological development[8], was in itself understandable: Technological progress is characterized by an advancing process of division of labor and specialization, and since Adam Smith every economist knows that division of labor and specialization require some form of economic organization that one way or the other facilitates market differentiation.

Neoclassical economic theory, as North contended, is in essence a theory that explains how markets *ideally* operate and in what way market forces stimulate technological development and by extension, the process of economic growth. The word 'ideally' is italicized for a good reason, because neoclassical theory does it in a very special way, which demonstrates affinity with the model of Newtonian mechanics: It assumes an abstract world in which *every conceivable impediment to the free operation of markets is ignored*.

Simply formulated one could say that the point of departure of neoclassical theory is situated in the question as to how economic allocation would come about in an imaginary world, in which there is no impediment whatsoever to the operation of free market forces. The consequence of that point of departure is that the neoclassical theory is well-equipped to explain just those historical processes of economic development that most closely approach the assumed ideal. But the other side of that coin is that the more the historical process to be explained, diverges from the ideal assumed by theory, the worse neoclassical theory can handle that. Neoclassical economics, in other words, is a very strong theory when it concerns answering the question about the operation of market forces, but it is useless when it concerns finding an explanation for the phenomenon that in some cases a market economy did prosper, yet in other cases not at all.

And if one is prepared to look beyond the economic *success story* of the Western world, it simply cannot be denied that history contains numerous examples of a market economy never having bloomed or, after an initial period of bloom, deteriorating at a later stage. Apparently there have been certain specific historical circumstances that were conducive to the emergence of a market economy, while in other cases the social context have evidently hindered such a development.

The implication of this line of reasoning is that only comparative research into the specific historical circumstances in which market economies have emerged (or rather have *not* emerged), may possibly provide an answer to the question why some countries have stayed poor. This induces the question in which manner one should approach such comparative historical research. The answer is self-evident: That was pre-eminently the strength of the Historical School and by extension, of traditional economic history!

The irony of history wanted that the new economic historians who so mercilessly polished off their traditional colleagues, in the seventies furtively became aware that the answer to one of the most fundamental issues in their field of study, could only be found by revisiting traditional economic history, the approach whose foundations they had rocked so happily and unanimously for years on end. Rutger Kopland had said it already: He, who thinks that he has found something....

Notes

1   About positivism, see for example: (Simon, 1963; Passmore, 1966). His twentieth century successor, neopositivism or critical rationalism, to which especially the name of Karl Popper is attached, really got it in the 1970s, particularly from a neo-Marxist corner (See for example: Nauta (red.), 1975), an ideological camp that in those years enjoyed a fair-sized following within the social sciences (Compare: Note 8 to chapter I, preceding). In retrospect it has to be recorded that neopositivism has survived the fight reasonably undamaged, which can hardly be said of neo-Marxism.

2   See Iggers (1983) about historicism as methodological basis for the study of history. About the methodological problems in which the historicists in the long run got entangled: (Brands, 1970; Klapwijk, 1970). To make it even more intricate and cluttered: 'Historicism' is sometimes also called 'historism'. But in Karl Popper's famous essay *The poverty of historicism* (1961), which mops the floor with the idea so-called 'laws of historical development' would be conceivable, the Popperian 'historicism' has an entirely different meaning

from that which almost everyone understands historicism to mean. That no 'historical laws' can be found in history, like there are 'laws' in natural sciences, is after all a stand in which Popper and most nineteenth century historicists do not give an inch to one another!

3   For a thorough outline of the emergence and development of the *Methodenstreit*, see: (Wentzel, 1999).

4   (Schumpeter, 1954) is and will be the absolute standard work when it concerns the history of economic thought. This naturally also goes for his masterly discussion of the evolution of the Neoclassical out of the Classical School.

5   The element which was regarded as determining the development process is dependent on the writer's views. Some adherents of the Historical School for example opted for the type of means of exchange that was considered to have been dominant in a certain era, which unavoidably yielded such classification as *Naturalwirtschaft — Geldwirschaft - Kreditwirtschaft*. Werner Sombart (1928), a late writer in the tradition of the Historical School, chose to hang his theory of phases to the concept of 'capitalism' and even the reader who never before read a word of Sombart can have a guess at the manner in which Sombart classified his magnum opus. Indeed: *Vorkapitalistische Wirtschaft — Frühkapitalismus - Hochkapitalismus*. For that matter, not all adherents of the Historical School held on so rigidly to the *Stufen* theories as is suggested here. Marx and Max Weber, for example, are generally also numbered among the Historical School, but their theories are nothing less than with the greatest of trouble to be squeezed into the inflexible straitjacket of a theory of phases. The essential point of whether certain writers should be rated among the Historical School or not is of course not whether the writer concerned, employed a theory of phases or not. The essential point is whether the writer was of the opinion that economic theory had to be built up via an inductive-historical method or via a deductive-mathematical approach.

6   The bloom of the traditional economic history is reflected by a real tide of economic history monographies which were published in the first half of the twentieth century and which finally resulted in a huge number of general to highly-specialized economic history handbooks. A representative summary may be found for example in the bibliography of (Clough, 1968: pp. 559-592).

7   See the preceding chapter I, paragraph 1.4.

8   Take note: It does *not* say here that technological development in a centrally planned economy is in principle impossible. Seen from a historical perspective this would be utter nonsense: The Soviet Union knew after the Second Word War for example periods of tempestuous technological development; remember that the first satellite — then still designated with the beautiful word 'artificial moon' — that was successfully sent into earth orbit was not launched by the United States but by the Soviet Union. At the same time, by

the events of the last decade of the twentieth century one cannot escape the impression that technological development in the communist world led to a highly unbalanced process of growth, which finally resulted in the collapse of the Soviet empire. The undeniable implication of that conclusion is, that historically seen we do not know any other successful example of modern economic growth driven by technological development than that of Western countries in the nineteenth and twentieth centuries. And in that example the operation of market forces held a key role.

3 The *École des Annales* as historical avant-garde

3.1 Criticism of Bloch and Febvre on the then accepted historiography

Before immersing ourselves in the post-war developments, we should pause a short while at the innovatory movement within history, as it was practiced in the faculties of arts. This historical avant-garde movement came about in the 1930s in France and was heralded by the founding of the journal *Annales* in 1929 by Marc Bloch and Lucien Febvre.

Bloch and Febvre had a critical attitude in common toward the then accepted practice of historiography. Their objections concentrated on two main points: In the first place history, in their view, was an elitist matter. Owing to the - in those years - dominant position of political, c.q. diplomatic history, it almost exclusively concerned a small political and diplomatic elite and moreover, historiography at that time limited itself also to a minimal part of their life, namely to those aspects which in one way or the other had had political consequences. Both the history of the majority of the population, the 'ordinary' people, and the history of 'ordinary' life (how did people in the past support themselves, what was their social life like, what was their attitude towards marriage and sexuality, how did they deal with death, et cetera) remained almost completely off the picture in official history.

As a result, the major part of the 'total' history of the human race was consequently disregarded by accepted academic historiography. The larger part of the history of the human race, Bloch and Febvre argued, was in fact 'forgotten history'.

Secondly, they concluded that the manner in which in history explanations were given for historical developments, differed completely from the manner in which other life and social sciences (such as in economics, sociology and geography) attempted to interrelate the phenomena. Was it not obvious, Bloch and Febvre argued, to consider the insights developed in other branches of knowledge as analytical instruments that the historian could employ, perhaps fruitfully, to explain developments that had occurred in the past?

That Bloch and Febvre, in first instance, had no chance of success with the French academic establishment is, in retrospect, not surprising: Their criticism was, from a methodological viewpoint, clearly rooted in positivism[1], and that is incompatible with the basic principles of historicism[2], which in the first decades of the twentieth century indeed had increasingly been the subject of severe critique, yet still influenced the study of history.[3]

The founding of a scientific historical journal of their own, was for the time being the only opportunity for Bloch and Febvre to have their voices heard. The subtitle they gave to their journal, *Economies, Sociétés; Cilivizations*[4], illustrated that they in fact advocated that economic and social aspects be granted a more important place within general history than was customary until that time.

Initially, the influence of the *Annales* was apparently slight in the historical world, but that changed after the Second World War. That was especially because a number of brilliant young French historians, such as Pierre Goubert, Emmanel Le Roy Ladurie, Jacques Le Goff and Fernand Braudel, from the very beginning felt attracted by the ideas which were promoted by the journal and these very historians, in the post-war years ultimately without exception ended up on the most prestigious and influential chairs at the French universities.

Over the course of the years within this 'second generation' of *Annales* historians, what is now known as the *Annales* paradigm, crystallized out; the catechism, to put it irreverently, according to which history, in the view of this group, should have to be rewritten.[5]

3.2 The *Annales* paradigm (1): Development processes instead of facts

The innovatory programme that the *Annales* historians pursued for the — note - *entire* study of history, was characterized by great ambition. This is obvious already from the motto under which they went to war: They wanted, in the words of their most prominent representative, Fernand Braudel[6], via their specific approach realize a *Histoire*

Totale, with which it was en passant implied that all their predecessors at best achieved only a *histoire partielle*. The question of course is how that 'total history' should look like. That very Fernand Braudel laid down in a number of methodological articles the 'credo' of the *Annales* historians. Its main points together provide a good picture of the objections they had against the manner in which at that time history was practiced and how they thought to address such objections.[7]

The most important objection of the *École des Annales*[8] was that the historians allowed themselves too much to be guided by historical events (*événements*, in Braudel's terminology). This reproach at first sight seems to be neither here nor there: What else could historians concentrate on, but placing historical events in a mutually coherent perspective? The criticism becomes understandable when we are willing to consider for a while Braudel's view on the nature of historical development processes in general (See: Figure 3.1). He distinguishes three kinds of developments which he designates with the names *structures*, *conjunctures* and *événements* respectively. The distinction between the three kinds is determined by the *pace* at which historical changes have occurred. *Structures* are then

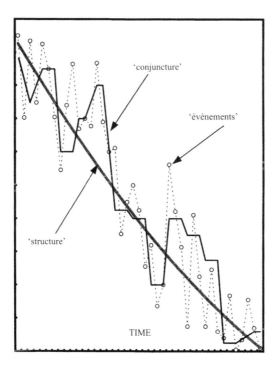

Figure 3.1 Diagram of the Braudelian development model

developments that are so slowly taking place that the untrained eye of the contemporary observer 'sees' no change at all.

An example might actually help: In retrospect we know that Carthage at the time of the Roman Empire was an important grain supplier to Rome. Who nowadays travels in the vicinity of the excavated remnants of that city, wonders how that was possible: On all sides around the ruins of the once so proud metropolis, stretches until the horizon a completely barren wilderness and nothing indicates that there has ever been any form of large-scale farming. Most modern visitors, however, know the answer to this riddle: Climatic changes combined with erosion have changed the geographic condition around the city to such an extent that in the course of the centuries intensive grain cultivation gradually came to be impossible, but — and that is essential in Braudel's view — that process occurred so slowly that it could not be directly observed by those who found themselves in the middle of things.

In Braudel's own words, in structural changes it is about *l'histoire quasi-immobile*, that is: *Apparently* stationary historical development processes. Such structural changes are in his view decisive for the progress of cyclical changes: Developments in which the 'surge' manifests itself over a period of a few years. Those cyclical changes in turn are decisive of the processes which, so to speak, change 'by the day' and which — note, in the realm of thought of Braudel — pre-eminently form the totality of historical facts on which history customarily concentrates.

In the acceptable historiography it is continuously tried to interrelate those 'events by the day' one way or the other, while it is ignored that they do not stand alone, but are inexorably determined by fundamental processes of change which, as it were, form the undercurrent, but are hidden to the eye of the traditional historian because they develop ever so slowly, and because the men of history refuse to call in the insights from other branches of knowledge which have a better eye for the explanation of such processes.

3.3 The *Annales* paradigm (2): Groups instead of individuals

The starting point that structural processes of change ultimately and decisively set the course of history has far-reaching consequences for the manner in which one would subsequently want to 'rewrite' history. Logically one of those consequences is that the role the individual plays in history, shifts to the background. If in traditional history a key role was often reserved for persons of influence, whose conduct was deemed to be of great influence on the course that history had ultimately taken (the Dutch Liberation War as a titanic struggle between William of Orange and Philips II, for example), the *Annales* historians rigorously reject such a picture. As far as they are concerned, it is rather that even the most powerful and influential historical personalities in their actions are subjected to the restrictions imposed by the structural and cyclical developments that took place in the world in which they lived. This change of perspective has had great consequences on the phrasing of the questions that historians try to answer. Within the traditional historical point of departure it may be well defended that it is of great importance to try to discover what the motivation was and what the considerations were of the historical *dramatis personae* as regards the things they decided, but as far as the *Annales* historians are concerned, things are just slightly different. In their answer to the question why certain things have happened, they look in first instance for the anonymous forces and circumstances that pushed the actions of the leading figures in a certain direction from necessity, whether they wanted it or not.

This is for example clearly expressed in the monumental thesis of Braudel (1949), *La Méditerranée et le monde mediterranéen sous l'époque de Philips II*, in which, different from what the title leads one to expect, for the King of Spain himself, no more than a role in the background is reserved and where — if the king comes to the fore already — it is emphasized time and again, that the course of events was not determined by Philip's autonomous decisions, but that the king was *forced* to take certain decisions, due to anonymous circumstances and developments of which he unwillingly was no more than a plaything

Now it is one thing to want to reduce the role of the individual in history, but the question of course is what the *École des Annales* put in its place. The answer is simple: In the *Annales* tradition the emphasis is put on the history of specific *groups*, which may be distinguished from others on the basis of economic, social or sometimes geographic criteria. It is a history that describes the adventures of farmers, merchants, intellectuals, vagrants, et cetera, usually in a certain, closely defined era and in a certain, geographically delineated region.[9] And even when in such a history certain individuals are introduced, this is invariably *not* to reconstruct the adventures of this or that particular individual, but that particular individual is put on stage as a typical representative of the *group*, to which he or she belonged. In the famous study *Montaillou* by Le Roy Ladurie (1977), for example, a meticulous sociological analysis of a mountain village in the Pyrenees around the beginning of the fourteenth

59

century, almost all inhabitants are mentioned by name, and their mutual relations are also described in such minute detail, that the reader is under the impression that about seven hundred years later, he is better informed of the relations in the village than the villagers themselves at the time. But that does not alter the fact that the central theme of the book is how the village as a whole reacted to the heretical ideas which reached this isolated village from the outside and to the measures the church took in its efforts to quash heresy.

3.4 The *Annales* paradigm (3): Regions instead of national states

The most common geographic concept of the traditional history, the national state, was rejected by the *Annales* historians as useless. Two reasons play a role in this. In the first place, until then, in their eyes, history had too often been abused for purposes of a nationalistic nature, whereby 'the motherland' was awarded a heroic role, which especially was intended to blow up the concept to mythical proportions, in order to rouse patriotism in any way whatsoever, so that subjects would actually be prepared to give their lives for their country if the political elite thought it opportune.
The second reason originated — again — from the Braudelian development model. The territory of every national state, in the view of the *École des Annales*, was only a more or less accidental — and in any case temporary — result of international relations of power politics of the past[10] and the concept therefore was totally unsuited to serve as delineation of the area on which structural developments exerted their influence: Geophysical entities do not bother about borders and erosion is not stopped by a customs office with a barrier.

Instead, *Annales* chose for a regional demarcation of the research area, whereby a region was especially considered to be defined by geophysical and/or structural economic characteristics. At times this could be a single village (Montaillou[11]), a town (Romans[12]), sometimes a region (Beauvais[13]), but — dependent on the phrasing of the question — the concept of region could also be so broadly interpreted that it would comprise the territory of several national states: Consider the earlier mentioned thesis by Braudel[14] where the entire area around the Mediterranean is regarded as one great, geophysical, climatic and economic entity.[15]

3.5 The *Annales* paradigm (4): *Mentalités* instead of anachronisms

The fourth fundamental point of departure of the *Annales* historians turned on the anachronistic aspects of prevailing historiography. They tried to substitute these by another approach which was named *histoire des mentalités*. Its origin goes back directly to a famous study by one of the two patriarchs of the *Annales*, Lucien Febvre.

In his *Le problème de l'incroyance au XVIe siècle: la religion de Rabelais* (1942), Febvre intervened in a historical debate which had caused a great deal of controversy in France before the Second World War. The matter concerned was whether the writer François Rabelais, who lived in the first half of the sixteenth century, on the basis of his writings, should be characterized as an atheist or not. Febvre managed to cause this discussion to take a surprising turn, first and foremost by querying in his book whether this question could be asked at all. What so far had been passed over by everyone, was whether the concept of 'atheist' in sixteenth-century France would have had any meaning at all for someone *of that particular period of time*. If that would not have been the case — and Febvre succeeded in demonstrating convincingly in his book that this seemed highly plausible — the entire discussion, however learned and erudite the participants' contributions may have been, could be dismissed as pointless daydreaming.[16]

However obvious Febvre's conclusion may seem in retrospect, it enters upon a delicate problem for which to date there is no indisputable answer. The matter concerned is whether the historian should describe the past in the contemporary terminology of that past itself, or in the terms and concepts of his own culture.

In the first case one wonders whether the historian does not pull the wool over his own eyes by supposing that it is *at all* possible to describe the past simply and solely in terms of that past itself. For it is obvious that he cannot possibly dissociate himself from his own — likewise culturally determined — outlook on the world, and that outlook also determines, whichever way one looks at it, how he *perceives* that past. Moreover, suppose for a moment that he could become 'detached' to such an extent that his own world view would be of negligible influence on the manner in which he looks at the past, even then would the result of his work — the description of the past in terms of that past itself — be incomprehensible to everyone who is less 'detached' than that brave historian himself, and that could hardly be the intention. Finally, it cannot be denied that the unambiguous choice for this stand (again: Insofar as practically possible!) would bring the historian unavoidably in the camp of historicism.[17]

The second approach hides the danger — as convincingly demonstrated by Febvre — that the line between sensible and senseless historical questions becomes particularly faint. Indeed, the question whether Agrippina Minor, the mother of Nero, was Muslim — it is said that she frequently went veiled — can at most be cause for hilarity during happy hour, but will probably not be considered in a serious historical paper. I chance to doubt, however, if that would also be the case with the matter whether Plato was a pedophile — in any event, bookshelves have been filled with works on this issue — despite the fact that the concept of pedophilia in the Greek antiquity had a completely different meaning than the meaning modern Western culture now gives it.

The question now is how the *École des Annales* handled this dilemma, and it cannot be denied that in respect of this problem it is in two minds. On the one hand the *histoire des mentalités* in the long term evolved into a respected specialty that made an attempt to reconstruct the concepts and the ideas, as they were linked together, with which specific historical societies created their own perception of the world around them.[18] On the other hand, it were those same *Annales* historians who, to a greater extent than was customary, applied terms and insights from other areas of science to explain certain historical developments (see: Paragraph 3.7) and whichever way one looks at it, the implication of this is that historical development processes are explained in terms which were completely unknown in the period in which those development processes occurred.

It was totally unavoidable that this methodological dualism at times produced outright arbitrary standpoints as to what was, and what was not permissible in historical explanations. So *Annales* historians made abundant use of historical price ranges, for example to distinguish periods of economic malaise from periods of relative prosperity, for prices were variables which in those very periods were used as a source of information by the historical subjects themselves. On the other side, they categorically rejected the reconstruction of time series of historical national income (a popular activity among economic historians after the Second World War) for the same purpose, because the term 'national income' or 'national product' would have been an unknown term before the twentieth century.[19]

3.6 The role of statistics in the *École des Annales*

How does one describe the history of every-day life of large masses of people? Moreover, how can one map the excruciatingly slow structural processes of change (Braudel's *histoire quasi-immobile*) that have a decisive impact on every-day life? And finally, how do you place all of that in a perspective so that the results do not stick together like loose grains of sand, but are linked together into a solid 'history'? In fact, the *Écoles des Annales* chose a dual strategy to solve these problems.

In the first place, statistics was awarded a much more important place than had been the case before in history. Different from what many skeptics thought, it appeared possible, by means of labor-intensive and meticulous study of the historical records, to retrieve a wealth of statistical data concerning every-day life in the past. The goal of the *Annales* historians was to ultimately achieve an overview as complete as possible of the development at that time of variables that were deemed to have been of crucial influence on every-day life. These reconstructed time series formed in their eyes the empirical backbone of history.

This type of research was deemed of such great importance that it was regarded as a separate historical specialty within the circles of the *Annales*; the *histoire quantitative* or, more specifically focused on the development of time series, the *histoire sérielle*. Nearly endless historical statistical publications, sometimes published independently, sometimes added as *Annexe Statistique* to monographs or theses[20], about production data, prices, tax proceeds, the developments in the population in a certain region or town, birth and death rates, age at marriage and size of family, et cetera, were the result. It is for an important part thanks to the *Annales*, that France, especially as regards the *Ancien Régime*, historically-statistically is one of the best documented countries in the world.

3.7 The role of other scientific disciplines

The second part of the new strategy consisted of the central role the *Annales* historians attributed to the application of concepts and theories, stemming from all sorts of disciplines in order to explain historical developments. From the beginning of the movement onwards, geography was of paramount importance in this, which should not be very surprising, as both Bloch and Febvre came from a double historical-geographical background. This is the main reason why fields of study that are closely related to geography, such as demographics and climatology, were given a rather prominent place, while later on also sociological and economic aspects gained in importance.

Some *Annales* historians were able to develop completely new research methods and techniques within the fields of these disciplines that were especially well fit for the explanation of specific historical developments, while others succeeded to retool successfully highly specialized techniques from a wide range of other disciplines into analytical instruments that were especially suited for historical research.

Michel Fleury and Louis Henry, for instance, developed a new demographical research method, the so-called 'family reconstruction', in which, on the basis of individual data, often from parochial registers, the composition of families from a distant past could be reconstructed. These 'reconstructed families' for their part served as the starting point for the estimation of a number of macro-demographic key variables, such as average age at marriage, life expectancy, fecundity, and birth and mortality figures. In this way it proved to be possible to make reasonably reliable estimates of population figures for specific regions, yes sometimes even on a national scale, where little or no original national data were to be found (Fleury and Henry, 1965). [21]

The above mentioned Emmanuel Le Roy Ladurie is the ultimate *Annales* historian who derived from a wide range of different — sometimes quite exotic - disciplines a truly amazing set of brand new methods and techniques, that could fruitfully applied to cultivate hitherto barren historical territory. By using 'dendrology', for instance, where the analysis of annual rings of trees is used to shed light on climatological changes in the past, he was able to reconstruct climatic changes over an extremely long period (Le Roy Ladurie, 1967), which was an important contribution for the explanation of periods of relative prosperity and poverty in pre-modern societies. He was also the one who, as a historian, for the first time made use of insights from social medicine and human biology on issues concerning human growth. Within these specialized disciplines, it was generally known that fluctuations in the material conditions of certain population groups, are reflected in fluctuations in their average sex and age specific height. Roughly speaking: People who live in poverty are, on average, smaller than people who live in abundance. By using registers of conscripts, he managed, not only to reconstruct what regions in France in a certain period had been relatively 'rich', and what regions relatively 'poor', but also, by compiling a series of average sex and age specific height over time, how the pattern of good and bad years had evolved in the course of ages. These experiments by Le Roy Ladurie formed the basis of a completely new branch of economic history since the 1980s: The so-called 'anthropometric history,' where changes in the material conditions in the past are reconstructed by the analysis of quantitative indicators of the human physique, such as average height, weight, etc.

3.8 Explanations for processes of historical development: The role of the model

The main function that was assigned to the other sciences in the *Annales* research was to interrelate in a coherent development process the progress of various variables in the course of time, as these had been made visible in the reconstruction of time series of such variables (the result of the *histoire sérielle*). And even if the *Annales* historians, contrary to the later new economic historians, never explicitly introduced one specific model which formed the all-decisive framework to explain the development process in question, they did indeed think in terms of models.

Perhaps an example might help, because the above sounds quite vague. Imagine that in the case of a certain region in a dim and distant past (in any case in pre-modern times), you observed that in a certain period there were a great many exceptionally favorable harvest years in a row and you want to find out what the influence of this has been on the circumstances in which 'common people' in that region were living. An *Annales* historian would then set out to work as follows (see figure 3.2).[22] He would first of all wonder whether that series of exceptionally rich harvests could well have been the result of a climate shift, that is, a non-incidental change in the prevailing climate (in the diagram: 1 → 2). In theory, so he would continue his reasoning, these rich harvests should have had a favorable impact on the material conditions in which the population was living, in the sense that they could then dispose of more food than previously or of the same amount at a lower price (in the diagram: 2 → 3). The improvement in the material conditions would have lowered the death rate, because the people's physical conditions improved as well (in the diagram: 3 → 4), while at the same time the birth rate would have increased, because the rise in prosperity probably would have lowered the average age at which people got married (in the diagram: 3 → 5).

The higher birth rates and lower death rates in turn would have caused the size of the population to increase (in the diagram: 4 & 5 → 6). For that reason the farmland available per head of the population would in the long term have dropped (in the diagram: 6 → 7), so that finally the

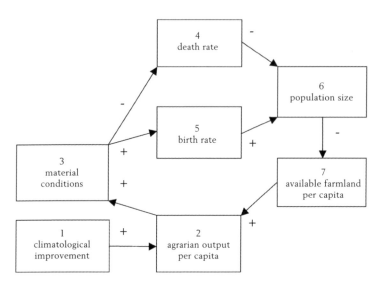

Figure 3.2 Malthusian explanatory model, typical for the *Annales*

total agricultural production per head of the population would again have declined (in the diagram: 7 → 2).

The implication of this reasoning is, that a non-incidental climatic improvement in a pre-modern society will lead to a temporary improvement in the material living conditions for the population, but that such improvement in the long term will again be undone by the population increase which is started off by the climate improvement, *even if such climate improvement itself is non-incidental in nature!*

This example clearly shows a number of things: First of all, it shows that thinking in model-like terms, as has happened here, gives a *possible* explanation for a historical development process. In the second place, it is important to realize that in using the model, hypothetical links between the different variables are introduced that are borrowed from different fields of science: Climatology and agronomy (1 → 2); agronomy and economics (2 → 3); economics and socio-medical sciences, c.q. human biology (3 → 4); economics and sociology of the family, c.q. demography (3 → 5); again demography (4 & 5 → 6), et cetera.

Most important, however, is to realize that a small change in the model is enough to turn the predicted final outcome completely upside down (namely: In the long run *nothing* changes in the material conditions, even if the climate has changed *permanently*). To make this clear, we glance at illustration 3.3 in which we have slightly changed the same model. As can

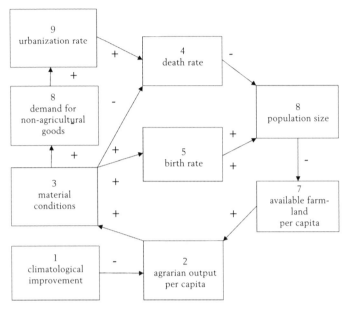

Figure 3.3 Non-Malthusian variation on the same model

be seen at a glance we have kept the connections in the original model, we only added two explanatory variables.

The original improvement in the material conditions that is the result of the improvement in the climate will not only have an impact on the mortality rate and the birth rate, but, as we now assume, it will also cause an increase in the demand for non-agricultural goods (clothing, appliances, et cetera) that are produced in the urban trades sector (in the diagram: 3 → 8). The increased demand for 'urban' products will cause the demand for labor in the cities to rise, which will exert an upward pressure on the wages. The increased wages will trigger a greater migration from rural areas into cities, which will cause a rise in the degree of urbanization (in the diagram: 8 → 9). The point at issue is that in pre-modern societies the death rate in cities is dramatically higher than in rural areas. Therefore, in those conditions increased urbanization will result in an increase in the *average* death rate of the *entire* population (in the diagram: 9 → 4).
It is not inconceivable that this latter increase is so high that it will compensate or transcend the effect of the assumed increase in the first model as the size of the population is concerned, which was the result of the decrease in death rates and the increase in birth rates. If this is indeed the case, then the climatic improvement will indeed bring about a *permanent*

improvement of the material conditions and not, as predicted in the first model, a *temporary* one.

The question it is all about, is of course which model (we have presented two here, but it is clear that we can effortlessly add a number of other models that will both relate entirely different variables in a different manner and predict completely different outcomes) is best to explain a specific historical development process, defined according to time and place. Because, after all, that is the sacred objective we aspire after, as imaginary followers of the *École des Annales*.

The answer to that last question should of course be looked for in the patterns that may be observed in the progress of the time series and from the comparison to other statistical 'snapshots in time' of the different variables that we have so arduously constructed.

To stay with our example: If we have indeed been able on the basis of statistical data to determine unequivocally that in a certain region during a certain period a long-term favorable climatic change had occurred and, moreover, we have indeed been able to observe that the average death rate afterwards did decrease, whereas the birth rate in that same time increased, and, in addition the numbers show that after some generations the death and birth rates had returned to their former levels, then, all these things taken together can be viewed as an — note, nothing more but *an* — indication that we are probably going in the right direction with our first, Malthusian[23], explanatory model. If we can further infer from the numbers that, for example, food prices had decreased shortly after the climatic change set in, but promptly had risen again when the death and birth rates returned to their original levels, then that is a second indication that our gamble on the first model was not so bad.

If our research furthermore involved a region in which in that time there hardly was a city of some importance, it seems little probable that the two extra explanatory variables which we introduced in the second version of our model have been of great weight, and that again points into the direction of our first model not being so bad at all.

In this connection it is crucial to remember that through a careful analysis of the numerical data and the other data, we are increasingly treading on firm ground in respect to the question whether the supposed model [24] offers a plausible explanation to the development process we have studied, but that the patterns observed in the data seldom if ever, point unambiguously in one certain direction. Generally the image coming forward from the numbers is so 'muddy' that it is open to several — often even logically mutually exclusive — interpretations.

In conclusion we must note that to forge the different patterns that are discernible in a great many different time series into a coherent development process, thinking in terms of a model that is composed of supposed relations between variables which have been borrowed from different areas of science can indeed to a certain degree offer something to hold on to, which we badly need in such an exercise. That is the good news.

There is, however, also less good news and that is, that there is almost never one single unique model that perfectly connects all patterns arising from the data, to the exclusion of other possibilities. A model offers some grip, so to speak, but different models offer different 'grips' and that makes the choice tough.

On the other hand, it is precisely that troublesome choice — which model best fits which development process — that is the core of the debate in economic history, and often one notices that more research into the same process, sooner on the basis of more and/or dissimilar data, in a large number of cases, indeed leads in the long run to a certain degree of consensus, with the inescapable result that the debate on that particular matter, subsequently cools down or even makes its exit for a long time.

69

3.9 The problematic quest for 'primal structures'

The problems broached above, namely that it is usually very tricky to infer, solely and only from the data available about a certain development process, in which direction the best applicable explanatory model to that development process should be sought, made it tempting to look elsewhere — that is, beyond the framework of the research proper — for a firm grip that could provide the pitiful researcher a guide for his desperate quest for the 'right' model.
Ideally this would be some sort of comprehensive view on the historical development process in its entirety. It cannot be denied that a number of respectable members of the *Annales* school have not been able to resist the temptation.

This is what I call the problematic quest for 'primal structures': Problematic, because one cannot get away from the impression that they were not always altogether happy with the final choice of their 'primal structures'[25], in the sense that they sometimes sought refuge in the hermetically closed ideological system that was quite *en vogue* within the French intellectual circles of those days. For example, the earlier work by Le Roy Ladurie is pervaded with an orthodox Marxism and to a certain degree — be it considerably more moderate — this goes also for certain studies by Braudel.

Another consequence of the problematic quest for a 'primal structure' was that in some studies, *a priori* a structure was imposed on the material, which in the long run took on the character of a straightjacket, after which little else could be done, but replace that structure with another one, that on further consideration started to pinch just as much, yet in different places. So Angus Maddison[26] in a criticism on the thesis by La Roy Ladurie (1966) about the agricultural society of Languedoc, pointed out that Le Roy Ladurie, apparently on aprioristic grounds, starts from a strictly Malthusian view in his analysis of the economic development (rather: The lack thereof) in Languedoc between 1500 and 1700, while his own data show abundantly clear that epidemic diseases and wars were much more important causes of the regularly recurring peak death rates than an acute shortage of food.[27]

In a later study (Le Roy Ladurie, 1977) in which data about a large number of different regions have been assimilated, he suddenly seems at a loss what to do with that Malthusian point of view. Now the emphasis is placed on suicide and infanticide as restraints on population growth, while a fairly vague ecological model in which human and animal demographic mechanisms seem to influence one another, appears to become his fundamental premise. In this latter study he, for that matter, admits frankly that he has exchanged his earlier Malthusian point of view for what he labels as a 'Ricardian'[28] view, meaning that it is now not population growth that is presented as the main explanatory factor for stagnation in the pre-modern agricultural society, but the lack of technological innovation.[29]

3.10 The influence of the *Annales* after the Second World War

Though Block and Febvre had difficulty before the Second World War to gain their place amidst the established French historians, and the second generation of *Annales* historians as well were not particularly received with great acclaim by the academic establishment, the influence of the *École des Annales* after the Second World War had grown so much that it is not exaggerated to say that the *Annales* have drastically changed the discipline of history and that change fits perfectly in the alternative that Bloch and Febvre had already suggested prior to the Second World War. That does not only hold true for the academic historiography: The influence of the *Annales* can clearly be noted in the history books used in secondary education. The supremacy of diplomatic and political history has been pushed back in favor of the history of ever-day life of 'ordinary' people; statistics as a tool to map certain developments has taken a much more prominent place in academic historical investigations, and any historian can nowadays tell what a 'Malthusian trap' is, whereas previously this term belonged almost exclusively to the field of economic and social history.

That the influence of the *Annales* in university historiography was of an importance that hardly can be overrated, may be supported by a few examples. In England the pioneering work of Fleury and Henry[30] formed the most important source of inspiration for a group of historical demographers and social historians at Cambridge University, who on the initiative of Tony Wrigley established the Cambridge Group for the History of Population and Social Structures.
This research center developed into one the most prestigious in the world and did pioneering work in the field of the reconstruction of the English population in the past and in the field of comparative research into family composition and social mobility in pre-modern societies.[31]
In Dutch historiography, the *Écoles des Annales* has left its marks through the work of Slicher van Bath[32], who exchanged his chair of economic and social history in Groningen after a few years for a chair in agricultural history in Wageningen. In this latter function, he developed a historical research center that became internationally authoritative[33] and formed the source of dozens of dissertations, which almost without exception were inspired by the *Annales*.[34] The striking postwar revival of cultural history[35] in the Netherlands, was also inspired by the *Annales*, especially by the *histoire des mentalités*. One of the reasons for this was that the later *Annales* historians thought that in the works of Johan Huizinga they recognized an important precursor of the *histoire des mentalités*.

In the United States, finally, Immanuel Wallerstein from the State University of New York at Binghamton established a research center that was named for one of the leading *Annales* historians of the second generation: The Fernand Braudel Centre for the Study of Economies, Historical Systems and Civilizations. Wallerstein's actual work, however[36], only had in common the broad approach and the emphasis on structural changes in the long term with the work of Braudel. In his explanation for the gradu-

71

Figure 3.4 Fernand Braudel (1902 — 1985) and Immanuel Wallerstein

ally increased dominance of the Western world over other 'civilizations', he reaches back to a modernized variant of the theories of imperialism of Lenin and Hobson and the so-called *dependencia* theories which in the 1970s were especially propagated by the Marxist *angehauchte* Latin-American economists, and the Braudelian view on history can hardly be found back here. To trace the unadulterated *Annales* impact in American historiography, one should look rather at the works of Simon Schama, (1987; 1995; 1999) who published exhaustively, among other things, on the bourgeois culture of the Republic of the Seven United Netherlands.

In conclusion, we have to state that the influence of the *Annales* on the study of history in the second half of the twentieth century has been greater than that of any other 'school': In essence, the gist of it is, that the *Annales* has made *general* history quite more 'economic and social'. At the same time we have to conclude that its influence on the specialist discipline of *economic* history, from an international point of view, initially remained very limited, as already appears from the fact that French economic history in the second half of the twentieth century was dominated by authors who did not have any ties at all with their *Annales* colleagues, such as Marczewski, Markovitch, Toutain and Lévy Leboyer.[37]
This seems more paradoxical than it is. The central issue concerned in those years in economic history was the explanation of modern economic growth, and because the *Annales* historians were almost exclusively occupied with the *Ancien Regime*, where modern economic growth was conspicuous by its absence, they had little to offer their economic-history colleagues. In line of the phrasing of the question, economic his-

tory in those years was dominated by reconstruction of historical national accounts. Apart from the fact that such reconstruction in first instance focussed on the nineteenth century (which the *École des Annales* was not even interested in) many followers of the *Annales* were extremely reserved about those exercises: In their eyes it was a classic example of applying modern concepts (national income, for instance) to explain historical processes from an era in which those very concepts had no significance and that came dangerously close to what many *Annales* historians scornfully named anachronistic historiography.

Finally, there was such a thing as a 'language problem': Through the rapid development of the new economic history from an international perspective, economic history in that period was dominated by American economic historians who, exceptionally, had enough mastery of the French language to inform themselves directly of French historical literature. Only in a later phase, when the most important *Annales* studies had been translated into English, the ideas of the *École des Annales* became widespread in the Anglo-Saxon academic world as well. This is the main reason why it was only in the last quarter of the twentieth century that there is a certain acceptance of and appreciation for the ideas of the *Annales* within American economic history. The deafening American violence with which the new economic history managed to secure a dominant place in economic history as of the second part of the fifties, so to speak, drowned out all other sounds for years on end.

73

Notes

1   Here, inadvertently the impression is given that I am confusing things. For, in many writings about the *Annales* it is stated that Bloch and Febvre are indeed opposed to the then positivist historiography. It's like this: One of the ideas emanating from positivism is that science should refrain from any form of metaphysical speculation, and must exclusively restrict itself to verifiable facts. In the course of time that idea gained in influence also in history — which after all did cherish scientific pretensions -. As a result, in historical research an ever-increasing emphasis was placed on the study of historical sources as main criterion for scientific status. This gradually turned the *interpretation* of the sources into an ever more precarious matter. To put it more boldly: The more interpretation — and especially the freer such interpretation — of the source material, the greater the possibility for speculation and thus, the slighter the 'scientific character' of the research. Understandably, this sometimes resulted in an almost endless unraveling of source material of

which the relevance in the light of the original phrasing of the question was unclear. This 'positivist' form of historiography, in which the relevance of the phrasing of the question was willfully sacrificed to the 'scientific nature' that apparently gained in exercises on the square millimeter, was condemned by Bloch and Febvre. That is correct. But that is a whole other matter than the idea of Bloch and Febvre that insights from fields of science other than history could — and should — be used to explain historical development processes. This idea is the essence of positivism and is at odds with the basic principle of historicism, which holds that it is an illusion to think that there could at all be some pattern in historical developments. For if there were no 'patterns' in history, it would be useless to try explaining historical developments with patterns that are the outcome of other scientific disciplines.

2   Compare: Paragraph 2.2 - 2.4, pp. 40-42, preceeding.
3   That the criticism by Bloch and Febvre on the then French historical establishment now seems very dated, is exactly the result of the great influence the ideas of the *Annales* have gained in the second half of the twentieth century. Without exaggerating, one can maintain that history in its entirety little by little has become quite more '*Annale*' throughout the western world after the Second World War.
4   To be precise, that subtitle did not appear until 1947. Prior to that time, the journal sailed two other — though in basic principle similar — flags, namely: *Annales d'histoire économique et sociale* (from 1929 until 1938) and *Annales d'histoire sociale* (from 1939 until 1946).
5   The expression '*Annales-paradigm*' is introduced in the title of a book by Stoianovich (1976), which title hardly covers the contents. If one would like to learn more about the point of views of the *Annales*, I find that the methodological articles of Braudel (1969) be best consulted directly.
6   The great impact Braudel had in his heydays on the discipline is shown by the nickname he was known by in French historical circles: 'Saint Fernand'.
7   Braudel's most important methodological articles are summed up in: (Braudel, 1969).
8   In the literal meaning of the word there has never existed any 'school' in which historians were initiated into the methods propagated by the '*Annales* historians'. Nevertheless, in the long run such a large number of French professors of history developed from the ranks of the *Annales* and through their Ph.D. students they exerted such great influence on French historiography that the expression '*École des Annales*' gradually became internationally established.
9   Of all *Annales* historians, Pierre Groubert is the one whose work meets this criterion almost perfectly as is shown by the very titles of a number of his most important studies: *Familles marchandes sous l'Ancien Regime* (1959); *La*

vie quotidienne des paysans français au XVIIe siècle (1982); *La prostitution et la police des moeurs au XVIIIe siècle* (1987).

10 There is some point in that: What should we understand by 'Austria' in the nineteenth century or by 'Belgium' in the eighteenth century? What to do with the GDR after 1990? Would anyone like to tell what the territory of Yugoslavia is? To say nothing about national states that, if we take a sufficiently long period, sometimes do, sometimes do not and then suddenly do again exist: Estonia and Latvia for example.

11 (Le Roy Ladurie, 1977).

12 (Le Roy Ladurie, 1979).

13 (Goubert, 1960).

14 (Braudel, 1949).

15 Admitted, in a number of later *Annales* studies, the strict choice of the region concept as geographic definition is abandoned. See for example: *Histoire économique et sociale de la France* (Braudel & Labrousse (Red.), 1979-1982). Does this show that the *Annales* historians have later abandoned this concept? Well, hardly, because the thing is that throughout the world it apparently has become at length an ineradicable tradition to define handbooks in the field of economic and social history along national (German, French, English, et cetera) or supranational (European, Latin-American, et cetera) lines. When at the beginning of the seventies the need for a new French handbook arose, that worldwide custom apparently was stronger than the basic principles of the *École des Annales*: It was in fact impossible to publish a new French handbook without falling back on the main exponents of the *Annales*. With a monographic study such as *l'Identité de la France* (Braudel, 1986), it is different. In respect of this book one must ask oneself, in all sincerity, whether French nationalism in the long run has not been stronger than the first generation of *Annales* historian assumed. The book was published one year after the death of the writer and the title is thus at odds with the original ideas of Bloch and Febvre that I wonder if the title was Braudel's idea or that his publisher had a hand in it.

16 The question posed by Febvre comes close to an issue which was broached in the seventies by Carlos Castaneda, a then very popular anthropologist, in so-called new age circles. To illustrate that the type of questions with which Western anthropologists approach the 'strange' cultures studied by them cannot but lead to completely meaningless answers, because those questions have no meaning whatsoever within that culture itself, he reversed the roles in a thought experiment: With what questions, he assumed, would imaginary anthropologists from an isolated region in the Andes, studying the 'tribe' of Manhattan inhabitants approach the subjects of their study? Of course with questions they themselves, the Andes anthropologists, considered essential from their living environment. In other words: 'How often has a spell been

cast on you? Do you know who cast the spell and how it was cast? In what manner have you managed to break the spell?' Indeed one may correctly wonder whether the answers of the average NY cab driver to these questions provide meaningful information about the culture of contemporary inhabitants of New York. Strangely enough, Castaneda is considered a first class charlatan by part of his colleagues only and that is, in my opinion at least, surprising in the light of the highly unlikely adventures with which he spices his 'anthropological studies', but — to be honest — with this thought experiment, he hit the mark. For the fans: (Castaneda, 1968) and (Castaneda, 1972) present a representative summary of his ideas.

17 One may recall the adage of Collingwood, cited in the previous chapter: '... The history of thought, and therefore all history, is the re-enactment of past thought in the historian's won mind...' That statement comes unpleasantly close to that which the *histoire des mentalités* had in mind.

18 Famous examples, besides Febvre's 'original study' in this domain, are for instance; (Le Goff, 1957; Le Goff, 1981; Goubert, 1987). For a general introduction in the *histoire des mentalités*, see: (Le Goff, 1974).

19 Apart from the fact that the point of view that the past exclusively must be described solely in the terms of that past itself results in an impossible situation, as I tried to demonstrate, there is indeed something to be said against the concept 'national income' which only got meaning in the course of the twentieth century. In the seventeenth century already there are writers who have tried to estimate the material prosperity of for example the Dutch Republic or of England in a number that comes close to the modern concept of 'national income'. Examples of these writers include: William Petty, whose estimates date from 1665 and Gregory King who published in 1696. For an overview of national income estimates from before 1900 of England, France, Russia, the United States, Austria, Germany, Australia, Switzerland, Greece, India, Italy and Norwegian, see: (Studenski, 1958).

20 The unintended result was that dissertations prepared within the *Annales* tradition had the tendency to grow into an irrepressible size: The thickest book about the most minuscule regions, critics used to mock.

21 Remarkably enough, Fleury and Henry have themselves (as far as I know) never published in the *Annales* itself. Yet, the historical and demographic technique they had developed was of such great influence on a great number of other *Annales* historians that they nevertheless are generally rated among the *École des Annales*.

22 The model, with slightly adaptations, is adopted from Wrigley (1969).

23 Models are often named for the writer whose view they more or less represent in a structured form (remember the 'Keynesian model' from the textbooks). The term 'Malthusian' refers to Thomas Robert Malthus (1766-1834), an economist of the classical school who became famous for his population

theory, laid down in his *Essay on the principles of population as it effects the future improvement of society* (1789). He argues in that work, on the basis of two 'laws of nature' supposed by him (namely that the human population growth would grow via a geometric progression, while the means of existence could only increase arithmetically), that humankind is doomed to continuously balance on the edge of overpopulation. Every economic demographic model that assumes that improvements in the material circumstances in which people live will in the long run 'automatically' be undone by the population growth which is triggered by such improvement itself, is since then termed 'Malthusian'. The Malthusian theory is a classic example of a theory which has become world famous in economics and demographics despite the fact that it is based on demonstrable erroneous assumptions.

24 Ideally a careful analysis of the data should, as it were, gradually disclose to the researcher in which direction he should look for his explanatory model. A model embodies indeed no more and no less the connections of one certain view on a historical development process. Precisely because a researcher in principle can choose from an almost infinite number of different models (the saying 'so many men, so many options' applies just as much to 'views' and 'models') in practice it often boils down to the researcher's having one specific model in his mind in advance and — whether or not desperately — trying to squeeze the patterns which are observable into the frame of his more or less aprioristic model. See also the preceding paragraph 3.9 of this chapter.

25 Quite apart from this, one can also wonder in all seriousness whether it is at all advisable to go search for a comprehensive view on the historical development process as ultimate guideline in the quest for the right model. Personally I cannot escape the impression that such total views on history (Hegel, Marx, Toynbee, to mention a few) in the mild light of eternity seem to have been considerably more bound to time and place than their followers pretended. On the other hand, it cannot be denied that historians who allege to be completely free from such ideological dead weight, are also telling fibs a little. Everyone (not only historians) has something that one could label a perception of the world, however private, germinal, incoherent, self-contradictory, et cetera, and impossible to stick a particular label (Marxism, liberalism, conservatism, et cetera) to it. This perception of the world naturally helps determine the way one looks at the past and even the most professional aloof historian cannot escape this.

26 (Maddison, 1982: pp. 11-12).

27 Will the Malthusian model in fact really falter? Actually Malthus did not at all deny that epidemics and wars (he called these *positive checks*; which today sounds rather cynical) are among the most important causes of demographic crises? Yes, the Malthusian model indeed will falter here because in Malthus'

view such epidemics and wars are the inevitable *result* of a shortage of food and this is precisely the point which Le Roy Ladurie cannot prove!

28 Named for the 'classic' among the classical economists, David Ricardo (1772-1823), one of the first writers who in the tradition of the Classical School has given ample attention to the role of technological development in economic development. In the third edition (1821) of his magnum opus, *The Principles of Political Economy and Taxation* (1817), he added a separate chapter on this subject, 'On Machinery'. A 'Ricardian' view on economic development processes implies that technological development is considered the ultimate, decisive factor that can prevent that, as a consequence of diminishing returns, an on-going economic development process will inevitably result in stagnation.

29 One can indeed wonder in all honesty whether those are not two sides of the same coin: Malthus' supposed maximal growth of the available quantity of foods via arithmetical series after all, starts from — if indeed it is founded already on anything — a situation in which there is no technological development in agriculture. If one abandons this assumption, Malthus' arithmetical series will at the same time loose the very last remnant of reality value.

30 Compare: p. 64 ff, preceding.

31 See for example: (Wrigley, 1969, 1973; Wrigley & Schofield, 1981; Wrigley *et.al.*, 1997; Laslett, 1965; Laslett, (Ed.) 1972).

32 Slicher's own dissertation, *Een Samenleving onder Spanning: Geschiedenis van het Platteland in Overijssel* (Slicher van Bath, 1957) is one of the earliest examples in Dutch historiography which fits perfectly in the *Annales* tradition: Regional history about pre-modern times in which the 'common people' stand central, massively resting on statistical data for the foundations of his arguments, utilizing concepts adopted from the social sciences, and... very, very sizeable in form and elaboration.

33 In Dutch historiography the term 'Wageningse School' is applied to designate the institute of Slicher and his successors, which indicates that the studies from Wageningen are indeed about a very specific approach which is, for that matter, so strongly inspired by the *Annales*, that it is not exaggerated to speak of a Dutch *École des Annales*.

34 The large majority of the studies from the Gronings-Wageningse School were published in two series published by the institute itself: The so-called *A.A.G. bijdragen* and the series *Historia Agriculturae*.

35 Recall for example the work of Willem Frijhoff (1981; 1984; 1996) and Klaas van Berkel (1990).

36 See for example: (Wallerstein, 1974; 1980; 1983).

37 Compare: Chapter 4, following, in particular note 41, p. 117.

4 The advance of the new economic history in the United States

4.1 Two economic issues are essential after the Second World War

In the years following the Second World War two issues pressed to the forefront in macroeconomics, both of which emanated from social problems. In the first place, the issue whether a market economy tended towards equilibrium 'naturally' or whether this could only be realized through 'adjustments', in this case by the government. The background was formed by the spectrum of the persistent, worldwide depression of the thirties that had seriously damaged neoclassical confidence in the self-regulating capacity of markets.

In the postwar years the pioneering study of the English economist John Maynard Keynes, *A General Theory of Employment, Interest and Money* (1936), which was already published before the war, started to play a central role in this. Keynes had successfully demonstrated that as a result of a few minor, yet essential, changes to the current neoclassical model the reassuring performance of a freely functioning market economy that automatically restored equilibrium, disappeared like snow in summer. His theory implied that the government was granted an important, adjusting role. Imminent overspending should be counteracted by the government through tax increases and/or a reduction in government spending; in case of imminent under-spending, the government would then have to encourage domestic demand by reducing the tax burden and/or by decisively increasing government expenditures.

Now it appeared that the recently developed methods and techniques of mathematical economics and its empirical counterpart, econometrics, were pre-eminently suitable for research into the correctness of the Keynesian view on the economic process and moreover, that the results of such research (especially when the possibilities for the analysis of huge amounts of quantitative data increased at a great pace owing to the development of computers in the 1960s) yielded a 'byproduct' of utmost importance: Econometric simulation models of a country's economy for which basically a connection was established between the development of the national income, unemployment and the price level, and which appeared to be extremely useful to assess the effects of various government measures.

For the development of such econometric models one had to dispose of — preferably over as long a period as possible — time series of the various macroeconomic variables which were interconnected in the model, such as consumption, investment, government revenue and expenditure, export and import, price level and interest rates, labor force and unemployment level, et cetera.
Fortunately, before the Second World War already in a large number of Western countries various national statistical research bureaus had conducted substantial studies in this field, inspired by the work of the American economist Simon Kuznets, one of the founding fathers of the meanwhile internationally standardized system of national accounts.
Building on the work of Kuznets and others (in the Netherlands a central role in this was played by Jan Tinbergen, who later together with his Norwegian colleague Ragnar Frisch became the first winner of the Nobel Prize in Economics), in the 1960s in a great number of Western countries the first mature macroeconomic models were created with which the consequences of various economic and political measures could be simulated and for that reason, fulfilled a key role in the economic policy of the central government.

The second social issue that in the postwar period had a fundamental influence on economic science was the issue of economic development. The issue was acute in Europe itself in the first place: As a result of the acts of war, many European countries after 1945 were in a state of disaster. Their capital stock (including infrastructure) had been destroyed for a major part and the millions of victims claimed by the war, had caused a dire need of workers. It was generally feared that a period of prolonged poverty and want would offer a fertile soil for political radicalism, a development that had occurred in Germany as well after the First World War and that had already then been predicted in 1919 with an eerie precision by that same John Maynard Keynes in his *The Economic Consequence of the Peace*, the book he had written after he, as a high-ranking English diplomat, had walked out of the peace conference in Versailles, in protest against the plan — he considered disastrous — to ruin Germany as economic power by forcing it to pay a strangling amount in reparations.

Against the background of the rapidly deteriorating relations between the then Soviet Union and the rest of the allied countries, which heralded the Cold War, and the rapidly growing influence of the Soviet Union in Eastern Europe, a recurrence of the political instability which had arisen in Germany during the period between the wars, had to be avoided at any price, such was the view of the United States. In practice this, among other things, led to the establishment of NATO and the implementation of the Marshall plan. For economics this meant that economic development issues (how could one successfully encourage a process of economic development and what are the causes of prolonged economic stagnation and decline?) were placed high on the agenda.

A second factor (also emanating from the international political situation) was connected with the fact that in these years a growing number of countries in Asia and Africa, that before the Second World War often had had colonial status for many centuries, saw their aspirations for political independence crowned with success. Partly, because the relations with their former oppressors in the initial years of their independence for obvious reasons left much to be desired (to word it carefully), partly because the communist ideology in the form of various imperialist theories stated that in postcolonial times as well exploitative relations with the highly developed capitalist countries would determine the economic fate of the former colonies, and finally, because a relatively large number of the new political leaders in Africa and Asia had been trained in Moscow or Beijing, many of the countries that had recently become independent in Asia and Africa, drastically rejected the capitalist West and took refuge in seeking a rapprochement with Russia or China.

81

This development as well, against the background of the Cold War, was suspiciously looked upon by the United States. For economics, this meant a second reason to place the issue of economic development with top priority on the research agenda.

4.2 Accepted economic theory of those days is left empty-handed

Oddly enough, mainstream economic theory of these years was left empty-handed as far as the explanation of long-term economic development was concerned. The neoclassical paradigm had not much more to offer than the conviction that free markets in the long run offered the best guarantees for as great prosperity as possible for all countries. Even though the message of the *Wealth of Nations* (note the plural!) was formulated in a totally different manner in the years after the Second World War, than Adam Smith had in 1776, the essence of the message had not changed. And the annoying thing of course was that the neo-Marxist theories of imperialism had designated precisely the unrestrained operation of free market forces as the root cause of economic exploitation by the rich West of that which then was still insouciantly called 'underdeveloped countries'.

But even Keynesianism whose popularity was rapidly growing in those years, gave little to go on for the explanation of economic development. Unlike their neoclassical colleagues, the Keynesians thought the government had to fulfill an important adjusting role in maintaining economic equilibrium in the national economy; the matter, however, was that in a Keynesian theory, in essence it involves the conditions in which a cyclical equilibrium (that is a balance on the short term) can be maintained.[1]

The urgent need for an empirically soundly substantiated development theory for the long term, added to the fact that neither the neoclassical theory nor its Keynesian counterpart had much to offer in this respect, brought about a renewed interest on the part of theoretical economics in economic history. Although the meanwhile mathematically and econometrically heavily armed economists had looked down with some disdain on their historical colleagues who worked, in their eyes, with little accuracy, they could not deny that in the domain of economic history, the issue of economic development had been at the center of attention since its beginnings in the second half of the nineteenth century. Of course, it was hardly probable, but still, who knows, economic history might offer some clues for the foundations of a long-term theory for economic development.

4.3 Help from the side of economic history: Rostow's *Stages*

One of the first studies that resulted from this renewed rapprochement between theoretical economics and economic history was the book *The process of economic growth* from 1953 by Walt Withman Rostow, who in that same year was appointed professor of economic history at the famous *Massachusetts Institute of Technology*. In retrospect this book could be considered a — rather exhaustive — preliminary study for his — in terms of size considerably slimmer — *The Stages of Economic Growth* that appeared in 1960 and pre-eminently marks the change from traditional economic history (say, the offspring of the historical school) to the *new economic history*, the approach which in the sixties and afterwards, initially especially in the United States, and later on elsewhere in the world as well, would to an increasing extent predominate the domain.

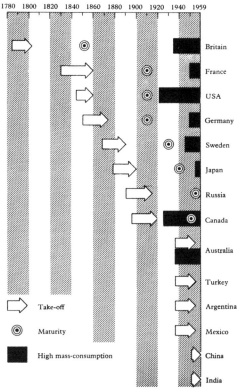

Chart of the stages of economic growth in selected countries. Note that Canada and Australia have entered the stage of high mass-consumption before reaching maturity. [By courtesy of the *Economist*.]

Fig. 4.1 Main chart of Rostow's *Stages of Economic Growth* (1960)

This hinge function of *The Stages* originates in two conditions: In the first place, Rostow, as is already suggested by the title of his book, in his approach obviously revived the tradition of the historical school. The standard method of the Historical School was to make use of the so-called phase theories in analyzing economic development processes[2], which otherwise rather had the character of exhaustive descriptions of typical characteristics of the different phases and, at best, the specification of the conditions in which one phase could change over into another. That tradition was carried on by Rostow. In his book he distinguishes five consecutive stages of economic development that a country would necessarily go through to become a modern, prosperous economy:

1   Traditional society;
2   Pre-conditions for take-off;
3   Take-off[3];
4   Drive to maturity;
5   The age of high mass-consumption.

What was new about Rostow's approach was that both in his choice of
the characteristics that distinguished one stage from the other and in
his specification of the conditions in which one phase would pass into
another, he fell back on concepts and theoretical insights which had been
derived directly from the modern economic theory, and at that point
precisely the Historical School had failed invariably. Basically, Rostow's
stages are distinguished from one another by different levels of real national income, while the main condition for transition from a modern
economy is formed — in his view — by a sudden increase in the ratio
of investment to national income, which implies an acceleration of the
growth of the capital stock, which in turn will result in an increase in
labor productivity.

The fact *The Stages* had been conceived on purpose to fill the gap that
arose as a result of the lack of an own 'capitalist' theory of economic development as counterpart of the various neo-Marxist exploitation theories which enjoyed great popularity in those years in western university
circles as well, is shown by the pugnacious subtitle Rostow endowed the
book with: *A non-communist Manifesto*. Rostow's book generated vehement discussion, among — and particularly between - economists and
economic historians, and intensified for that reason only the above-mentioned process of rapprochement between pure economics and economic
history.
This could not conceal that Rostow's view on the process of economic development had not emerged entirely undamaged from the debate. What
it came down to basically, was that he was told by his fellow economic
historians that his model was too rigid a straightjacket to do justice to the
great differences which, historically seen, seemed to have characterized
the long-term economic development of different countries. It cannot be
denied indeed that in this respect the shoe pinched unpleasantly here and
there: Rostow's own scheme, represented at the beginning of his book,
(see figure 4.1) shows that his consecutive stages are shuffled miserably
when he lets his model loose on countries where the development apparently transpired completely different than in the United Kingdom or in
the United States. Australia, for example, had already landed in *the age of*

high mass-consumption before there even was a proper *take-off* and similar anomalies may also be observed in other countries.

On the economics side, the main criticism on the contrary was that Rostow's theory of stages was not rigid enough: The conditions for one phase to pass into another were insufficiently specified according to theoreticians who were thinking in inflexible models, and would therefore in practice offer too little hold to the view developed in *The Stages* in the choice of the package of measures which in a specific situation would promote a successful economic development process.

4.4 Growth theory, national accounts and .... new economic history

The renewed interest — especially, as mentioned, in the United States — in economic long-term analyses within the economic theory generated at the American leading universities (the so-called *Ivy League Universities*) and at large economic research institutes, such as, for instance, the *National Bureau of Economic Research*, a tide of new research initiatives which may be divided into three categories.

In the first place, it concerned the development of (generally expressed in strict mathematical form) new economic theories aimed at the long-term explanation of the phenomenon of economic growth. The starting point for this was a study that was already published in 1928 by Cobb and Douglas (1928), entitled 'A Theory of Production', in which a so-called production function is introduced, that is to say a mathematical equation in which the output of an economic system (say, the annual production of a country) is related to the inputs, that is the quantities of production factors deployed (labor, land and capital) with which such production was achieved. On the basis of these (or similar) production functions it appeared that several growth theories could be developed. While in some cases a link was made with a Keynesian view on the economic process (the growth model of Harrod and Domar[4], for instance), resulting in a most unstable growth process, in other cases the neoclassical paradigm served as starting point, as in the growth theory of Robert Solow (1962), which yielded a much more balanced growth process. A problem with these first growth theories was that empirical testing of hypotheses derived from the theory, often was difficult, due to the complex mathematical form in which they were formulated.

Secondly, feverish activities were developed in the field of gathering, re-constructing and analyzing quantitative data which could throw light on the manner in which the economy had developed in the past. This was a field *par excellence* in which economists and economic historians, with their experience in searching archives for quantitative data, could work together productively. The development of econometric models became an essential analytical instrument for the economic policy of central gov-ernment during the 1960s in many western countries, and this required — preferably as long as possible — time series of the macroeconomic variables that in the model are related to each other. As a result of the painstaking work for many years by large numbers of collaborating re-searchers, gradually the national accounts of many countries since — ap-proximately — the beginning of the twentieth century, were published.

In the wake of this type of research, series were established that, strictly considered, did not belong to the national accounts, but that indeed were essential for the reconstruction of the course of economic development in the past, such as the development of the labor force and unemployment, the growth of capital, interest rates, et cetera.

The successful quantitative reconstruction of the economic development in the twentieth century, made it tempting also to examine whether it would be possible to go back further in time. The gloomy predictions on the part of many traditional economic historians, namely that such quantitative reconstruction for the nineteenth century — let alone for periods even further back in time — were doomed to fail, because of the lack of sufficient, reliable historical numerical data, proved to be without foundation.

After a modest start in the fifties by a small number of pioneers around the Russian-American economist Simon Kuznets[5] (1953; 1961; 1966; 1971; Kuznets, Moore & Spengler (Eds.), 1955), such as Moses Abramo-vitz (1956; Abramovitz & Eliasberg, 1957) and John Kendrick (1956; 1961; 1973)[6], in the 1960s and thereafter, a real upsurge in publications in which, first for the United States, then for many European and even for a number of South-American and Asian countries, the national accounts, sometimes in a rudimentary form, sometimes even surprisingly detailed, for a long series of years consecutively (in some instances even for the entire nineteenth century) were reconstructed. In some cases, it was pos-sible to even make a global quantitative outline of the economic situation in the second half of the eighteenth century.[7]

Thirdly, the renewed interest in long-term issues of pure economics had the effect of a rapidly increasing popularity of economic history (a subject which had previously had a marginal existence at economic faculties because of the diverging opinions resulting from economic theory that had come into existence in the first half of the twentieth century[8]) among economists (and students of economics!).

The new crop of economists were thoroughly trained in the methods and techniques of mathematical economics and econometrics, and that was exactly the reason why this renewed interest from the part of economics in economic history, started a methodological revolution within economic history: The ultramodern methods of mathematical economics and the advanced econometric techniques, to everybody's utter astonishment — and to the bewilderment of more traditionally oriented economic historians — apparently could be successfully applied to a multiplicity of economic history issues. The baffling result was that a great many traditional views on essential issues of economic history that for a long time had been cherished as being more or less firmly established, had to be rejected as incorrect.

The first signs of an approaching revolution in the domain, announced themselves more or less simultaneously: In the mid 1950s within a number of economic faculties of high ranking universities in the US.

4.5   The breakthrough (1): Conrad and Meyer's "The Economics of Slavery"

There are good reasons to consider the economic history workshop given by Alexander Gerschenkron in those years at Harvard University, as the starting point of the revolution. In the framework of this course, two of Gerschenkron's Ph.D. students, Alfred H.Conrad and John R. Meyer, had written an article entitled *The Economics of Slavery in the Antebellum South* (Conrad & Meyer, 1958) which immediately after its publication had triggered an unprecedented harsh debate.

In this study the two young authors had tried to answer the question whether the production of cotton by means of slave labor on the plantations in the south of the United States during the years preceding the Civil War, had been profitable. The question was of old politically seen to be highly emotionally charged in the United States: A major source of conflict in the American Civil War was indeed the abolition of slavery, and the Southerners had defended the preservation of the abject system continuously — but, as history teaches, in the end in vain — by arguing that the production of cotton by means of slave labor, from an economic point of view, was the mainstay of the South. Abolition of slavery would have meant, in their view, the definitive downfall of the, then, rich southern states.

After the Civil War this argument had fully disappeared under the table, but even a fledgling student of history would not have been surprised about it: Official historiography has indeed been always viewed from the perspective of the victors. In addition, the Abolitionists thought they had an argument that could pull the rug out from under the southern view in one fell swoop: The cotton price had shown a declining trend in the United States already since the end of the thirties of the nineteenth century and that decline had continued even after the end of the Civil War. How would it ever have been possible to base a flourishing economy on a sector in which apparently, given the price development, structural overproduction existed?

In other words, however politically tense the matter might be, the answer to the question Conrad and Meyer asked themselves in their study, for every right-minded economic historian was as sure as God made little green apples: The production of cotton by means of slave labor was not only utterly morally condemnable, but, from a strictly economic point of view, on the eve of the Civil War, it was meanwhile also obsolete, archaic and unprofitable. Slaves, so ran *communis opinio*, were held by the quasi highborn elite in the South, especially for reasons of prestige and grandeur, and that made the moral argument all the more pertinent.

To all appearances it would seem that Conrad and Meyer could attain little else with their study then, for the umpteenth time, to labor an obvious point; but... nothing could be further from the truth. The odd thing about it was that their study did not concern the interpretation of previously unknown file data: The records they had used, had been known for a long time already.

In fact, the only really new thing they introduced in their study was the method with which they approached the problem: Conrad and Meyer considered the problem simply and solely from a mathematical economic and econometric angle. Would it be possible, they wondered, to construct a mathematical economic model of the average cotton plantation and — supposing that it would be possible — what would simulations with that model yield when provided with quantitative data from the period immediately preceding the Civil War?

From that perspective, a slave could be considered simply as a capital good, employed in a firm. Just as any other means of production, slaves had an average life span, and within it, a certain productivity. Just as means of production, costs for energy supply and maintenance were also attached to slaves, even though such costs in this case were not called fuel, maintenance and repair, but: Food, clothing, housing and medical facilities.

And if it were possible — and against expectations it indeed appeared very much possible — to find reliable historical data on the average life expectation of slaves; the expenses that on average were incurred for food, clothing, housing, et cetera.; the costs for sowing seed for cotton growing; the storage of cotton, the means of transport needed to take the cotton to market and — certainly not insignificant — the quantity of cotton produced per year per slave on average, then the model would neatly compute whether the total number of activities — again, on average — would have been profitable or not in the period from which the data had derived.

To everyone's amazement, the model by Conrad and Meyer predicted, even with exceptional simulation parameters, that the production of cotton by means of slave labor in the years preceding the Civil War had been highly profitable. To align the thoughts: The best yielding agricultural firms in the United States about the mid-nineteenth century were the large grain farms in the Midwest. According to the computations of Conrad and Meyer that view had to be reviewed urgently: The vast cotton plantations in the South seemed to have been *at least* as profitable as the legendary grain farms in the Corn Belt. In all fairness, it should be added that in the model by Conrad and Meyer a second source of profit for the plantation economy had been built in, which — however odd it may sound — before that time had been overlooked by all authors on the subject.

89

Slaves, so they reasoned, produced not only cotton, but also... little baby slaves who, in the long term, could either be put to work on the plantation, or be sold by the owner. And because slave families on average had a surprisingly large number of children, this 'by-product' produced a high degree of profitability.

The *Economics of Slavery* was a bombshell in the field of economic history. In September 1967 the annual congress of the American Economic History Association was for an important part devoted to the economic aspects of slavery and, of course, the controversial study of Conrad and Meyer was the central point. In no time it appeared that the critics were divided into two camps. On the one side were the mainly very young economic history rebels trained in mathematical economics and econometrics, who attacked the two authors on the validity of their model and the accuracy of their calculations, but who were not per se opposed to

TABLE 11

ANNUAL RETURNS ON A PRIME FIELD WENCH INVESTMENT (WORKING ON LAND
WHICH YIELDED 3.75 BALES PER PRIME MALE FIELD HAND, ASSUMING A 7.5-CENT
NET FARM PRICE FOR COTTON AND FIVE "SALABLE"! CHILDREN BORN TO EVERY
WENCH)

Year from Purchase Date	Personal Field Returns	Child Field Returns	Child Sale Returns	Personal Upkeep	Child Upkeep	Net Returns
1.............	$56	....	....	$20	...	$ 36
2.............	40	....	....	20	$50	−30
3.............	56	....	....	20	10	26
4.............	40	....	....	20	60	−40
5.............	56	....	....	20	20	16
6.............	40	....	....	20	70	−50
7.............	56	......	....	20	30	6
8.............	40	$ 3.75	....	20	80	−56.25
9.............	56	7.50	....	20	45	−1.50
10.............	40	15.00	..	20	95	−50.00
11.............	56	22.50	....	20	60	−1.50
12.............	56	37.50	....	20	60	13.50
13.............	56	52.50	....	20	65	23.50
14.............	56	75.00	....	20	65	46.00
15.............	56	97.50	....	20	75	58.50
16.............	56	127.50	....	20	75	88.50
17.............	56	157.50	....	20	85	108.50
18.............	56	191.25	....	20	85	142.25
19.............	56	225.00	....	20	90	171.00
20.............	56	180.00	$875	20	75	1,016.00
21.............	56	210.00	....	20	75	171.00
22.............	56	157.50	875	20	60	1,008.50
23.............	56	180.00	....	20	60	156.00
24.............	56	120.00	875	20	40	991.00
25.............	56	135.00	....	20	40	131.00
26.............	56	67.50	875	20	20	958.50
27.............	56	75.00	....	20	20	91.00
28.............	56	....	875	20	...	911.00
29.............	56	....	....	20	...	36.00
30.............	56	....	....	20	...	36.00

Figure 4.2 Table from "The Economics of Slavery" by Conrad & Meyer (1958)

the econometric approach. On the other side stood the often somewhat
older, traditional economic historians, who were either baffled because
they simply did not grasp the essence of the method applied by Conrad
and Meyer, or felt deeply hurt by the nature of the study.

The latter is not completely incomprehensible: In retrospect one cannot
escape the impression that a certain desire to provoke was not strange to
the two young authors. What to think, for example, of their formulation
in the title of a notorious table from their essay (see Figure 4.2) in which
is calculated the net profit of a 'prime field wench' (read: Female slave),
during 30 years after purchase, assuming that during her 'productive life',
she bears five 'salable' children?

The lack of understanding on the part of the traditional economic historians culminated in a burning issue that repeatedly was put to the two
writers: To what plantation did the data used by them apply? Where had
that plantation been and to what years did their data refer? The his-

torically oriented reader will recognize these questions immediately as bearing on the reliability of the source material used, and he will not be surprised either that Conrad and Meyer caused their critics disbelief and desperation with their answer that such plantation did not exist at all and had never existed either, but that their calculations were based on the averages that had been computed for a large number of plantations. In econometrics the application of averages to estimate the course of certain developments is an absolutely normal practice, but historians still had (certainly in that time) a holy respect for the individual source, and estimating trends on the basis of averages was looked at with Argus' eyes, even so much so that according to some, the method applied by Conrad and Meyer did not belong in the field of economic history.

Furthermore, by passing over the moral aspect of slavery, "The Economics of Slavery" could not be judged otherwise, according to them, than a basically immoral and therefore improper paper, apart from the conclusions whether or not the plantation economy was profitable. The authors' response, through Alfred Conrad, was that they fully agreed with their critics as regards the moral impropriety of the system of slavery but that this was not discussed in their study, simply because it was beyond the problem definition, understandably added fuel to the flames. In the course of the afternoon, the discussion escalated into an ordinary quarrel, in which the exchange of abuse mounted to such an extent that the chairman, Moses Abramovitz, had great difficulty preventing the learned discussers from actually coming to blows. At the end of the meanwhile completely chaotic debate, both camps parted embittered and infuriated, without having come even a millimeter closer to each other.

On one point — but that had nothing to do with their research — Alfred Conrad and John Meyer had been completely mistaken. As they regularly told later on, it was their honest opinion that their "Economics of Slavery" was the definitive answer to the question about the profitability of slavery, and they expected that practically no one, after their study, would feel the need to once more analyze the matter on the basis of other data or another model. On the contrary. Already in the beginning of the 1960s, when the results of "The Economics of Slavery" were only known to a limited circle of insiders, the issue of the economic aspects of the system of slavery appeared to have become the topic *par excellence* for dissertation research into the American economic history, and after the tumultuous congress in 1967, an actual tide of new, cliometric research into the same subject arose, which finally resulted in the summarizing two-volume study by Robert William Fogel and Stanley Engerman, *Time on the Cross: The Economics of American Negro Slavery* (1974). The tumult surrounding the publication of this book did not remain limited, as with Conrad and Meyer, to the circle of American economic historians but even reached the columns of general periodicals such as in the United States *Time Magazine*, in England *The Times Literary Supplement*. The conclusions of that research were indeed so shocking that the commotion raised by this study was at least understandable. Don't let us run ahead of the story: Below I will come back to this.

4.6   The breakthrough (2): Fogel's *Railroads*[9]

Imagine that in a study on the economic development of the United States in the nineteenth century you would find a map in which a large number of canals are drawn and the accompanying text would analyze with great precision which differences in heights had to be bridged in their construction, what the costs of construction of those canals would have been and what regions would have been opened up by their construction (see Figure 4.3).

You leaf back and yes, the map, the hydraulic speculations and the financial calculations appear to refer to a system of inland waterways which was never *constructed*, but *probably would have been constructed*, had there been no railroads. You realize that there were indeed railroads in the United States around 1890 and resentfully you conclude that the person who came up with all those bizarre calculations probably cannot be denied a certain sense for the absurd, but that all this was certainly not intended to make a serious contribution to the history of the economic development of the United States in the nineteenth century.

That conclusion is wrong: The above study, Robert William Fogel's *Railroad and American Economic Growth: Essays in Econometric History*[10] (1964) was indeed intended to make a scientific contribution to the analysis of economic growth in the United Stated during the last decades of the nineteenth century.

A number of economic historians (among whom the above-mentioned Walt Whitman Rostow was the most prominent) put forward with certainty that the amazingly high growth rate of the American economy in the nineteenth century for an important part had been caused by the role the railroads had played in this process. The construction and the exploitation of the railroads, according to them, would have exerted a not to

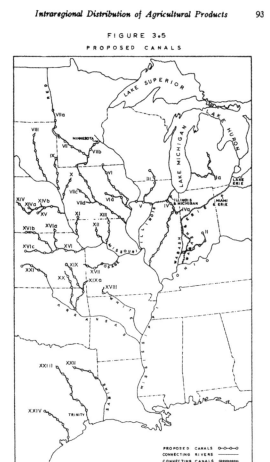

FIGURE 3.5

PROPOSED CANALS

Figure 4.3 Map with imaginary canals from Fogel's *Railroads* (1964)

be underestimated demand on American industry, and furthermore the reduction in transport costs caused by rail transport, had brought about a reduction in the prices of agricultural and industrial products that in the course of time had resulted in a sharp increase in sales.

Now Fogel had done nothing else in his *Railroads* but with iron logic expose the consequences emanating from the acceptance of this hypothesis, and test such consequences against quantitative evidence.

For what was the implication of the proposition that railroads had been an *indispensable factor* — a term coined by Rostow — in the economic development of the United States? Nothing more and nothing less, according to Fogel, than that the economic growth of the United States would have evolved less rapidly in the absence of railroads, and the only logical manner to test that, was to create an imaginary nineteenth-century America that was a dead ringer for the historical example, except that an elaborate system of waterways with canal boats had, in the imaginery example, taken over the role of the railroads.

A comparison of the economic growth scored in reality to a reconstruction of what might have been the economic growth in the imaginary counter-example, would give an indication of the importance of the railroads in the growth process. If that difference was substantial, the railroads had indeed been an 'indispensable factor' in the process. A small difference or - what in principle was also possible — if the reconstructed growth in a 'trainless' America would have been higher than the economic growth measured in actuality, than railroads would not have been a crucial factor in the economic development or would even, in the second instance, have been an impediment to growth.

Fogel calculated that in the United States, had there not been railroads, but if the existing country roads had been improved and a system of inland waterways had been built in those places where such had been technically possible and economically profitable, in 1890 a gross national product would have been obtained that as a consequence of the less efficient transport system would have turned out approximately 1 percent less than the actually scored figure in that year. Hence his conclusion read: "...Cheap transportation rather than railroads were the necessary condition for the emergence of the north Central States as the granary of the nation. The railroad was undoubtedly the most efficient form of transportation available to the farmers of the nation. But the combination of wagon and water transportation could have provided a relatively good substitute for the fabled iron horse...'

Fogel also attempted to answer the question to what extent the construction and exploitation of the railroads had increased industrial demand. The conclusion was that the railroads in 1859 at its highest would not have taken even 4 percent of the total industrial production and this made the proposition defended by *inter alia* Rostow that the construction of the railroads in the United States had played a crucial role in the American *Take-off* appear dubious, to say the least. Even for the iron industry, the railroads had been of only limited significance, which was primarily caused by the fact that after 1839 over 40 percent of the demand for rails was met by melting down old, worn-out rails to manufacture new ones.

The reason for the great expansion of the iron industry between 1845 and 1849 could hence, according to Fogel, better be attributed to the great demand for nails than the use of rails. In Fogel's own words: '...Nails rather than rails triggered the 1845-1849 leap in iron production. Indeed, the domestic production of nails, probably exceeded that of rails by over 100 percent...'

Immediately after its publication, *Railroads and American Economic Growth* was sharply criticized from various sides. The essential innovation Fogel had introduced in his book, the so-called *counterfactual analysis*, that is to say, the creation of an imaginary counterexample to determine the impact one specific factor had on the development of a complex historical process, particularly for the traditionally-oriented economic historians was like a red rag to a bull. One of them (Redlich, 1965) labeled the book in an uncommonly scathing review bluntly as *non-history:* The *counterfactual analysis* was considered to be in flat contradiction to the respect every historian should have for *facts*, if he wants his work to be eligible for serious study by his colleagues.

But Fogel also got it from his new economic history colleagues. Lance Davis (1968), Peter McClelland (1968; 1972), Albert Fishlow (1965; 1966) and Paul David (1969) passed severe criticism on Fogel's study, whereby — remarkably enough — not the counterfactual method applied by Fogel was the central object (apparently that was not denounced as non-historic at all by the new economic historians), but the manner in which Fogel, by means of this method, had arrived at his spectacular conclusions.

In essence their criticism was that Fogel had relied too much on the principle of 'big strides; home quickly'. Often, according to his critics, he had drawn so-called incontrovertible conclusions which, on further consideration, were based on appallingly few statistical data.

That Fogel's *Railroads* subsequently is to be considered pioneering research, is not so much a matter of the results — which on second thoughts proved to be far from unassailable, but of the methods and that precisely was the point on which he — just as Conrad and Meyer — had been fiercely denounced by the traditional economic historians.

It was, against this background, little surprising that the fight between traditional economic history and new economic history in the initial years was especially waged in the methodological area.

4.7 Methodological skirmishes with the traditionalists

In retrospect the methodological battle between the tradition-oriented economic historians and the new economic historians that was rather intense in the 1960s (an almost endless number of articles, yes, thick books were written on the subject[11]) strongly reminds one of the proverbial tower of Babel. The vehemence with which the warring parties harassed one another can only be understood when we realize that both camps sincerely believed to have a monopoly on the 'true' economic history and that both approaches, as was genuinely believed at the time, were mutually exclusive.

The most important reproaches the new economic historians heaped on the traditional economic history concerned the role economic theory played in the traditional approach and the matter that in traditional economic history there was little, if at all, testing of hypotheses. In one of the most understandable studies in this field, an article by Georges Murphy (1965), this criticism is based in outline as follows.

A traditional economic historian, when he makes a study of a certain subject, prior to his research will always have several more or less vague ideas about the course of the historic process and the reasons why that process went as it did. Those ideas, according to Murphy, should be regarded as a whole of implicit hypotheses regarding the course of the historical process in question. The fact that such hypotheses are not made more explicit, holds two risks.

In the first place, it is very well possible that the whole of implicit assumptions the researcher starts with, contains internal inconsistencies. Making the hypotheses explicit, preferably in the form of an economic theory, could bring to light the internal inconsistencies of the *a priori* selected assumptions.

Secondly, the danger looms (again: Precisely because the hypotheses remain implicit) that the set of hypotheses with which the research starts, will gradually change in the course of the study, under the influence of the interim results the researcher finds and — what is worse — such changes will occur largely unnoticed, so that the researcher invariably ends with that set of ideas (read: Hypotheses) which best fit the material he has studied. And again: Whether that new set of —unnoticeably changed — hypotheses in its entirety is logically consistent, is something that most researchers will hardly spent any thought on: For, his (most recent) ideas on the process 'explain' it excellently, and that was what it was all about, wasn't it?

It will be clear that in such a research strategy there is no room for the formal testing of hypotheses. The researcher ends — as already said — with exactly the set of assumptions which to his taste best match the material researched, thus: How would one be able to reject such a set, without throwing out the baby (one's own view) with the bath water?

There can be no doubt that the literary narrative method of which history (and hence the traditional economic history as well) avails itself, is miles away from the formal analytical method that is applied in the natural sciences[12], and if you are of the opinion that only those latter branches of sports merit the qualification 'scientific', than traditional economic history will be exposed, if only because of that literary narrative method, as non-scientific.

It should hardly be surprising that Murphy points out the use of 'the language of ordinary people' as main culprit for, in his opinion, the unscientific character of traditional economic history. That is why, he argues, it often happens that essential concepts ('Industrial Revolution', to name only one) remain vaguely defined, so that as the argument unfolds, the concepts may undergo an imperceptible shift in meaning, or may be used in an entirely different meaning by different authors. Likewise the use of words that in fact are used for reasons of style (for instance 'so'; 'therefore; 'it was crystal clear'; et cetera) often suggest causal connections that have not been verified on their tenability in any way, other than that the researcher himself is convinced that X is the result of Y, whereas further in the argument it is suggested that Y was the result of X: The word 'so' is, in a manner of speaking, so quickly typed that you don't even need the proverbial paper that won't blush.

It is, in short, in Murphy's opinion, the lack of exact character of the language of which the traditional economic history avails itself, that leads to different (and logically mutually exclusive) explanations for certain developments to coexist for a while, without it being very well possible to make an unambiguous choice on empirical grounds, while it also happens more than once that every explanation in itself shows internal inconsistencies.

Of course it is correct — and that is where Murphy undoubtedly scores points — that 'the language of ordinary people' offers more room for intrinsically inconsistent explanations than a formal analysis in the form of a mathematical model (mathematics has been called upon by the natural sciences and humanistic studies to expose logical inconsistencies in reasoning and argumentation!), but is it not true that from this line of that — in itself correct — conclusion Murphy starts to exaggerate?

Surely, it is by no means a feature specific to traditional economic history that different, mutually exclusive explanations coexist for a longer period. Indeed, without much difficulty, one could maintain that this is pre-eminently typical of science in general: As soon as there is universal consensus (perhaps plane geometry is a good example) every scientific discipline is doomed to become a dead science.

Furthermore, Murphy does not make it easy for his readers to follow him in his position that traditional economic history par excellence is teeming with inconsistent explanations, because he does not mention one single practical example in support of his theory. Nonetheless it could have been easily done. Let me try to give a concrete example of what Murphy apparently had in mind.

As already known, the Republic of the Seven United Netherlands was the wealthiest country in the world in the seventeenth century. Not only contemporaries were unanimously convinced thereof, but also modern research in which reconstructions of the real income per head of the population of the Netherlands and England (the second obvious candidate in that respect) are compared (Maddison, 1982), unambiguously points in that direction. An explanation for that evident wealth, which to this date is popular, considers two factors to be of decisive importance: First, the favourable geographical situation on the junction of the most important international European trade routes of that time and secondly, the mentality of the Dutch, which supposedly could be characterized as 'working hard and living frugally.[13] The highly developed work ethic would have led to a high labour productivity, whereas the proverbial frugality would have brought about a high saving rate and hence, a high investment rate. The two latter factors would in turn have been largely responsible for that which Van der Woude and De Vries (1995) have named 'the first round of modern economic growth'.

Somewhere in the last quarter of the seventeenth century this prosperity ended: The Dutch economy landed in a long process of economic stagnation[14], that would have been caused, among other things, by a general spirit of apathy, which would have seriously affected the work ethic and entrepreneurial vigor, with fatal consequences for the once so exemplary economic development process.

It may be clear that here the shoe badly pinches in the sense Murphy refers to: First the Dutch mentality is pushed to the fore as one of the important reasons for the economic revival in the seventeenth century, and the next thing is that this mentality — to which apparently something bad has meanwhile happened — is dug out again to explain the subsequent economic stagnation. This way, you can explain everything, but the reasoning is totally unsound: If you want to guard this 'explanation' for the Dutch economic development between the beginning of the seventeenth century and the first half of the nineteenth century against any inconsistencies, you would have to at least make plausible *why* that mentality has changed so drastically in the course of time, and that is precisely what is lacking in the story.

The followers of the new economic history, now, thought that economic history — at least for the greater part — could be protected against such unscientific, faulty reasoning by fitting its practitioners in a straightjacket: In the first place, every argument suggesting an explanation for a given development, in their opinion, should be based on connections taken from economic theory, whereby the theory used would have to be explicitly raised in advance, preferably in the form of a mathematical economic model. This would, according to the new economic historians, in any case protect economic history for the two points of which Murphy had accused the traditional variant: Vague and hence ambiguous definitions and inconsistent arguments. In the second place, the explicit use of the economic theory would open the possibility to test, on the basis of connections predicted by the theory, the assumed relations against historical statistical material, in fact in exactly the same manner as in econometrics the accuracy of certain economic theories are tested against recent statistical data.

99

The inevitable consequence of this approach is that the supposed explanation is always expressed in averages[15]: The model describes at best how the system *as a whole* is set up, but this has absolutely no effect on the fact that *individual* elements in the system can show behavior that diverges from the tendencies described by the model. And the consequence of that is, in turn, that the importance of the individual historic source as the empirical foundation par excellence for historiography is reduced immensely. The careful study of the original sources, that in traditional economic history plays a key role in the assessment for 'scientific quality', fades into the background, simply because the interest of the individual historic source is pushed to the background by the model-based approach. Instead, another question pushes itself to the fore: Is the entire historical statistical evidence (in practice almost always a sample survey) against which I want to test a given economic theory indeed representative for the system the model is supposed to describe?[16]

This was basically the last item on which the tradition-oriented economic historians denounced new economic history. Did the youthful revolutionaries tell them that their method was not scientific? According to them there were still some things to be said about that, but on one thing there could be no two ways about: Whatever the new economic historians did — at best perhaps an eccentric form of applied economics — it was not in any case history, because *not the exact historical facts* were central to the analysis, but *the properties of the system within which these facts had been interrelated* by the researcher. [17]

Around the beginning of the 1970s, when the methodological skirmishes in the United States had more or less subsided and the new economic history had gradually also gained in popularity outside the US, a similar scrimmage took place all over again in Europe. In The Netherlands as well a number of articles was published in which adherents and opponents crossed swords with each other and the Dutch *Tijdschrift voor Geschiedenis* (Journal of History) in 1969 even devoted a complete theme number to that subject, entitled: *Nieuwe wegen in de economische geschiedenis* (New ways in economic history).[18] In that framework, an adherent of the traditional view summarized the difference between the two points of view in nicely measured words: '... A historian is a portrait painter and an economist is not...'

A second point of criticism of the new economic history from the traditionalistic side was the explicit use of *counterfactuals* in research[19] (I already briefly touched upon this when discussing Fogel's *Railroads and American Economic Growth*). Again it concerned the point that historians, according to the traditionalists, should strictly limit themselves to historic factual material, and to create an imaginary historical world to assess the influence of one single factor on a certain development process would be inadmissible in serious historical research, if only for that reason. The response of the new economic historians[20] was that always and everywhere the existence of a causal connection is assumed, in fact a counterfactual is also implicitly or explicitly introduced and that certainly is not exclusive to the new economic history. An example might help.

He who claims that the decisive reason for the victory in the battle of Azincourt was formed by the infantry of the British (archers on foot), who because of their relatively lighter weapons could operate much faster than the French army of cumbersome, heavily armored mounted knights — and to the best of my knowledge you cannot find one historian who doubts this — also implicitly introduces an imaginary historical world: *If* the British had not had their archers on foot, *then* the battle of Azincourt would have had a different ending. The gist of the matter, according to the new economic historians, is not the use of counterfactuals per se — because this is, as already said, inextricably bound up with every statement in which a cause-effect relationship is suggested — but whether the counterexample forms a plausible alternative that from a historical perspective would have been equally possible: That the British at Azincourt would not have had archers at their disposal, but had also brought armoured knights on the field, is a totally reasonable alternative over which no historian has ever stumbled. The allegation, however, of a kind such as 'if the French had had machine guns (and the British had not), they would have won the battle of Azincourt', is bizarre dreaming which has nothing to do with the serious study of history.

Hence, the key question is whether Fogel in his *Railroads* — for that was *ad nauseam* the bone of contention in this connection — with his counterfactual in the form of an expansion of the carriage of goods by water in the supposed absence of railways had offered a reasonable historical alternative. The answer to this latter question could not be other than affirmative: The carriage of goods by water was indeed done at that time in the United States and the assumption that in the absence of railways greater use would have been made of this possibility appears to be a completely reasonable historical alternative.

The debate about the admissibility of counterfactuals after all did yield a clear response, despite the rather obscure character of the discussion itself: The question about the admissibility in itself is pointless, because every causal connection implies a counterfactual. The heart of the matter is whether or not the counterfactual introduced, offers a reasonable historical alternative. And the only difference in this matter between the traditional economic history and the new economic history is that the new economic historians have the tendency to make their counterfactuals explicit, whereas the traditional economic historians usually refrain from doing so.

In the first half of the 1970s the methodological conflicts between the traditionalists and the new economic historians gradually faded into the background. This had not so much to do with the fact that in the long run a certain degree of consensus had arisen.[21] That was, given the fact that indeed two fundamentally divergent approaches of economic history were involved, not very well possible either. It had more to do with the fact that the new economic history, after the sixties had come to an end, began to supplant traditional economic history at a high speed, at any rate in the United States. Chairs in economic history which fell vacant (that is to say, for the time being exclusively chairs linked to economic faculties) at American top-class universities, were given, almost without exception, to new economic historians, whereas (again through appointment of new economic historians to the editorial staff) also leading scientific journals in the field of economic history, such as the *Journal of Economic History*, gradually put aside their initial reserve against the new approach. Without exaggeration, you could maintain that the new economic history, at least in the United States, started to play a predominant role in the discipline in the course of the seventies.

4.8 The new economic history becomes a hot topic

In the foregoing, I have spent rather much attention on the study by Conrad and Meyer on the economic aspects of slavery and Fogel's analysis of the role of railways in the economic growth of the United States in the nineteenth century, which may be justified on account of the fact that both, in retrospect, are pre-eminently considered milestones in the early historiography of the new economic history, as appears from the heated and lengthy discussions which both studies triggered among their colleagues.

It would, however, be a misrepresentation to conclude from the above that the publication of their work and the subsequent debate all at once created a new approach in the discipline.

Figure 4.4 The *Hermann C. Krannert School*, faculty of economics of *Purdue University*, cradle of the New Economic History

In the above, I already pointed out that since the the the end of the 1950s, say, since the publication of *The Stages of Economic Growth* by Rostow, a number of economic faculties in the United States had started economic history research that in terms of methods and techniques made a clean break with the past. The academic institute that was the most outspoken cradle of the revolution, was *Purdue University*. At Harvard, Alexander Gerschenkron's workshops produced a genuine torrent of new economic history talent. In addition to the already mentioned Alfred Conrad and John Meyer, others were also trained there, including Peter Temin, Albert Fishlow and Paul David. A second important source were the students of the earlier mentioned Simon Kuznets, among whom one finds the names of Richard Easterlin, Robert Gallmann, Lance Davis, Robert William Fogel, Stanley Engerman and Douglass North. The surprising thing about this list is the circumstance that all these names put together with that of the already somewhat older Moses Abramovitz, who played some sort of father role; present a rather complete picture of the young economic historians who in the 1960s started a methodological revolution in American economic history.

In the first years, two research centers were of crucial importance to the development of that which soon was to be called *new economic history*: The *National Bureau of Economic Research (NBER)* in Cambridge (Mass.) and the already mentioned *Purdue University* in the small town of West-La-fayette in the State of Indiana. At the end of the fifties, the NBER launched a big research program devoted to quantitative long-term analysis of American economic development, for which a long and intensive cooperation was established between a large number of prominent economists and mostly young, quantitatively trained economic historians.[22]

Purdue University in the sixties was a true hotbed of revolutionary activities in the field of economic history. Two new economic historians of the first hour, Lance Davis and Jonathan Hughes, who were connected to the economic faculty of this university, worked together on this with a mathematician, Stanley Reiter[23], who developed statistical procedures with which large quantities of quantitative historical data could be analyzed with the help of a computer.[24] The cooperation between Hughes, Davis and Reiter and others at Purdue led to a number of studies in which elaborate experiments with the new methods and techniques were conducted.[25]

The incidental meetings at Purdue University gained an institutional character in December 1960, when Lance Davis and Jonathan Hughes, on the basis of the reputation their group had meanwhile built in the field of that which then was still called *quantitative economic history*, were granted by the university a budget to annually organize a small conference at which young economic historians of other universities who engaged in the same work, were invited to West-Lafayette to exchange thoughts with each other and present new work. The performance of Robert William Fogel — before that time an unknown within the small world of new economic historians — at the first Purdue conference did not fail to make a stunning impression: '...Always early in the morning he would start a discussion,' one participant still remembers, 'and always at the end of the afternoon he was still engaged in the same debate...'[26]

That something special was going on in American economic history gradually became apparent also beyond the small circle of insiders. In 1964, the *American Economics Association*, during its annual congress in Chicago, for the first time dedicated a separate meeting to recent developments in American economic history. The meeting attracted over 200 interested people, an extremely large number, compared to other sessions. Samuel Williamson, at the time research assistant of Jonathan Hughes, who was charged with organizing the annual Purdue seminars, discovered on that occasion that some highly prominent economists were deeply offended when they found they had not been invited to the annual new economic history meetings in West-Lafayette.[27] New economic history apparently had become a *hot topic* among economists within a few years' time.

4.9 The long march through the institutes:
The NEH sweeps through the USA

That the new economic history among economists during the 1960s so rapidly gained prestige, had as a consequence that the fight between traditionalists and economic history modernists, in the United States at least, in the course of the 1970s definitively turned out to the advantage of the latter group.[28]

The success of the new economic history was so overwhelming that the movement by the end of the sixties had outgrown her main cradle. Purdue University is a modest member of the Ivy League — the informal, but highly prestigious club of American top universities — and the demand for new economic historians from other, more famous, universities was so great that finally even at Purdue there was not a single new economic historian to be found. Lance Davis went to the California Institute for Technology, Jonathan Hughes left for the Northwestern University in Chicago, and Nathan Rosenberg, who had also been connected to Purdue for some years, following a visiting professorship at Harvard University received an appointment at the university of Wisconsin.

Even the new economic historians, who had never been connected to Purdue, but who did participate in the annual Cliometric Seminars, throughout the years in surprisingly large numbers landed on the most prestigious chairs. Douglass North, who was older than the rest of the group, in the initial years of the new economic history already was professor of economic history at the University of Washington: In fact, he was the guru of a large number of later new economic historians, among whom Lance Davis and Jonathan Hughes. At Harvard the *éminence grise* of the discipline, Alexander Gerschenkon, was succeeded by the most revolutionary new economic historian of all, Robert William Fogel, who nevertheless some years later still gave preference to what was then the Mecca of pure economics, the economic faculty of the University of Chicago. The person who had worked together most frequently with Fogel, Stanley Engerman, received an appointment at the University of Rochester. Paul David became, next to Moses Abramovitz, the second economic historian at Stanford University, while Peter Temin accepted an appointment at MIT. In less than 10 years' time, after the first meeting at Purdue in December 1960, there was hardly a chair in economic history at the Ivy League economic faculties that was not held by a new economic historian.

For the same reason — the new economic history became 'too big' for the modest West-Lafayette - the annual Cliometric Seminars were moved in 1970 to the University of Wisconsin, while as of 1979 the University of Chicago became the temporary home base. Because the conference meanwhile could count on structural financing from the National Science Foundation, the venues changed regularly afterwards.

In 1983 it was decided to establish an own — that is, separate from the already existing Economic History Association — professional association, the so-called Cliometrics Society, which soon had a few hundreds members and began to publish its own newsletter, *The Newsletter of the Cliometric Society*. Two years later, in the spring of 1985, the new economic history had become so popular in other countries besides the United States, that it was decided to organize an international congress for the first time. Joel Mokyr, Donald McCloskey and Samuel Williamson (in fact already a second generation of new economic historians) organized at Northwestern University *The First World Congress of Cliometrics*, which attracted over ninety participants, 20 percent of which from outside of the United States. In the following years it became apparent that the new economic history had obtained a firm footing within economic history elsewhere in the world as well. The second World Congress was held in

1989 in Spain, while the third was organized in München in 1997 by John Komlos. The last congress had about a hundred participants of which the majority (63 percent) did not come from the United States.[29] The fourth cliometric world congress, in terms of organization much more modest than the congress in München, was held in Toronto in 2000.

4.10   The 1970s and 1980s: The cliometric colonization of the western world[30]

The rising star of the new economic history in the United States in the 1960s did not stay unnoticed in the rest of the world in the long run, but because in most European countries after the Second World War, economic history became increasingly popular in especially the faculties of arts[31], whereas in economic faculties it managed with the greatest difficulties to hold out at best[32], the process of acceptance got of the ground with difficulty[33], despite the fact that a large number of American new economic historians often delivered guest lectures outside of the United States. Only in Canada[34] and — but here only in part — in the United Kingdom there was a reasonably easy acceptance of the new methods.

The result was that, while in the United States new economic history had already become the order of the day, the revision of the economic history of European countries on cliometric grounds was made primarily by Americans, sporadically in cooperation with their European colleagues: A sort of cliometric colonization process of Europe by the United States. In fact, this had started already in the sixties: Many of the first cliometric studies done by the group surrounding Jonathan Hughes at Purdue University (1967) related to English history.

In the 1970s this development became much more visible. For the eighteenth and nineteenth century England the traditional view on the origin and development of the Industrial Revolution was brought up for discussion by several American economic historians.[36] A vehement discussion arose about the question to what extent the fact that England by the nineteenth century from an economic point of view had been surpassed by the United States and Germany could be attributed to the failure of English entrepreneurs from the Victorian era. The new response was — against all accepted wisdom of the time — : Hardly[37], but that response was again considerably put into perspective in the second round of the debate.[38]

In the long run there was hardly any branch of English economic history where the American new economic historians were not one way or the other attempting to undermine the traditional views with new methods

and techniques and — as happened earlier in American economic history — often this indeed led to interpretations divergent from the generally accepted views to such an extent, that by analogy with what had earlier happened in American economic history — the famous *Reinterpretation of American Economic History* edited by Fogel and Engerman (1971) — in 1981 a revision of English economic history on the basis of the recent research was published (Floud & McCloskey (Eds.), 1981).[40]
The 'colonization' by the new economic history of other countries did not remain limited to England. In the seventies and eighties, the sphere of activity of the cliometricians extended to almost all European countries[41], with the exception of the Eastern bloc: The intellectual climate which in those years was still dominated by Marxist historians was hardly conducive to the spreading of this type of pseudo-historical exercises perverted by capitalism. The contacts of the American new economic historians with the East-European and Russian colleagues were for that reason scarce; it was rather a bother to obtain quantitative historic data on these countries and even if one did get them, it was extremely difficult to form a well-founded opinion on the reliability of such data.[42]

By the end of the 1970s and in the 1980s, also the economic development of non-western countries was gradually submitted to a cliometric examination. The fact that in general[43] the wash was considerably poorer here, was caused by the fact that historical statistical data for these countries usually are more scarce than in most western countries[44]. The flood of cliometric studies by — primarily — American authors on non-American countries, gradually brought about an increase in the interest for new economic history among the Europeans — and even later still — non-western economic historians, in any case, insofar as they had an economic background. In part because of the European-American exchange programs, which in these years could boast an increasing popularity, the cliometric methods and techniques finally took hold also outside of the United States.

It is, I think, not an exaggeration to state that by the end of the 1970s, the academic economic history research outside of the United States was dominated by a rigorous quantitative analytic approach, which pushed the earlier prevalent literary history method at least to the background. The split in economic history between those with an economic training and those with literary history training in the United States — the result of a second *Methodenstreit* which in the United States had heralded the beginning of the cliometric revolution — had thus become a fact in the rest of the world as well.

Notes

1 Think of the phenomenon that in the so-called simple Keynesian model, investment indeed does play a role in the analysis, but its effect on the capital stock, is left out. In other words, only the effect that the volume of investment has on national income is reckoned with in the Keynesian model. The fact that net investment means an increase in the capital stock and that such in the longer term could produce an increase in productivity, is purposefully disregarded '...In the long run, my dear Marshall, we are all dead...,' Keynes is supposed to have replied, according to reports, when his master, the great neoclassical economist Alfred Marshall, pointed out to him this deficiency in his theory.

2 Compare chapter 2, par. 2.9, p. 46 ff, preceeding.

3 The metaphor is derived from the take-off of an aircraft and the importance of the metaphor is that Rostow assumed a rather abrupt transition from the second to the third phase. Subsequent research showed that this abruptness in practice is usually not all that obvious.

4 Roy Harrod (1939; 1948) and Evsey Domar (1947) had already published a similar Keynesian growth model prior to the 1950s. Only by the end of the fifties, when growth theory started to occupy a place of ever higher importance in economic theory, that part of their work still became the focus of attention.

5 Simon Kuznets was awarded the Nobel Prize for economics in 1971.

6 However important the work of these pioneers may have been, it is not that they, either in the United States or elsewhere, from the absolute nothing had to gather their series in general. Often there were much older estimates which at the time when they had been published, were given little attention because in the then accepted economic paradigm, this type of data was not considered of high importance.

7 Angus Maddison (1982) has brought together most of such estimates conveniently arranged and moreover, he has made them mutually comparable. He adapted the material into annualized estimates of the real gross domestic product, the size of the population, employment, sectoral employment structure, and average labor productivity, volume of capital, price indices for consumer non-durables as approach to changes in the cost of living, and the export volume of Australia, Belgium, Canada, Denmark, Germany, Finland, France, Italy, the Netherlands, Japan, Norway, Austria, the United Kingdom, the United States, Sweden and Switzerland for the period 1870 up to 1979 inclusive. In a limited number of cases he even expands his estimates to 1700(!). In later work by Maddison (1989) estimates are also given to six Latin-American (Argentina, Brazil, Chili, Colombia, Mexico and Peru) and nine Asian countries (Bangladesh, China, India, Indonesia, Pakistan, the Philippines, South Korea,

Taiwan and Thailand), as well as some series for Russia. Much of this material was adapted by himself and by his Ph. D. students during his professorship at the University of Groningen. After his retirement, he extended his research for an even larger number of countries for an even larger period of time, while his work was also continued under the leadership of his student Bart van Ark in the *Groningen Growth and Development Centre.*

8   Compare chapter 2, par. 2.9, and further, above.

9   This paragraph is in part derived from (Drukker, 1980a).

10 Remark: There is no *economic* in the subtitle, but *econometric* and that was certainly no coincidence. The new economic historians wanted to distinguish themselves clearly in these years from 'ordinary' economic history. The compilation in which the famous study by Conrad and Meyer was reprinted and which also appeared in 1964, was entitled *The Economics of Slavery and other studies in econometric history.*

11 A small selection: (Andreano (Ed) 1970; David 1964, 1971; Davis 1966, 1968; Desai 1968; Fogel 1964a, 1965, 1966, 1967, 1970, 1979; McClelland 1975; Murphy 1965, 1969; Murphy & Mueller 1967; North 1963, 1965; Redlich 1965, 1968).

12 And who, in imitation of natural sciences, in the course of the nineteenth and twentieth century increasingly gained influence also in most human sciences. See chapter 2, paragraph 2.2 to 2.4, above!

13 The second factor (mentality) is not based solely on popular ideas on the Dutch national character, as is often illustrated by national songs of the high strapping-fellows-tough-guys calibre. Max Weber (1905; reprint 1992) wrote at the beginning of the twentieth century *Die protestantische Ethik und der Geist des Kapitalismus*, in which he argues that an essential precondition for the emergence of capitalism was the very specific pattern of standards and values, whose origin he sought in orthodox Protestantism about the beginning of the seventeenth century. He supported his view by pointing out that the earliest forms of a capitalist economy in the western world originated precisely in those communities where strict variants of Calvinism played a dominant role, whereby he mentioned seventeenth-century Netherlands as the most important example. Weber's study became world famous: The relation he supposed existed between the capitalist mentality and the Calvinist morality to this day is known as 'Weber's thesis'. And although by no means unchallenged, it is not that Weber's supposed relation between Calvinism and capitalism whereby indirectly a connection is made between the mentality of the Dutch in the seventeenth century and the conspicuous wealth of the Republic (for capitalism created the preconditions for a remarkable fast economic development for that time) has meanwhile landed on the historical rubbish dump of old rarities. A modern — and renowned — historical study on the Republic in

109

the seventeenth century as *The Embarrassment of Riches* (Schama, 1987), for instance, is really full of it. See also the foregoing Introduction, pp. 13-17.

14 Johan de Vries (1959) was the first to show that the economic stagnation process in the eighteenth and the beginning of the nineteenth century probably had a relative rather than an absolute character.

15 An economic model is after all nothing more than a schematic representation of the manner in which various variables in a certain economic system are supposed to influence one another and that explicitly does not imply that *every individual element* in that system will have to behave strictly as predicted by the model: If in a certain model a positive connection is assumed between, for example, the level of expenditures and income, this does not mean that every consumer expands his consumption by y percent if his income increased by x percent, but only that the *average* level of consumption expenditures increases by y percent if the *average* income increases by x percent.

16 Perhaps unnecessarily and also, to emphasize the contrast, a bit of a caricature serves as an example: Suppose that a traditional economic historian and a new economic historian both conduct research into the development of assets in the past on the basis of notarial inventories. The question on the foreground for the traditional-oriented researchers is whether inventories constitute a correct description of the estate of the deceased. The new economic historian will in first instance wonder about the size of the population group at that time that was so poor that no notarial inventory at all was made upon their death.

17 The criticism from the traditional side on the new approach is considerably less than the other way round. The best known criticism on the new economic history is from Redlich (1965; 1968). The first words in the title of the article by Lance Davis (1968) '"...And it never will be literature...": The New Economic History: A Critique', beautifully expresses the essence of the traditionalist criticism in short, but smartly puts the reader on the wrong track. The quotation is to be interpreted ironically, because the tenor of Davis' article is pro new economic history and not contra.

18 See, for example: (Schöffer, 1965; Slicher van Bath, 1969; De Jonge, 1969; Drukker 1973; Van der Wourde, 1973; Van Stuijvenberg, 1977; Baudet & Drukker, 1977).

19 The problem is analyzed in great detail in: (McClelland, 1975, particularly chapter 4).

20 Through, among others, Fogel (1967), Green (1968), North (1968), Cochran (1969) and Davis (1971).

21 The most extreme attempt to reconcile, came, surprisingly enough, from the side of Fogel (1979), who in earlier publications had showed himself to be one of the fiercest critics of traditional economic history. In the article entitled '"Scientific" History and Traditional History', he argues that the method of

traditional history greatly resembles the manner in which in legal proceedings it is endeavoured to furnish evidence that something has happened exactly in this or that manner, where the structural context within which those events transpired, at best play a background role. In 'scientific' history (needless to say: New economic history, among other things), this is exactly the other way around. Both approaches have a right to exist, but the essential difference is that they each try to respond to a different type of question, which explains their difference in method. This, according to Fogel, does not mean, however, that they are mutually exclusive or even that they have an antagonistic relation: "..Thus, while "scientific" and traditional history are different, and in some respects, competing modes of research, they are neither mutually exclusive, nor intrinsically antagonistic. Quite the contrary, precisely because each mode has a comparative advantage in certain domains of research, they supplement and enrich each other. It seems reasonable to believe that as the tendency toward the interpretation of the two modes continues, the intensity of the cultural conflict between the two will diminish...' (Fogel, 1979, p. 43). Remember, Fogel wrote these words in 1979. Ten years earlier, when the battle between the traditionalists and the new economic historians was at its height, his position was considerably more uncompromising.

22 The *Conference on Income and Wealth* in 1957 which was organized jointly by *NBER* and the *American Historical Association* may be considered one of the first meetings at which it became clear that a revolution in American economic history was about to set in. During the sessions on economic history, Walt Whitman Rostow (1957) presented a paper on the relation between economic history and economic theory, in which the traditional point of view evidently predominated so that the conclusion was the two camps had little to part with each other. However, also up for discussion during that same session was the famous paper by Conrad and Meyer (1957) entitled 'Economic Theory, Statistical Inference and Economic History', which may be considered as the methodological basis of the new economic history.

23 It was this mathematician who has coined both the words *new economic history* and *cliometrics* for the new approach in economic history. *Cliometrics*, a bizarre contraction of the name 'Clio' and the suffix '-metrics' which suggested that something was measured, was initially meant as nickname — derived from another, not seriously intended, discipline *theometrics* which, according to reports, would engage in issues such as the problem of how many angels could at the most sit on a pin-head —, but took root in the United States, besides *new economic history*. Elsewhere in the world, only the term *new economic history* found acceptance.

24 Statistical computer programs, as we know them, were then still unknown, just as PCs. The data had to be entered beforehand on punched cards, after which for every statistical test an individual program had to be written to

analyze the information in question at the one big central computer — the so-called *mainframe* - that the university had at its disposal. Computer time at such a mainframe was so costly and scarce that it was divided in units of seconds over the members of the university, whereby the amount of computer time allotted was determined by the status of the discipline and of the scientist in question: A professor of mathematics was allotted considerably more computer time than an economics lecturer, for instance. Thus, how it was in that respect with a few lecturers who engaged in something as obscure as economic history goes without saying. A small unnoticed error in the software was in those circumstances a real disaster: Costly computer time was lost, without workable results coming out.

25 The most important ones of these early studies were compiled in (Purdue, 1967). A special place is occupied by 'The First 1945 British Steamships', an article by Hughes and Reiter (1958), which according to tradition would have been one of the very first studies in which a computer was used to analyze quantitative historical data.

26 See: (Williamson, 1991: p.20).

27 (Williamson, 1991: p.22).

28 That is to say, for the time being exclusively within economic faculties. The chairs in economic history which had their home base in the faculties of arts, remained firmly in the hands of the traditionalists. That is understandable: In the faculties of arts, the very language in which the new economic historians were communicating with one another was often not understood. The result was that in fact a division in economic history occurred, whereby from a scientific angle the representatives of the traditional variant were gradually marginalized because the new economic historians with revolutionary drive started to occupy key positions in the American professional association of economic historians (the American Economic History Association) and in the editorial staffs of leading scientific journals. So, John Meyer (who together with Alfred Conrad had written the controversial *The Economics of Slavery in the Antebellum South*) had joined already in 1955 the editorial staff of *Explorations in Entrepreneurial History*, which turned this journal (the name was later changed into *Explorations in Economic History*) into the first leading publication possibility for the new economic history within the discipline of economic history. In 1960, Douglass North, a new economic historian from the very beginning, and William Parker, an older economic historian who later had converted to new economic history, constituted the editorial staff of the most important economic history journal, *The Journal of Economic History*. Nevertheless it took until the second half of the sixties before *The Journal of Economic History* regularly published work from new economic historians. Until that time, the publication opportunities of the group were mainly restricted to the *Explorations* and the specialist journals in the field of economics. In a

cliometric (!) study of the acceptance of cliometrics in the leading economic history journal, *The Journal of Economic History*, Robert Whaples writes: '... The data validate the conventional wisdom, showing that the cliometric revolution swept the profession, as indicated by this JOURNAL's articles, in the 1960s and 1970s. Annual data show that the period of most rapid growth was between 1965 and 1970, when the cliometric portion of pages grew from one-eight to one-half. (...) By the 1980s cliometrics dominated the field, making up over 80 percent of the pages in regular articles..'(Whaples, 1991: p.294).

29 That the new economic history at the moment had also caught on beyond Europe, is shown by the fact that the *Third World Congress* attracted participants from, among other places, Russia, Israel, Brazil, Argentina, South Korea, Australia and Japan.

30 This paragraph is partly based on (McCloskey, 1987, in particular pp. 77-84).

31 This was for a major part attributable to the growing international influence in these years of the *École des Annales* on the entire history discipline. Compare chapter 3, par. 3.10, p. 70 and further, above.

32 In the Netherlands, for instance, in the 1960s, any academic training in economic sciences had an obligatory course of economic or socio-economic history for all students, as part of the then B.Sc. examination. Through the subsequent educational reforms (the abolition of the B.Sc. examination and the reduction of the duration of the studies from 5 to 4 years), economic history often disappeared from the programme as a compulsory subject. As a result, when subsequently rigorous cutbacks were made on university education, the chairs in economic history which had their home base in the economic faculty were almost always the first on the list to be cut.

33 Two recollections — admittedly! strongly personally tinted —from the time illustrate the situation: In the beginning of the seventies Douglass North held a guest lecture at the *Vrije Universiteit* (Free University of Amsterdam). At that time, the professor of economic history was a specialist in the field of pre-modern agriculture in the Netherlands, and North's lecture related to the developments in American agriculture in the colonial era: One would expect that such would at least have produced an interesting comparative perspective. Nothing was further from the truth: During the discussion it became painfully clear that both specialists had little to share with each other for the simple reason that they did not understand each other at all. In the same period Robert William Fogel had a guest appearance at the university of Leyden, where he started his lecture with the legendary sentence: 'There are still people who think that a new economic historian is someone, who, when asked to re-write the history of the crucifixion of Jesus Christ, starts by counting the nails in the cross.' The Leyden history department, which was prominently present, appeared hardly amused, to say the least. Fogel was lucky not to have

reserved this lecture for the *Vrije Universiteit*, which — in contrast with its name — was in these years dominated by orthodox Calvinism .

34 Fairly soon a strongly quantitative analytic tradition in economic history arose in Canada, but that was mainly because Canadian academic education, traditionally spoken, had always already been under strong American influence. The most used economic history manual about Canada by Marr and Paterson (1980), for instance, shows a striking new economic history bias.

35 In England there was a not unimportant tradition in the field of historical statistics (Mitchell, 1962; Mitchell & Jones, 1971; Mitchell, 1988). Moreover, the reconstruction of historical national accounts in England under the direction of Phyllis Deane and Arthur Cole (1967) had blossomed in the same period that the new economic history had come into existence in the United States, and as far as that was concerned, the developments in the United Kingdom paralleled the American one. Later English researchers who expanded, refined and revised the numerical data of Deane and Cole, such as Feinstein (1972; 1978), later in collaboration with another British pioneer in this field, Matthews (1954) and Odling-Smee (Matthews, Feinstein & Odling-Smee, 1982) and Nick Crafts (1985), or who reconstructed those parts of the historical national accounts of other countries (Crafts, 1983; Maddison, 1982; 1989; 1991) could effortlessly join in with the new economic history. Another distinctive aspect of the new American approach, the explanation of economic development processes by the explicit application of economic theory, often of a neoclassical nature, does not really match the English tradition, with as a result that this latter type of research, as held true for other European countries as well, initially was mostly conducted by Americans.

36 Almost everything that was generally accepted prior to that time in respect of the Industrial Revolution, was again held up against the light, which at least unsettled a large number of established ideas. The primary protagonists in the discussion: Hyde (1977) about technological change in the English iron industry; Harley (1971) about the revolution in sea transport from sailing ships to steamships; about human capital and technology (Harley, 1974) and about the probable rate of economic growth during the Industrial Revolution (Harley, 1982); Hausman (1984) about the significance of coal in the Industrial Revolution; Lyons (1977) about the textile industry; Hartwell & Engerman (1975), Mokyr (1977) and Williamson (1981) about the development of the standard of living during early industrialization. A summary of the debate is to be found in (Mokyr (Ed.), 1985). All authors mentioned in this note are Americans, except for Hartwell.

37 See, for example: (McCloskey, 1970; 1973; 1981; Mc Closkey (Ed.), 1971; Floud, 1976; Harley, 1971; Sandberg, 1974; Lincert & Trace, 1971,; Edelstein, 1976; 1982).

38 See: (Kennedy, 1974; Allen, 1979; Lazonick, 1981a; 1981b; Webb, 1980).

39 A — perforce — relatively random selection: Jones (1973) analyzed the role of the small-scaled English industry in the initial phases of the Industrial Revolution. Two Australians (yet tried and tested in the methods and techniques of the new economic history) Von Tunzelmann (1978) and Hawke (1970) examined the role of the steam engine in the English industrialization process. Von Tunzelmann wrote about the impact of the steam engine on factory production, while Hawke (1970) wrote a study inspired by Fogel's work on the role of the English railways in the British economic developments in the nineteenth century. Foreman-Peck (1979) wrote about the English automobile industry. The economic and social effects of the modification of the *Poor Law* were examined by Easton (1978), Boyer (1985) and McKinnon (1986). Paul David went ahead and did his famous study into the mechanization of American agriculture in the nineteenth century (David, 1966) all over again for England (David, 1971). Lance Davis and Robert Huttenback (1982) called into question — on good grounds — whether the British Empire had on balance yielded any profit for the mother country. The causes of the crisis of the 1930s tested against the English economic development were the subject of fierce controversies (Moggridge, 1962; Howson 1975; Benjamin & Kochin, 1979; Eichengreen, 1981; Eichengreen & Sachs, 1985). The pre-industrial economic history of the United Kingdom did not escape the theoretical scalpel of the new economic history either, although statistical data to test the hypotheses derived from theory in this case were conspicuous by their absence: McCloskey (1975) wrote a treatise based on neoclassical insights about enclosures. He did not even hesitate to set neoclassical theorems loose on the medieval economic history issues (McCloskey, 1976; McCloskey & Nash, 1984). The application of insights, derived from the neoclassical economic theory, to explain structural economic processes of change in periods for which statistical data in fact were conspicuous by their absence, was in the mid-1970s distinctly exceptional still. Apart from the work by McCloskey mentioned, Gerald Gunderson (1976) hazarded an explanation based on neoclassical insights, for the decline of the Western Roman Empire. In the eighties, however, these types of analyses, under the influence of the pioneering book by Douglass North (1981), *Structure and Change in Economic History*, became a popular activity among cliometricians. In this book, North presents a — somewhat modified — neoclassical explanation for the most important structural economic processes of change for sedentary agriculture, for the revival and decline of Greek-Roman civilization; feudalism and for — what North calls — the First and the Second Economic Revolution. The book signified a breaking point in the new economic history: Until then the rather unquestioning acceptance of the neoclassical paradigm within the new economic history was increasingly put up for discussion and in the long run this led to an approach in the economic history in which more than before, room was offered to the

115

important role which institutions play in economic development processes. This recent development within economic history will be dealt with exhaustively in chapter 7 of this book.

40 The first edition only referred to the period 1700 — 1860. In the subsequent years, two other parts were added. The second edition consisted of three volumes (Floud & McCloskey (Eds.), 1994) which in their entirety cover the complete period from 1700 until 1992.

41 Again, because of the abundance of publications in this field, a necessarily restricted selection: The economic history of Ireland, dominated by the dramatic famines in the nineteenth century, was revised by the Irishman Cormac Ó Gráda (1975; 1981), who was strongly influenced by the new economic history approach, and later by Joel Mokyr (1980a; 1980b; 1980c; 1985). For Sweden, the market development in the nineteenth century was analyzed by Lars Jorberg and Tommy Bengtsson (1975), whereas the role of human capital in the Swedish economic development was scrutinized by Lars Sandberg (1979). Jonung (1983), finally, studied the impact of the rate of circulation of money on the Swedish economy in the final quarter of the nineteenth century. The other Scandinavian countries, Norway, Finland and Denmark, got less attention from the American new economic historians but that is not to say that the traditional approach in economic history remained predominant here. The most important journal in the field of Scandinavian economic history, *The Scandinavian Economic History Review*, distinguished itself in the 1970s by publishing a conspicuously high number of modern quantitative analytical articles, while the Danish economic historian, Karl Gunnar Persson, later played a key role in the establishment in 1997 of the first European journal with a strong cliometric orientation, *The European Review of Economic History*. Furthermore, in all Scandinavian countries there existed a strong tradition in the field of the reconstruction of historical national accounts, as is expressed in the work by Hansen (1974) for Denmark, by Olle Krantz (1988) for Sweden, by Riitta Hjerppe (1989) for Finland and the many publications of the National Statistics Bureau of Norway in this field. Owing to the pioneering work of Hoffmann (1965) there existed in Germany an important tradition in the field of the reconstruction of historical national accounts. Hoffmann's work, however, was especially placed at a premium by economic circles; the German economic history had been strongly traditionally determined for a long time. The result was that, as elsewhere, the new economic history of Germany had been dominated years on end by Americans, such as Tilly (1982) and Webb (1980; 1984), a Scot who for ages had been oriented on the United States, like Angus Maddison (1986), and a few German economic historians who had mainly trained in the United States, such as Fremdling (1977) and Dümke (1977). Studies concerning the Habsburg Empire (or parts thereof) were made by Eddie (1977), John Komlos (1983), Rudolph (1983) and Good

(1984). In the Netherlands as well, the traditional approach long prevailed in economic history, for which reason cliometric-oriented work in the seventies was produced predominantly by two Americans: Jan de Vries (1984) — a full-blooded American who, however Dutch his name sounds, lectures at Berkeley — and Joel Mokyr (1976) who is of Dutch origin but emigrated to Israel and from there to the United States. Only sporadically did there appear in those years a few economic history articles with an obvious quantitative analytical slant written by autochthonous writers: Bos (1979), De Meere (1979) and Drukker and Harbers (1979a; 1979b). Drukker, too, in part was trained in the United States and during his stay at Purdue University he came into contact with the new economic history. Belgium in the seventies did no attract very much attention from the new economic historians, but there the new economic history started to prosper as of the eighties around the research group of Herman van der Wee at the University of Leuven. Van der Wee, himself originally an economic historian from the traditional school, through his contacts in the United States had become enthusiastic about the new approach and since then greatly promoted the quantitative analytical research. Some of the most important results: (Van der Wee, 1981; 1984; 1986; Peeters et.al., 1986; Soete, 1989; 1991; Solar & Cassiers, 1990; Van der Wee & Van Meerten, 19992; Scholliers,1991; Aerts *et.al.* (Eds.), 1992, 1993a; Van Meerten, 1996). In France, in the seventies the situation was comparable to that of Germany: There was an active tradition in the field of the reconstruction of historical national accounts as appears from the work by Marczewski and Markovitch (1965; 1966), Toutain (1987) en Lévy Leboyer (1968; Lévy Leboyer & Bourguignon, 1985), but these authors operated rather isolated from historical tradition in France which in those years was fully dominated by the *École des Annales*. The *Annales* historians stood extremely aloof from the new economic history, despite the fact that both approaches strongly emphasized quantification (see: Chapter 3, par. 6, p. 63, preceding). The point at which the views of the two schools differed greatly concerned the matter of the admissibility of the application of theories and concepts which derived from modern economic theory to explain historic development processes. The new economic history did nothing else and for the followers of the *Annales* this was a typical example of the 'anachronistic historiography' that they abhorred (see: Chapter 3, par. 5, p. 61, preceding). As a result, cliometric studies on France in the seventies and eighties were written primarily by Americans, for instance Grantham (1975; 1980) and Hohenberg (1972) about French agriculture; Roehl (1976) about industrialization; Barry Eichengreen (1982) about the destabilization of the French franc in the twenties and David Weir (1984) about the backgrounds of demographic crises in pre-modern times. For Italy and Spain the same holds: You will find a sole autochthonous new economic historian (in Italy, Giovanni Toniolo (1977) for instance; in Spain, Gabriel Tortella-Casares (1975) and later Cesar Molinas and Leonardo Prados de la Escosura (1989)), but for the major part it is once again the Americans who dominate the field in the seventies. Flynn (1978) builds on the classic studies by Earl Hamilton (1934; 1936; 1947) about the role of Spain in the European Price Revolution. For Italy, in 1962 already, the legendary Alexander Gerschenkron (1962) had published an index for the industrial production development for the period 1881-1913 of which Stefano Fenoaltea (1969; 1984a; 1984b) — an American despite of his Mediterranean sounding name — later made mincemeat. Later still, Maddison (1991) published revised estimates of Italian economic growth over the period 1861-1989. Richard Rapp (1976) wrote about the economic crisis of the seventeenth century in Italy, while Jon Cohen (1979) wrote an article on the impact of fascist agricultural politics on Italian agricultural development in the days of Mussolini.

42 A few exceptions which prove the rule: Gregory (1974; 1984) and Metzer (1974) wrote studies with a cliometric slant about Russian economic history.

43 An exception is the Caribbean region about which a conspicuously high number of new economic history-like studies have appeared. The explanation is obvious: Because the economic aspects of slavery in the United States from the very beginning were at the centre of attention in new economic history, in the last-mentioned research field the need was gradually growing for comparative studies to answer the question whether slavery in the South of the United States was showing exceptional characteristics or whether more or less the same patterns could be found elsewhere as well. The quest for historical material for comparison led as it were 'automatically' to the Caribbean. By consequence, in proportion, a conspicuously high number of cliometric studies about different aspects of the Central-American plantation economy have been published. So, Robert Paul Thomas (1968) and Philip Coelho (1973) studied whether the English colonies in that region that were dominated by the sugar plantations had made a profit or loss for the mother country. Gemery (1980), starting from colonial population statistics, showed the migration from England to the American colonies and also published, in conjunction with Hogendorn, exhaustively on the Atlantic slave trade (Gemery & Hogendorn, 1974; Gemery & Hogendorn (Eds.), 1979). Also Stanley Engerman, after the gigantic research into the economic aspects of slavery in the South of the United States that he conducted together with Robert William Fogel (Fogel & Engerman, 1974), deeply immersed himself in the economic and demographic history of the Caribbean. See, for example: (Engerman, 1984; Engerman & Klein, 1979).

44 Comparatively much has been published on Australia in the field of cliometrics, a consequence of the fact that Australian universities of old were strongly focussed on the United States. So, Ralph Shlomowitz (1979), who completed his training in the United States under the supervision of Robert William

Fogel, published on the history of the sugar industry in Queensland; Barnard, Butlin and Pincus (1982) wrote about the relation between the public and private sector in Australia in the twentieth century; the same Butlin (1962; 1964) reconstructed also the size of the domestic product, the investments and the volume of the foreign loans in Australia in 1861 and 1939, while he also conducted a historical demographic research about Aboriginals (Butlin 1984). Pope (1976) reconstructed Australian immigration patterns in the past, while Forster edited a manual on the economic development of Australia in the twentieth century (Forster (Ed.), 1970). Brian Haig and Neville Cain (1983) published figures on the productivity in Australian industry in the twenties and thirties of the twentieth century. Japan as well, like Australia, enjoyed relatively great interest from the field of cliometrics. Saxonhouse (1978) published about the Japanese labour market in the past, whereas Yamamura (1974; 1976) alone and together with Susan Hanley (Yamamura & Hanley, 1978) wrote a number of quantitative-oriented studies about several aspects of Japanese economic history and also edited (Yamamura Ed., 1978) the theme edition that *Explorations in Economic History* dedicated especially to the economic history of Japan. Allen Kelley and Jeffrey Williamson (1974) together wrote a manual with a cliometric slant to it about the economic development of Japan, while Hugh Patrick (Ed. 1976) edited a similar compilation. Mosk (1978) researched the relation between certain demographic variables and the quantity and quality of food consumption in Japan in the past. The conspicuously rapid economic growth of Japanese economy following the Second World War was analyzed by Denison and Chung (1976). Quantitative research into the Chinese economy in the twentieth century was done by Thomas Rawski (1980) and Loren Brandt (1985). A comparative study between China and India was published by Latham (1978), whereas Maddison (1998) wrote a strongly quantitatively oriented general work about the history of the Chinese economy. Persistent stagnation phenomena in agriculture in South Asia were analysed by Heston and Kumar (1983), while Morris (1983) portrayed industrialization in that area from the beginning of the nineteenth century until the end of the Second World War. The development in agriculture in Thailand in the first half of the twentieth century was the subject of a study by Feeny (1979). As regards India: Leonard Carlson (1978) published about the decline in Indian agriculture in the first half of the twentieth century, while the earlier-mentioned Morris (1965) described industrialization in India in the second half of the nineteenth and the first half of the twentieth century, in relation to the development of the cotton industry in Bombay. A number of studies with a cliometric slant also appeared sporadically about South-American countries in this period. Nathanlie Leff (1968) published about the industrialization of Brazil, while in 1979 a general survey written in the Portuguese language about the economic history of

119

Brazil was published (Neuhaus Ed., 1979). John Coatsworth (1981), finally, wrote a study about the economic importance of the railways in the economic development of Mexico.

5 *Sadder and wiser:* The Socratic contribution of the NEH

5.1 Socratic economic history: To know that you don't know[1]

At one point Socrates in any case did not suffer from exaggerated modesty, if we can believe Plato: He thought he could maintain on good grounds that he was wiser than other people and this, not because he knew more than others, but precisely because he knew less, as shown by his statement, οιδα οτι ουκ οιδα: 'I know that I don't know.'
For, others thought they knew something, but Socrates always managed to expose such knowledge by shrewd reasoning as pseudo-knowledge. To the question, which was understandably posed following such exposure, namely "tell us, how is it *really*, then?" he usually also had no answer.

The picture Plato draws of Socrates perfectly applies to the new economic history during its first hey-days, say, the 1960s and 1970s. The explicit application of economic theory in explaining processes of economic development and — if possible — the quantitative testing of hypotheses about such development processes, derived from the theory applied, led to it that in American economic history, a large number of fundamental ideas and insights, whose accuracy before had not been challenged by almost all economic historians, were unsettled. The empirical accuracy could simply not be proven, or, worse still, meticulous analysis of the available historical statistical material pointed in a completely different direction than anyone had ever assumed. But, just like Socrates, the new economic history often had no answer ready to the question which naturally followed — well okay, so it wasn't like that, but how was it *really*, then? — certainly not in the first phase of its existence: Many answers were possible in principle, but the standard, traditional reply, which everyone agreed on, usually appeared untenable.

What was this mysterious exposing force of cliometrics? Had traditional economic historians always been so lazy and idle, that they often had not taken the trouble to closely examine a certain assumed relationship between the phenomena, and had they, when an authoritative colleague had suggested a certain explanation for one or other development, unthinkingly accepted such explanation on the basis of his authority? Not at all. That exposing force was in fact not that mysterious at all; it stemmed from three conditions.

In the first place, the application of economic theory to explain a given development, had often as a result that the theory left open the possibility of a number of different relationships between the variables involved, which had been overlooked in the implicit or intuitive application of the theory. McCloskey (1987) gives a good example - which she in turns takes from West (1975a; 1975b).

In 1870 the English government established free and — up to a certain age — compulsory education, while until then a system had prevailed under which private institutions provided education against payment. Almost everyone will intuitively be of the opinion that the total quantity of education in England after that government measure would have increased: Why would you consume less of something for which you previously had to pay yourself and which now was offered 'for free' by the government?[2] West was the first to make an analysis of that problem explicitly on the basis of some — surprisingly simple — theoretical insights stemming from microeconomics, and the answer was: No, the total quantity of education did not need to have increased per se.

A small exercise on the basis of a simple graph (figure 5.1) shows that he — against our intuitive feeling — is indeed right. In the graph the horizontal axis depicts the quantity of education provided and the vertical axis, the quantity of other goods and services (everything except education, that is) an average English family could consume around 1870. The line AE, the so-called 'budget line', is the set of all combinations between quantities 'education' and 'other goods' which the family can afford at the most, within the limitations of its total budget. Every point within the triangle OAE is budgetwise attainable for the family and as long as the point is 'to the southwest' of AE, the family has money left; every point 'to the northeast' of AE is budgetwise unfeasible. If, for the sake of convenience, we put 'have money left' for a moment also under the category 'all other goods and services', this means that the family in making its choice in the relation of quantity of education to all other goods will always find itself somewhere on the line between A (the family spends nothing on education) and E (the family spends its entire budget on education).

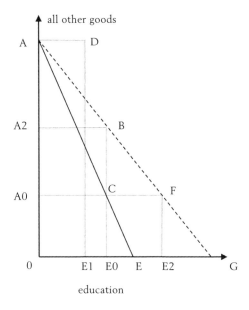

Figure 5.1 Microeconomic analysis of the 'education problem'

Suppose that the family before 1870 was at point C: It then consumed a quantity of education the size of OE_o and spent OA_o on all other goods. It is quite conceivable now that the quantity of education which the government makes available 'free' and 'compulsory', on average per family is less that the quantity the family itself spent prior to that date. This can be illustrated by assuming that the quantity of free and compulsory education after 1870 per family gets to OE_1. The family then suddenly, necessarily (education is compulsory!), lands[3] at point D, where it spends its entire budget OA on other goods and services, while it perforce consumes a compulsory quantity of education the size of OE_1.

The work by West actually appeared to be more than just an elegant theoretical exercise: His empirical research suggested emphatically that the average quantity of education in England, following the introduction of 'free' and compulsory education, had indeed declined!

Not only can insights from applied economic theory draw our attention to relations which we otherwise would have easily overlooked, the theory can also sometimes suggest to us the effects which probably might have ensued if the historical process researched, in this case of another education policy, had taken a different course.

Now, suppose that the English government had proceeded in 1870 to subsidize the existing private schools, instead of introducing 'free' and compulsory state education. What is likely to have happened in that case?

Figure 5.1 again brings help: Following the introduction of educational subsidies, this implies that for the average family the price of education drops, in other words, that with the same amount of money more education can now be obtained, whereas the prices of other goods and services have meanwhile not changed. In the graph this means that the original budget line AE changes into the new budget line AG. What new spending possibilities this opens up to our family? The possibilities lie between two extremes: The family could have spent the extra spending possibilities resulting from the decline of the price of education in full on other goods and services. Then, budgetwise, it shifts from C to B where it still consumes the same quantity of education OE_0 and now spends OA_2, instead of OA_0, on other goods and services. In the other extreme, the family uses the decline of prices in full for additional education. In that instance it moves from C to F: It continues consuming the same quantity of other goods and services as previously (OA_0), but now consumes a larger quantity of education, namely OE_2, instead of OE_0. With education subsidies, so the theory predicts, the average quantity of education enjoyed per family would at least have remained the same, or else, increased. In other words, had the English government in 1870 wanted to promote with its measures that the average quantity of education enjoyed in England would increase (which is indeed what it wanted), it would have been better if it had subsidized private schools instead of introducing 'free' and compulsory state education.

The interesting thing about this example is, that the application of the simplest economic theory apparently provides us with insights in the possible course of historical processes, without us having actually made an in-depth study of such a process, for instance, by extensive research of the sources. Of course, this does not mean to say that this renders the study of source material superfluous. The theory helps us to get a better idea of the various possibilities along which the process in question could have evolved, and so gives us at least an indication of the direction in which we should look for the sources that are likely most fertile in answering the questions we started with.

Secondly, the success of the new economic history in the sixties and seventies resulted in an explosive increase in the number of — mostly young and ambitious — researchers in the United States who launched into economic and historic issues. In the foregoing, I already pointed out[4] that the economic history within the economic faculties in the first half of the twentieth century had gradually been marginalized by its — in the eyes of the economists — often inadequate theoretic substantiation. This changed dramatically with the arrival of cliometrics, and the result was that, in the 1960s, the number of students at economic faculties who chose a Ph.D. training in economic history increased tremendously. The intellectual elite of that same student population, after having completed their thesis, in part landed finally on the chairs in economic history that had fallen vacant, and they in turn, via their Ph.D. students, produced new impulses. Moreover, these 'new' economic historians, in view of the special character of cliometrics, were often more focused on collecting and analyzing historical quantitative data than the older generation. Finally, owing to the rapid development of computer hard- and software in these years[5], they were often better able, compared to their predecessors, to process gigantic quantities of statistical material within a relatively short period.

Thirdly, the development of econometrics in this period created a boom of ever more sophisticated statistical testing procedures, with as a result that the possibilities to discover relations between variables that were concealed in the data set (or, to invalidate earlier assumed relations) increased enormously throughout the years.

These three conditions, in addition to the fact that in the new economic history intensive cooperation between researchers was more accepted than in traditional economic history (cooperation was inspired if only by the extreme labor-intensive nature of historical-statistical research), resulted in the very same issue, which before was investigated by one or two experts, was now all of a sudden analyzed by as many as dozens of researchers, on the basis of gigantically more data than had previously been available, and also with the help of superior analytical techniques. The result was, as said earlier, that a huge number of views on and explanations for a lot of issues, concerning the American economic development in the past, that had been considered as rather conclusive, and that had been passed down from generation to generation, perished en masse. Let us try to get a better view of the battlefield.

5.2 'Industrial Revolution' and *'Take-off'* are fictions from a quantitative viewpoint

Perhaps the most fundamental attack of the new economic history on the traditional economic history lay in the fact that the idea that the industrialization of the western world had been the consequence of a revolutionary economic process of change, that had instantly manifested itself, was an illusion. The term 'Industrial Revolution' for ages has been undoubtedly the pre-eminent central concept within the economic history discipline and above all, a concept with a respectable historiographic tradition: "...The term Industrial Revolution was probably for the first time used in the first half of the nineteenth century, among others by the French economist Blanqui. Friedrich Engels used it in his book *Die Lage des arbeitende Klasse in England* which was published in 1845. The term became widely accepted through Arnold Toynbee whose *Lectures on the Industrial Revolution*, were published in one volume after his death in 1883, and through Paul Mantoux, who in 1906 published *La révolution industrielle au XVIIIième siècle...*'.[6]

In the course of the twentieth century until the 1970s the term is given an ever more central place in economic history literature[7], despite the fact that in that same period it gradually becomes clear that the term, from a quantitative viewpoint, cannot be given an empirical underpinning.

In the narrowly defined meaning of an instant structural transformation within the economic process with a clearly historically perceptible starting point, which has the effect that economic growth, defined as a steady increase in the real income per capita gets a permanent character, while before that time 'growing pains' which were always followed by a drop to the former level of income, occurred only sporadically, the term 'Industrial Revolution' has proven to be fiction. This assumption is the most striking conclusion from the enormous research devoted since the fifties of the past century[8] to the reconstruction of historical national accounts. The result of those research efforts was indeed that gradually, for a large number of countries, the real national income since the beginning of the nineteenth century — for some years the starting point even lies somewhere in the eighteenth century — became available on an annual basis. And however much those series differed from each other in terms of level and growth rate, at one point they showed a surprising similarity: There was in fact never a clear marking to be observed between a pre-industrial and an industrial period, in the sense of the sudden start of a modern 'era of economic growth'. Quite the contrary. All countries clearly showed the same pattern of initially fierce, and in the long run declining annual fluctuations around an extremely gradually increasing trend in economic growth. To illustrate this, I have represented in a graph the Real Gross Domestic Product (RGDP) of the Netherlands and the annual increase in terms of percentage of the Dutch RGDP in the nineteenth century, both as an aggregate (Figure 5.2A & B) and per head of the population (Figure 5.3A & B).

A. Dutch real gross domestic product, 1807-1913

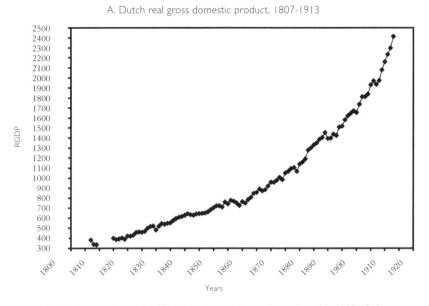

B. Yearly annual growth of Dutch real gross domestic product (%), 1808-1912

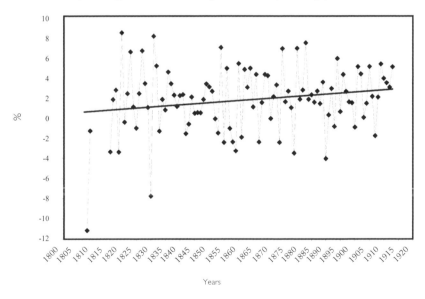

Figure 5.2. Dutch Real Gross Domestic Product, 1807-1913 (A) and yearly annual growthrate (B) (Source: Smits, Horlings & Van Zanden, 2000)

From the two graphs of the RGDP (aggregate and per capita) the image of a very gradual increase in the course of the nineteenth century clearly shows up [9]: Nowhere can a breaking point be found where production

A. Dutch real gross domestic product per capita,
1807-1913

B. Yearly annual growth of Dutch real gross domestic product per capita (%),
1808-1912

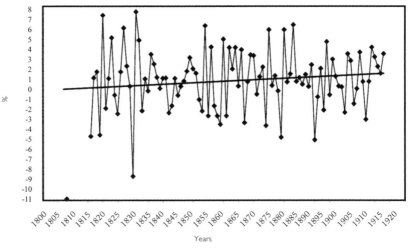

Figure 5.3. Dutch Real Gross Domestic Product per capita, 1807-1913 (A) and yearly annual growthrate (B)
(Source: Smits, Horlings & Van Zanden, 2000)

suddenly starts to increase, after it had fluctuated around a horizontal trend before that time. That image is confirmed by the two graphs of the annual growth in percentage: Especially at the beginning of the period, there are hefty fluctuations which seem to abate in the long run, but again it can be noticed that it concerns annual fluctuations around a gradually increasing trend. This agonizingly slow, increasing trend is also noticeable at the beginning of the nineteenth century, in other words: Again we see that there is no instant change, but something we would be almost inclined to call an 'evolution', instead of a 'revolution', were it not that the first terms calls up associations with a biological evolutionary process that involves natural selection and for that reason could easily put us on the wrong track.

That the term 'Industrial Revolution', in a quantitative sense at any rate, was misleading, gradually became clear more widely since the *XI International Historical Congress* held in Stockholm in 1960 and where the *Stages of Economic Growth* by Walt Whitman Rostow that was published that very same year, was briskly discussed, and during an international congress in Konstanz that was entirely devoted to the Rostow's *Stages*. It was no coincidence that the names of Simon Kuznets, Phyllis Deane and Robert Solow are among those of the most important critics: The first two belong to the leading pioneers in the field of the reconstruction of historical national accounts (Kuznets and Phyllis Deane), while the third

Dutch investments as a percentage of gross national product, 1808-1913

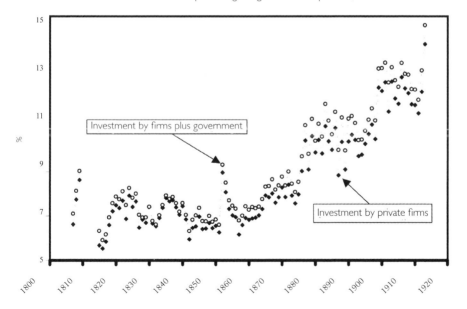

Figure 5.4 Investment in The Netherlands as a percentage of Gross National Product, 1808-1913 (Source: Smits, Horlings & Van Zanden, 2000).

is one of the founding fathers of modern growth theory in theoretical economics.

Rostow's *Take-Off*, his translation of the term 'Industrial Revolution' in modern economic terminology, bit the dust, simply because in quantitative sense no empirical underpinning could be found for it.

A similar fate has fallen to the idea assumed by Rostow that his supposed *Take-Off* would be accompanied by a sudden increase in the investment rate of less than 5% of national production to 10% or more of GDP.

To illustrate I have again chosen the Netherlands (Figure 5.4) but — again — other countries could just have well served as example. Here as well an overly clear image comes up that conflicts with what according to Rostow should have happened during the *Take-Off*: There is, so the graph shows, no once-only sudden increase. What we see is again the image of hefty fluctuations — just as many premature *Take-Offs*, invariably followed by *Touch-Downs*, so to say — which in their entirety form a cyclical pattern around an — again — agonizingly slow increasing trend of the investment rate.

The reconstruction of historical national accounts of dozens of countries and frantic attempts to make its results mutually comparable (probably the most extensive statistic drudgery that has ever been done in economic history) in any case produced one clear conclusion, even if it could hardly be labeled positive: If during the economic modernization of the western countries such a thing as an 'Industrial Revolution' had taken place at all, not a trace of it could be found in the national growth figures.[10]

5.3 The myth of colonial exploitation

Another field in which the new economic history made matchwood out of the generally accepted view within the discipline, concerned the economic effects of the relation between the western countries and their colonies. It all began with a discussion about the economic relations between England and the colonies in North America, prior to American independence. This relation, part of the mercantilist policy of the British empire, would have caused serious damage to the economy of the colonies in favor of the mother country, something that in the leftist jargon of the 1960s was known as 'colonial exploitation'.

In a nutshell, this relation boils down to the following. On the basis of the *Navigation Acts*, the foreign trade of the North American colonies was entirely and exclusively conducted via England: Any export from America was first shipped by English or colonial ships to the United Kingdom and thereafter locally used or re-exported to the rest of the world. The reverse applied to import: All imports in the colonies originated from England and direct import out of other countries was prohibited. Furthermore, there was a whole array of subsidy and tax measures in respect of the colonies. The colonial production of the products deemed of importance by England (for example ship chandlery and timber) was encouraged with subsidies, while the mother country levied tax on a myriad of imports.

The generally accepted view within American economic history for years had been, that this relation had seriously damaged the colonies in an economic sense.[11] The proud settlers — thus the story went — exasperated by the merciless exploitation by the mother country, would rightly have revolted and so have launched the American revolution that finally heralded North American independence. Throughout the centuries this theme from American history played a successful role in stimulating nationalist sentiments: To this day, the term 'Boston Tea Party' and the slogan 'No taxation without representation' will sound familiar even to the reader who is no expert in this matter. Amidst such patriotic verbal assault, however, one crucial question had been forgotten: In retrospect, how severe had that exploitation been exactly? It was this question that stood central in the discussions that started within the new economic history.

In this debate, use was made of practically the only author who, prior to the emergence of the new economic history, had tried to reconstruct the size of the economic damage of the *Navigation Acts* to the North American colonies: Lawrence Harper (1943; 1964 reprint). His calculations referred to one randomly chosen year (1773), for which he, as best as he could, given the then available data, and starting from different assumptions respecting the volume of the foreign trade of the thirteen colonies from that time and the possible effects of the English trade policy, directly made a low, an average and a high estimate of what the financial consequences had been for the colonies' export and import, as a result of the mandatory transport via England. Moreover, he had also made an estimate of the financial advantages the settlers had enjoyed from the English subsidy for certain colonial products. All this resulted in an estimated loss of colonial income in the year selected by him of between 2.5 million — the low estimate — and 7 million dollar. The most plausible would have been a loss of 3.3 million dollar (the average estimate), which he considered a heavy loss: The amount was higher than the overall government budget of the American government in the nineties of the eighteenth century.

The first who had doubts about the results of Harper was Robert Paul Thomas (1965). Basically, he attacked his opponents on two items: He made a recomputation of the loss of income estimated by Harper by placing the estimates in an economic theoretical framework and an explicit counterfactual and secondly, he placed the question of what in this context would have to be called a big or a small loss in an entirely new perspective.

The theoretical framework in which Thomas placed the problem, in fact was nothing more than a simple model of demand and supply (Figure 5.5)[12], but no matter how simple, it offered a careful analysis of the impact of the English *Navigation Acts* on the foreign trade of the North American colonies in a nutshell. Let us see how Thomas approached the problem.

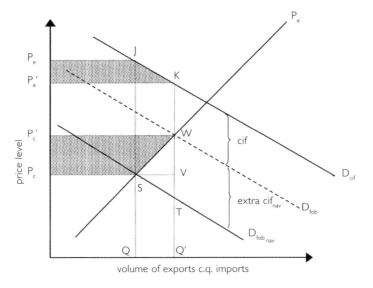

Figure 5.5 The Supply & Demand Model by Robert Paul Thomas: Export and Import of the North-American colonies under influence of the 'Navigation Acts'
Source: (McClelland, 1969)

The supply curve of American manufacturers of export commodities is represented in the figure by the line Sfob. Here, the subscript 'fob' stands for the expression 'free on board' which indicates that it concerns of the price level at which the export commodities are delivered on board ships in American ports. The line Dcif represents the demand curve of European importers for American exports under a regime of international

P

free trade, thus in the hypothetical case in which England would not have taken restrictive measures in respect of the international trade of its colonies. The term 'cif' stands for 'cost, insurance and freight', in other words, the price level of American exports in the final European ports of destination applies to this curve, this means, including *any costs* attached to transport from America to the final destination. By subtracting all 'cif costs' per unit of product (line segment KW in the graph) of those prices, the dotted demand curve Dfob emerges, that is the demand curve for American export commodities at the quays of American ports, still on the assumption of international free trade. Supposing, now, that *all additional costs* per unit of product that resulted from the English trade policy are represented in the graph by the line segment WT — because the *Navigation Acts* stipulated that colonial exports first had to be transported to English ports, and only then from there to the ports of destination (for example, think of the additional transport costs this would entail) then this means that as a result of the trade policy pursued by the United Kingdom, the demand curve for American export commodities (still: In American ports) shifts from Dfob to $Dfob_{nav}$.

After all this shifting, the graph suddenly offers us a surprisingly clear picture of the problem. Under market equilibrium ánd the English trade policy followed, American suppliers of export commodities will now indeed export a quantity OQ at an export price level of P_c (remember, that is the price they receive in American ports!). Under exactly the same circumstances, *but then without the trade policy followed*, they would have exported more (namely OQ') at a higher price level, namely P_c'. On first thoughts it now seems that the additional income the settlers would have received under free trade is the difference between the rectangle OP_c'WQ' and OP_cSQ. This, however, is not quite correct: For the settlers would have had to deploy additional production of goods to have the supply of export commodities increase from Q to Q'. Again, under market equilibrium, this additional deployment of production would have had to be withdrawn from their original production destination, so that the settlers would have remained deprived of such original production under a regime of free trade.

These so-called alternative costs (*opportunity cost* in Anglo-Saxon literature) are depicted in their entirety in the graph as the trapezium QSWQ'. On balance, the income difference from export between a supposed free trade regime and the trade restrictions imposed is the gray area P_c'WSP_c. It probably seems as if this analysis is little more than a load of theoretical chatter, but that is only on the surface. The consequences for this practical research are far-reaching: The size of the gray area P_c'WSP_c (the net additional income from exports for the settlers under free trade, that is) is determined by the inclination of the supply curve Sfob and of the demand curves Dfob and Dfob$_{nav}$ — remember, those last two run parallel under the assumptions of the model — and furthermore, through the size of the difference between P$_c$' and P$_c$ as well as Q' and Q. The inclination of the curves is a graphic representation of what in economic theory is called: Price elasticity, which roughly means the extent to which the price reacts to a change in the quantity supplied c.q. demanded. Robert Paul Thomas, now, on the strength of historical American trade statistics from before and after the independence, seemed able to make concrete estimates of the difference between Q' and Q. On the basis of similar archival material he also estimated the difference between the American export price level before and after independence. Finally, he endeavoured to make as reasonable an estimate as possible of the price elasticity of the American supply of export goods and that of the European demand for American exports. Once he had those data, he could make a theory-based estimate of the loss of income from 'missed' exports resulting from the English trade policy.

He followed the exact same reasoning with respect to the consequences of the trade policy for the imports by North American colonies: Supposing that Sfob represents the supply curve of European suppliers of export commodities to the colonies in European ports. As a result of the trade policy pursued by England, the total 'cif costs' per unit of product consist of the 'ordinary' 'cif costs' — the costs per unit which have had to be made in the event of direct transport from the ports of origin — plus all additional 'cif costs' which emanated from the English trade restrictions. In other words, under free trade, the colonial demand curve, measured in American ports would have been Dcif and the same demand curve in the ports of origin Dfob. As a result of the English trade policy the European exporters, however, were confronted with a colonial import demand curve Dfob$_{nav}$. As a result of the English trade policy the settlers thus demanded OQ import goods, for which they pay a price P$_e$ in the colonies, while under a free trade regime they would have demanded more import goods (namely, OQ'), for which they would have paid a lower price (namely, P$_e$'). The loss of income resulting from the English trade policy insofar as it concerns the imports of the colonies may therefore be represented as the difference between that which they would have bought in the event of free trade (rectangle OP$_e$'JQ') and that which they have actually bought (rectangle OP$_e$JQ), plus the opportunity cost of the higher import price level, that is, analogous to the export example, what they would have been able to buy in additional goods if the lower 'free trade import price level' had been applicable. This loss of income is represented in the figure by the gray trapezium P_eJKP_e'. In the same manner as he succeeded to calculate the loss of income from the smaller exports, Thomas calculated the size of the loss as a result of the higher priced income. Adding the two, brought him to an estimate of the total loss of income for the colonies as a result of the English trade restrictions.

The American colonies did not only have an economic disadvantage from the fact that they were a part of the British Empire, however; there were also advantages. Through the mercantilist policy of the mother country not only exports from England to the colonies were protected against foreign (read: Non-English) competition — which, as we have just seen, resulted in smaller colonial imports at higher price levels — but also American exports to England were protected from non-English competitors, which resulted in greater exports at a higher price level than would have been the case in international competition. Besides, the English government subsidized the production of a number of colonial products it considered to be of strategic importance, such as indigo, timber for the construction of ships and other ship chandlery. The ingenuity of the demand and supply model used by Thomas was that he could now apply that very same model as pattern of thought in respect of the consequences all this could have had, on balance, for the income of the American colonies. In the event of subsidies for strategic products, for instance, the line segment WT can be interpreted as the amount of the subsidy per unit of product which causes a shift in the European demand curve for colonial exports from $Dfob_{nav}$ to $Dfob$. The gray trapeziums now suddenly represent the increase in colonial exports that is the result of the subsidies, and the deduction of the relevant differences in price and volume from the trade statistics as well as the assessment of the elasticities at issue, yields an estimate of the consequences for the colonial income.

Of course, the key question now is how big the loss of income estimated by Thomas really was. At first, the answer seems surprisingly disappointing: Despite his careful substantiation and the application of much more precise estimation methods than Harper, the loss of income resulting from the English trade restrictions as estimated by Thomas did not differ all that much from Harper's middle average. Harper estimated the annual loss of income as a result of the *Navigation Acts* at 3.66 million dollar, whereas Thomas arrived at 3.1 million dollar. Because the economic advantages for the settlers emanating from the fact that they compulsorily formed part of the British Empire were higher in Thomas' calculations than Harper's (0.44 versus 0.32 million dollar respectively), Thomas, who himself arrived at an annual net loss of income of 2.66 million dollar, concluded that Harper's lowest estimate of the total loss of income (2.56 million dollar) on balance had been closer to the truth than his middle estimate. If it had stayed at that, the results of Thomas' research, in spite of his revolutionary approach to the problem, would hardly have been called spectacular.

The most essential point in Thomas' revision of Harper's figures, however, was to be found in the answer to the question whether the ultimate amount of over 2.5 million dollar should be considered as large or rather as small and in that respect Robert Paul Thomas and his predecessor differed greatly from each other. Harper had labeled the loss of income as great, putting forward as an argument that the amount was more than the total American government budget in the last years of the eighteenth century. That Harper came with this rather out of the blue criterion, strikes us as compelled by necessity: When he published his study, hardly any macro figures on the colonial economy were known. Well over twenty years after Harper, Thomas did have relevant figures at his disposal, to which he could compare the difference in income: In 1965 there were reasonable estimates of what had been the total income of the North American colonies in that period and on the basis of that Thomas concluded that the loss of income calculated by him amounted to less — considerably less even — than 1% of the colonial income.

The study by Robert Paul Thomas formed — as usual within the new economic history[13] — the starting point of an intense debate in which two questions were the central point. In the first place, Thomas' estimate was held up against the light from all sides: Had his estimation methods been correct? Had he used the most reliable and relevant data? Secondly, the question was tabled again whether the economic damage suffered by the North American colonies as a consequence of the British mercantilist policy had been big or small.

The debate about the first question produced two conclusions. Further study showed that the use of other data than those which Robert Paul Thomas himself had based the research on, did indeed affect his final estimates: It was, in other words, not difficult to arrive at a higher amount of the loss than Thomas had calculated, but — and most critics had to hand it to Thomas — the differences were not spectacular. In line with this, a number of critics wondered whether Thomas had been sufficiently skeptical about the assumptions he had built in his model. This had become a popular trick among the cliometricians in the preceding years, which in the literature is known as *counter-biasing*: To play the devil's advocate for one's own research. The idea is that you do good, if you are forced to rely on highly incomplete information, in picking exactly choosing those assumptions to include in your model, as to make every effort possible to reduce your own hypotheses to rubble. The idea of Robert Paul Thomas was that Harper's estimates of the colonial loss of income had been too high and he would have had to, according to the principle of counter-biasing, make every effort to attain himself as high results as possible. It was in particular Peter McClelland (1969) who lectured him on this and in fact did his homework all over again. If Robert Paul Thomas indeed had selected his assumptions consistently as strictly as possible, he would have arrived at, according to McClelland, an economic loss of about 60% of the colonial income and that, of course, is considerably more than the less than 1% Thomas himself left it at.

With some difficulty one could maintain that the entire matter about the size of the colonial loss of income in the end boiled down to the rather meager conclusion that it has turned out to be darn bothersome to make a reasonable estimate, but that everything pointed to a loss in the order of 1 to 5% of the colonial income. And then the second question immediately presented itself: Had that been little or much? Surprisingly, the answer to that second question has, indeed, been of great importance in a much broader context.

In the debate about the Harper-Thomas controversy, initially only the question about the size of the direct loss and the economic advantage for the colonies as a consequence of the *economic* policy of the mother country was of importance. In the question as to whether that loss should on balance be interpreted as great or small, gradually other aspects were also taken into consideration. Thomas himself had pointed out already that the North American colonies in the years concerned were actually in a state of war: They were threatened by the French and a large number of Indian tribes (this episode in colonial history in the United States is still known as the *Franco-Indian Wars*) and there was no one who doubted that the settlers military-wise would not have stood a chance, had they not been actually protected by English army units. Within this framework the key question naturally took on a different aspect: Had the colonial loss of income been greater or smaller than the cost England had had to make military-wise to protects its colonies on the North American continent against the French and Indian troops? And however rough and approximate the different estimates of the economic loss for the colonies as a result of mercantilism, there was in fact no one who doubted the answer to this last question. If you would add the English military expenses for the protection of the North American colonies to the costs which were made any how in the mother country to maintain the exclusive trade relation with the North American colonies, only one conclusion was possible: Those costs would have been much higher than any estimate of the colonial loss of income whatsoever. In other words, on balance, England had sustained losses and the military protection of the settlers against the French and Indian 'invaders' had largely been financed by the English taxpayer. It was this conclusion that appeared to have far-reaching consequences for the thinking within the economic history about the economic relations between mother country and colonies in general during the period of western expansion.[14]

Lance Davis and Robert Huttenback elaborated on this line of thought in a different connection.[15] What would happen, they wondered, when you would try to answer that same question (how large was the profit from the colonies for the mother country?) for the relation between England and that territory that generally was considered its richest colony of all— namely, India - measured at the height of British imperialism, say, the second half of the nineteenth century.

The answer to that question was quite amazing, even though most readers will not be surprised after having read the foregoing: It could simply not be demonstrated that the English nation at the peak of its imperial power, on balance had had any economic advantage of the colonial empire in India, at least when you would take into account (and, strangely enough that had been systematically overlooked until then) the additional government spending (two armies, two fleets, two government apparatuses, etc.) which was needed to maintain the colonial relation. That conclusion was completely in conflict with the, in those days accepted views, on the economic aspects of western colonization. In the late sixties and early seventies of the 20th century, the body of thought of the radical left was fairly dominant in western intellectual circles, and that had not gone by economic history. In line with the then popular *dependencia* theories[16] in economics in which it was argued that the economic exploitation of the countries in the third world by the western countries, which had been characteristic of the colonial era, after the independence of the colonies albeit under changed political conditions, had simply continued, within economic history a modernized variant of the Hobson-Lenin thesis was the generally accepted view.[17]

The gap between rich and poor, according to that view, was to a decisive extent the result of the unequal distribution of power which had grown gradually during colonialism and which had reached a climax in the period of imperialism, roughly the second half of the nineteenth century and the first decades of the twentieth century. As a result of that unequal distribution of power, a disunity in the world economy would have developed, especially in the years of western imperialism, in which the colonies were forced to supply raw materials and labor to the western countries at a price level the rich west could extort from them, and which made any form of economic development in the third world impossible from the outset. As a result of this unequal division of power the gap between poor and rich counties — even after colonization, because the economic inequality was not altered by it — could only become bigger unless — that is where neo-Marxism entered the game — the former colonies were prepared to definitively break with the capitalist west by way of a revolution.[18]

The study by Davis and Huttenback was based on a very large sample (447 businesses) concerning the investment behavior of English enterprises in the period from 1860 until 1914 inclusive[19] and the results were disastrous for the credibility of the colonial exploitation theory.

In short, their conclusions boiled down to the following: In the first place the English investments in their colonies had been surprisingly slight at the height of imperialism. A much larger amount was invested by the British not in the colonial territories, but elsewhere in the world and furthermore, the amount of domestic investments was much greater than generally assumed. Only by the end of the period studied by them, did colonial investments take on substantial proportions but those years, oddly enough, were characterized by extremely low yields from colonial enterprises. The return on shares in colonial enterprises in the first period of their research — say, 1860 through 1885 — indeed had been much higher than that of both 'ordinary' foreign and domestic shares, but after 1885, owing to increased competition, the proportions had shifted around: Between 1885 and 1914 the colonial yield had without exception been considerably lower than the yield on domestic and foreign funds.

A second aspect of their research concerned the socioeconomic status of the English shareholders. They could demonstrate that investments in the colonies for the major part were made by a small financial elite (the traditional representatives of 'big business', so to speak), while for domestic investments precisely the 'middle class' (managing directors of small to medium-sized companies, managers, members of the professional services sector, etc.) ruled the roost.

The third aspect of their research concerned the costs to maintain the British Empire and the manner in which the English government had defrayed those costs. Davis and Huttenback calculated that those costs had been born in full by the English taxpayer. Those who had profited especially were chiefly the inhabitants of those parts of the empire where

139

white settlers had settled down in large numbers: Canada, Australia and New Zealand.[20] For other parts of the British Empire, in particular India, the balance was less clear: It could not be denied, indeed, that also for those parts *on balance* a considerable flow of subsidized goods and services had moved from the mother country to the colonies — and not the other way around — but on the other hand it could not be proved either that those areas would have chosen the *same* package of goods and services had they had freedom of decision.

All in all, the pattern of the flows of money as reconstructed by Davis and Huttenback in respect of the financial relations between mother country and colonies differed substantially from the *communis opinio* at the time they published their research: Seen from a macroeconomic perspective, there had not been any exploitation of the colonies by England; quite the contrary, on balance gigantic English subsidies had been required to maintain the empire.

This did not mean that there had been no 'exploitation', only, such exploitation was of an entirely different nature than everyone had always thought. A number of English companies that were operating in the colonies had managed to make enormous profits for decades, among other things as a result of the carefully protected relations within the English empire. Those who had had great interests par excellence belonged to the traditional financial elite in England. The costs for those protected relations were paid in full by the average English taxpayer. On balance, there had been a relation of exploitation *within the mother country itself*: All English taxpayers together had borne the costs of maintaining a system under which a small, immensely rich minority had succeeded in getting even more extravagantly rich than would have been possible under different circumstances, or, in the words of Davis and Huttenback themselves: '(...) *The evidence indicates that empire returns were as high as they were only because of substantial subsidies from the British. The imperial experience could therefore be viewed more as a redistribution of income within the United Kingdom than as a transfer from the empire to the mother country...*'[21]

5.4 Demythologizing American slavery[22]

If success in economic history would be measured against the attention given to cliometric studies by the popular media, then *Time on the Cross: The Economics of American Negro Slavery* (Fogel & Engerman, 1974) undoubtedly to the present day would be recorded as the most successful cliometric study of all times. Immediately upon its publication, the book was exhaustively discussed in the United States in *Newsweek, Time Magazine, The Atlantic Monthly, The New York Times, The Wall Street Journal* and the *Washington Post* and both writers, time and time again, appeared in nationwide television talk shows.[23] Also in other places in the world the book came as a real bombshell: In England the *Times Literary Supplement* devoted considerable attention to it, while in The Netherlands a lengthy article appeared in the cultural supplement of the respectable Dutch newspaper, the NRC *Handelsblad*. This overwhelming media interest could not disguise that the study by Fogel and Engerman was by no means undisputed in professional circles: Immediately following its publication a sharp debate broke loose, which qua tumult was a match for the squabbling which the cliometric 'basic' study on slavery 'The Economics of Slavery' by Conrad and Meyer had raised at the time.[24] The book was cheered by some *("...destined to become a classic...'* one reviewer wrote) and ran into the ground by others ('...Time on the Cross *is a failure...'*, another wrote).

The odd thing was that *Time on the Cross* was largely based on earlier research, the results of which were known already in cliometric professional circles. In the foregoing I already stated[26] that in the years following the publication of the controversial article by Conrad and Meyer, an avalanche of new research on the same subject, against the confident expectations of the two first authors, who really thought to have published the last word on the economic aspects of American slavery. The result was, that within a few years a formidable quantity of monographs, based on new records, had appeared, which in themselves were all extremely interesting, but as a result of which, virtually no one could see the wood for the trees anymore.

For that reason Robert William Fogel and Stanley Engerman decided that it was high time to try to compile all research efforts in this field, whereby bookcases full of new quantitative data had surfaced, in one comprehensive study. That meanwhile this subject was indeed listed high on the agenda of the economic history forum appears, among other things, from the fact that in applying for (for that time, immense) research subsidies, they were so successful that in no time the pair among their colleagues, who were apparently not entirely devoid of jealousy, was nicknamed 'Fogel and Engerman Incorporated'.

The purpose of this extensive research was in principle, that all quantitative data on the history of American slavery, known at the time, would be gathered into one gigantic database, thus establishing the possibility to analyze all of the partial results that had been published so far in a large number of separate articles, in conjunction with each other. All this, re-

141

sulted in the subsequent years in dozens (!) of dissertations that had been prepared under the supervision of Fogel and Engerman, and, as a tail of the research, in the publication of the two-volume *Time on the Cross* in 1974.

The book was purposefully aimed at a broader public than only cliometric confrères: In the first volume, the conclusions of the research were summarized in simple language. The second volume was absolutely full of mathematics and technical explanations of how the writers had arrived at their results.

That this book, immediately following its publication aroused such tumultuous reactions, is not that difficult to explain in retrospect: The conclusions were, even for seasoned cliometricians, who since the article by Conrad and Meyer had become used to a lot in this field, absolutely shocking.

Firstly, the earlier conclusions of Conrad and Meyer regarding the profitability of cotton production with the aid of slave labor — for the umpteenth time — were more than confirmed: The purchase of a slave had just before 1860 been an investment which, from a viewpoint of profitability, could compete with the best investment possibilities available in the United States at that time. At the outbreak of the Civil War, slavery was by no means a form of activity that from an economic viewpoint was doomed to die. Quite the contrary; the abject system prospered as never

Figure 5.6 American slaves on an American cotton farm

before at the outbreak of the Civil War, and the development pointed in the direction of a further expansion rather than fragmentation.

The traditional image that the South of the United States on the eve of the Civil War had been a backward, stagnating economy, had to be radically adjusted, according to Fogel and Engerman. In fact, the real income per capita in the South had been higher than in the so-called 'modern' North, and the prospects of economic growth had been more favorable than elsewhere in the United States. The American planters had rightly held a very optimistic view of their own future during the decade preceding the Civil War, contrary to the later claims in this respect of Northern historiographers.

The stereotype image of the lazy, impassive Sambo was based, according to Fogel and Engerman, on prejudice and was not supported by facts: Slaves proved to have been more productive and more efficient than the average white farm worker and, on the whole, the efficiency of the cotton plantation was approximately 35 percent higher than that of the typical agricultural family business in the North of the United States.

Furthermore, contrary to the claims of official historiography in this connection, slavery had not been an impediment to industrial development in the South. Wherever slaves had been employed in the industrial sector, they could easily hold their own with white factory workers, as regards both manual skill and productivity. And, the fact that relatively few slaves had worked in the secondary sector was not caused by the unfitness of the slave for factory work, but simply because the production of cotton in the South brought in still higher profits than the manufacture of industrial products. Moreover, the demand for slaves in the urban areas in the years preceding the outbreak of the Civil War had risen faster than in the rural areas.

143

Fogel and Engerman's readers, whose picture of slavery in most cases had been formed by Harriet Beecher Stowe's *Uncle Tom's Cabin*, were most shocked by their conclusions regarding the living conditions of the slaves at the plantations. The food supply, for instance, in general had been over-abundant (on average over 4000 kilocalories per slave per day), and varied in composition.

Slaves had in general been housed in a manner which according to current norms would be rated sober, but which was still favorable compared to the slums in which the New York factory workers at the end of the nineteenth century had been forced to pass their days.

It appeared that slave-keepers had made medical arrangements for their slaves which, in the light of the limited medical knowledge of the time, could certainly not be considered to be poor. In general, slaves were dressed reasonably well up to very good. Anyway, that was the impression created by the surprisingly high expenses their owners had incurred for these household items, while the same picture was painted by archive material that showed that slaves had often been able to earn independently substantial amounts of money which was mostly spent on brightly colored fabrics.

Corporal punishments were indeed inflicted, but it could not be proven that slave-owners applied the whip more frequently or more cruelly than in the nineteenth century was the custom elsewhere (for instance, in education or the English navy).

The widespread ideas that sexual abuse of female slaves by their owners was the order of the day, and that a stable family life for the slaves was made impossible by the system, were relegated by Fogel and Engerman to the realm of fiction. Promiscuity among slaves was rather surprisingly low, than strikingly high, and forced sexual intercourse between female slaves and their masters occurred only sporadically. Of the purposeful "breeding of baby slaves for the purpose of selling them", no indication could be found in the material. On this point, Fogel and Engerman refuted the study of Conrad and Meyer who thought they had found the evidence of this in the data.[27]

For the strange fact that earlier already had attracted the attention of historians, namely that in the brothels of New Orleans hardly any female slaves were working as prostitutes, Fogel and Engerman had a simple explanation. The accepted explanation, namely that black women would not have been attractive to most prostituants, lacked any cohesion, of course: How could it be explained, then, that elsewhere on the American continent, in South America for instance, many female slaves were indeed exploited as prostitutes? Fogel and Engerman calculated that a female slave working on the plantation simply brought greater profits for her owner than if she had worked as a prostitute.

It was furthermore unusual that slave families were torn apart by the sale of various family members to different owners. Children were sold in general when they had reached the age that it would be natural for them to leave home. The social basis of slave society had been the traditional two-parent family which, in addition, showed a conspicuous stability.

One of the most contradictory conclusions in *Time on the Cross* was, that within the slave population in the United States, there had been a rather high degree of social mobility. Fogel and Engerman had regularly encountered situations in which it appeared that a slave was independently employed as a craftsman, whereby it had more then once happened that a

144

slave, as 'boss' of a smithy or timber workshop, had white wage laborers in his employment.

In brief, the writers of *Time on the Cross* to their own amazement had to admit, that the material circumstances (not the emotional, as they repeatedly emphasized) under which the slave population of the South of the United States had lived, had been much more favorable than any right-minded person had thought previously.[28]

This book had to bring a storm of critique down on itself. Hardly one year after publication, a entire conference at the University of Rochester was exclusively devoted to *Time on the Cross*, and in the following years an avalanche of magazine articles, two books and a special edition of *Explorations in Economic History* were published that were completely devoted to criticize the challenged study.[29]

Essentially, the gist of it was that the source material, on which the conclusions of Fogel and Engerman were based, according to their critics, would not be a random sample from the population of all plantations. For, only on the large plantations careful records had been kept of the economic activities and these *plantation records* were for the major part the sources of the data Fogel and Engerman had used. On account of that, the small plantations, which according to a number of historians had been more characteristic of the South, and where the living conditions of the slaves had probably been much worse, were not included in the picture. In addition, a somewhat other view of the source material painted a less cheerful picture. The infliction of corporal punishment might have been relatively infrequent, according to nineteenth century standards, but it still meant that, even if the number quoted by Fogel and Engerman — which was based on the data for one plantation(!) — came reasonably close to the historical practice, slaves on a big plantation witnessed the flogging of one of their own more often than once a week.

In a number of articles and in another book, Fogel and Engerman replied their critics.[30] The essence of their defense was, that the critique on their work was largely of a speculative nature. Of course, it was possible that the living conditions of slaves on small plantations — actually, that these would have been more characteristic of the South was opposed by them — might have been worse than on the big plantations, but the reverse was likewise also possible, and that controversy could only be truly solved by producing quantitative data which would support the first assumption with facts. And, given the fact that in *Time on the Cross* about all quantitative data that were known at the time about the living conditions of the slaves had been processed, their critics had not always managed to do so. Nevertheless, Fogel and Engerman, too, had to admit that from the avalanche of new research *Time on the Cross* had sparked off, a number of issues were raised indisputably, that at the very least were difficult to reconcile with the picture of the exceptionally favorable material conditions the slaves would have known. Further research into the physical characteristics of male plantation slaves and demographic analyses of their average life expectancy had indeed confirmed the optimistic image of a strong and well-nourished slave population, but how could this be reconciled with the extremely high infant mortality and the exceptionally low birth weight of slave babies?[31] It would seem that extremely hard physical labor for pregnant slaves until the birth of their baby had been normal on the plantations.

On other points as well, the historical picture seemed less unambiguous than Fogel and Engerman had initially suggested. Their position that the degree of exploitation of slaves (that portion of the income generated by a slave which the master appropriated) on average had not been more than 10%, was very susceptible to the manner in which one defined the degree of exploitation. Other authors arrived at much higher percentages on the basis of other definitions.[32]

Yet, it is hard to deny that *Time on the Cross*, given the fact that dozens of critics for years on end had done their utmost to make matchwood out of the book, has stood the test of time miraculously well[33], but again it seems as if the contribution of the book and the subsequent discussion to our knowledge of economic history can be summarized in negative rather than positive terms. *Time on the Cross* has unmistakably shown that the traditional image of the economic situation in the South prior to the Civil War with the North had been completely mistaken. Not the North was more prosperous, but the South, and the prospects of economic development had been more favorable at that moment in the 'traditional' South than in the 'modernizing' North. Also, Fogel and Engerman have ensured that every economic historian will react extremely cautiously to the question as to how the material living conditions of the American slaves were on the eve of the Civil War, while that question previously would have been answered by any and all with 'miserable to the point of inhuman'. *Time on the Cross* at that point has at least corrected the historical picture, albeit that the adjusted picture is inconsistent and not clear: On the one hand, there are no indications that such conditions had appeared to be surprisingly favorable in a large number of instances; on the other hand, closer scrutiny produced data (the high infant mortality and low birth weight of slave babies) that completely contradict that favorable picture.

Again: If one would like to speak of 'Socratic' economic history, the result of the discussion triggered by *Time on the Cross* is a classic example of that, even if in first instance you probably would not have surmised as much from the certainty with which Fogel and Engerman presented their findings in 1974.

Robert William Fogel and Stanley Engerman were, as said, themselves completely surprised by the picture that had emerged from the source material they had researched. And it must be said: In the years following the publication of *Time on the Cross* they both had not just attempted to stubbornly hold on to the picture they had painted. Of course they tried to defend themselves against their critics by endlessly explaining why they selected the sources, methods and techniques they had used. In the long term, however, they both, individually, tried to nuance the picture that emerged from their work. Engerman did so by researching slave economies in other countries and through this work indeed succeeded in introducing an important nuance: Practically everywhere in South America and the Caribbean, as was shown time and again by quantitative historical research, the living conditions of slaves had been worse than in the South of the United States. In other words, put in a slightly broader perspective, it would seem that the favorable material conditions of the slaves on the cotton plantations in the South of the United States had been the classic exception to the rule.

147

Fogel took another course. He came in contact with the work of the French historians of the *École des Annales* — more in particular that of Emmanuel Le Roy Ladurie — who, separate from the cliometric revolution in the United States, had built a rich tradition in the field of quantitative historic research on the standard of living in the past.[34] In this research, following the nineteenth-century 'Hygienists', changes in the material conditions under which the masses of the population in the past had lived, were reconstructed on the basis of fluctuations in all sorts of anthropometric variables, such as the average sex-specific and age-specific physical height, for which they used historical data of colored persons or soldiers.[35]

5.5 Engels is rising from his grave: Anthropometric history

By integrating the methods and techniques of the French historians into cliometrics, Fogel reinvigorated an old debate in social and economic history[16] (the so-called standard-of-living debate) and while doing so he laid the foundations for a new specialty within economic history: Anthropometric history. Thus he managed for the umpteenth time to bring an important innovation to the discipline, as is evidenced among other things by the fact that one of the central A-themes of the world congress of the *International Economic History Association*, which is held every three years, in 1998 was fully devoted to anthropometric history.

The standard-of-living debate essentially deals with the question whether material circumstances of the great majority of the population during the economic modernization process that, true to tradition is indicated as 'Industrial Revolution', had improved or worsened. Of old, two camps are distinguished: The so-called 'optimists' who believe that the living conditions improved as a result of economic modernization, and the 'pessimists', who assume the contrary. The debate must be viewed against the background of the ideological controversy between Marxists and liberals about the social consequences of capitalist development. A central point in the Marxist development theory was the so-called *Verelendung* theory which predicted that the material conditions of the proletariat would worsen as capitalism further developed. This view that in the second half of the nineteenth century and in the twentieth century had a tenacious following in leftist intellectual circles, was based on a book by Friedrich Engels (1845), *Die Lage der arbeitende Klasse in England*, in which he depicts the extremely poor living conditions of the English industrial workers in the first half of the nineteenth century. Economic historical research after Engels concentrated on the reconstruction of the real wage development in industrialized countries in the nineteenth century and the inescapable conclusion was that the standard of living of the average worker, in any case since the second half of the nineteenth century, had generally shown a dramatic improvement and in any case no worsening. This implied that in the long term no empirical support could be found for the standpoint of the 'pessimists' and with this, the orthodox pessimist standpoint, so it seemed, definitively fell into discredit: The *Verelendungs-theory* was relegated to the realm of fiction. In line with this development, Engels' view on the worsening living conditions of British laborers in the first half of the nineteenth century also faded into the background: If on the long run it could be demonstrated unambiguously that the development of capitalism in the nineteenth century on all sides had led to an unprecedented improvement in living conditions, how could it then be explained that in the first stages of economic modernization a dramatic worsening would have occurred? That seemed most unlikely and that was the exit of Friedrich Engels.

Even so, the adherents of the optimistic view in the debate had spoken a little too soon. The point was, that the development of real wages and all other (mainly demographic) variables that could provide an indication of the development of material circumstances, such as average life expectancy, child mortality, *et cetera*, for the second half of the nineteenth century without exception pointed towards improvement, but those very same variables showed a less unequivocal image for the first half of the nineteenth century. For this period, data was much scarcer than for later years and, in addition, the conclusions from different data sets were often contradictory. That notorious data scarcity, however, did not apply to one specific variable which had hardly played a role in the debate until then. It appeared (also for that period) that an abundance of data existed concerning the average human physical length. Military medicals; lists, originating in prisons, which apart from physical characteristics also kept the exact height of the prisoners; archives of orphanages, *et cetera*, formed a rich source of data about physical height in the first half of the nineteenth century, which made it possible to reconstruct, also for this period, annual time series of the average so-called sex-specific and age-specific[17] physical height for a large number of countries.

From the socio-medical sciences and from human biology, it was known that changes in a population's material living conditions are reflected in changes in the average physical length of that population: In case of an improvement, people become taller on average, whereas in case of a deterioration, they become smaller. The overwhelming volume of quantitative data about the development of the average height of people in the first half of the nineteenth century therefore seemed an ideal possibility to examine whether the 'optimists' in the standard-of-living debate, were also right for the period of early economic modernization.

In the eighties of the preceding century, this type of research took such an enormous flight within cliometrics, that at the end of the twentieth century it had developed into an independent specialty within economic history, anthropometric history.[38]

149

The results of anthropometric history research into the standard of living, in the light of the fact that in that time the view of the 'optimists' was generally regarded as correct, were surprising. On the basis of the development of the average physical height in the industrialized countries in the first half of the nineteenth century, it had to be concluded that indeed there had been a dramatic deterioration in the material living conditions and that meant nothing more or less than a rehabilitation of the view Friedrich Engels had developed in his *Die Lage der arbeitende Klasse in England*.

At the same time that result was of course extremely paradoxical: The reconstruction of historical national accounts that had been realized for many a country for the nineteenth century in the years preceding the rise of anthropometric history, learned that such deterioration of material conditions generally had taken place in a period in which the real national income per capita had increased! Could it be possible that economic growth for a longer period was accompanied with a decline in the material living conditions of the great majority of the population? This strange phenomenon, that was named the 'early modernization paradox' or 'Komlos paradox'[39] in the literature, today takes a central position in anthropometric history, and despite a number of bold attempts to answer the paradoxical question, at the moment there is still no consensus on the matter. What the 'early modernization paradox' does indeed clearly show, is that in some instances economic growth over a longer period can bring along such a serious social disruption, that large groups of society may be worse off for a longer period in terms of living conditions. This latter conclusion seems difficult to reconcile with one of the basic thoughts of the neoclassical economic theory, that predicts that adjustments of a market system to exogenous shocks in general happen fast and smoothly.

150

5.6 The mystery of McCormick's Reaper

The physical size of a study is a reasonable indication of the diligence of the writer, but says nothing further about the importance of his work for the development of his discipline. Sometimes a study of very brief size can have an unbelievably great impact. A classic example of this latter is an article by Paul David, with the title 'The Mechanization of Reaping in the Ante-Bellum Midwest' (1966), which was first published in a *liber amicorum* for the *éminence grise* of American economic history in the 1960s, Alexander Gerschenkron, and was reprinted countless times since.

David's study in set-up was not much more than a case study into the introduction of the first harvesting machines in American agriculture in the nineteenth century, but without exaggerating one could maintain that the manner in which he analyzed the problem, forever changed the approach of technological change issues in economic history: There are not many articles of as few as 40 pages in our discipline that have found such a massive following, perhaps with the exception of the earlier mentioned 'The Economics of Slavery' by Alfred Conrad and John Meyer.

The problem that David attacked was — as so often in new economic history — not new. It basically involved a paradox that traditional economic history had never been able to solve, with the result that the matter laid dormant in traditional literature. What it involved, was that the first successful mechanical harvesters in the United States, the so-called *Reaper* (see: Figure 5.7), which in the beginning of the thirties of the nineteenth century had been developed by two inventive American farmers, Obid Hussey and Cyrus McCormick, initially was no commercial success at all, but about twenty to thirty years later, suddenly and completely unexpectedly became a topnotch bestseller.

In short, between 1833 and 1840 only 45 Reapers were bought by American farmers. At the end of 1846, McCormick decided to move production, which until then had taken place at his own farm, to a separate factory in Chicago, but until that moment, since the invention of that machine, no more than some 800 had been sold. From then on, things changed rapidly: About 1850 in the United States alone 3,373 harvesting machines had been sold since 1833, and some eight years later, that had become... 74,000!

The question naturally is why it had taken the American farmers so long (some thirty years, please note) to grasp that they could realize enormous savings by not, as had been done for thousands of years, bringing in the harvest by sickle or scythe, but with a simple harvesting machine, pulled along by one or two horses.

Figure 5.7: The Reaper (from 1833) of Obid Hussey & Cyrus McCormick

The answer that was previously given to that question put the blame on a deeply rooted conservatism of American grain farmers in the Cornbelt. They would have waited first to see which way the wind blew, so to speak, before they massively switched over to the new technology.

That explanation was highly improbable for two reasons: Firstly, the American grain farmers from the Cornbelt in that time were known for their unbridled urge for innovation. In innumerable studies people had been amazed at this great 'urge for innovation' of the farmers from the Cornbelt: Why would they have, as they did (and very successfully), experimented extensively with new hybrid crops, with new fertilization and irrigation techniques, etc., but shied away from an experiment with the new harvesting machine which — as appeared in the fifties — could imply a gigantic productivity increase?

The second reason why the traditional explanation seemed to cut no ice, was the sudden, overwhelming success of the Reaper since the beginning of the fifties. If the alleged conservatism of the farmers had been the decisive factor in the delayed adoption of the Reaper, a much more gradual adoption curve (if one sheep leaps over the ditch, all the rest will follow, but not all at once) would have been more natural.

David's analysis of the problem was bold, because he, solely by applying elementary price theory, could show that the grain farmers of the Cornbelt did not at all for irrational reasons had postponed the adoption of the harvesting machine, but rather because they had waited (with unerring precision, so to say) with purchasing a Reaper until the moment that the harvesting machine had indeed become economically lucrative.

His reasoning was as follows[40]: From an economic point of view the two technological regimes involved, can be distinguished from one another, because they embody different cost configurations (see: Figure 5.8). David started from the unavoidable fact that harvesting with scythe or sickle is a relatively labor-intensive technology; compared to the harvesting machine that *mutatis mutandis* embodies a relatively capital-intensive manner of harvesting. This translates in different total cost curves for the two methods. The old technology is characterized by a relatively slight share of the fixed costs in the production process and — in the event of an increasing quantity of harvested grain per time unit — a sharply increasing variable costs curve (graph A).[41] This is plausible enough in itself: The expenses on fixed capital per farm in the case of the old technology (scythes or sickles, grindstones, etc.) are a fraction of the expenses a farmer has to incur, to be able to buy a Reaper (OA in graph A is smaller than OA in graph B), but then again, if the farmer wants to harvest more within a

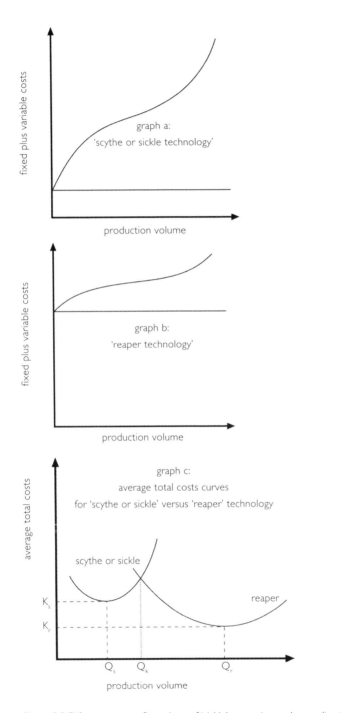

Figure 5.8 Diferent cost configurations of 'sickle' versus 'reaper' according to David (1966)

certain time limit (remember, the harvest is seasonal) the old technology rapidly gets into 'capacity problems'. The only manner to realize this, is indeed to 'man' the scythes available more intensively (from the crack of dawn until late into dusk and this, all days of the week) and this in turn means that the farmer in question must hire additional labor, and consequently, that he is confronted with increasing labor costs, which in the total cost curve are expressed by the sharply increasing curve AB.

Harvesting with the Reaper exactly contrasts with this (graph B): The share of the fixed costs in the total costs is relatively large, but on the other hand, when increasing the production volume, the rise in variable costs passes off much more flatly than when harvesting with the scythe (in graph B, AB is rather less sharp than in graph A). In simple words: The Reaper is very expensive, but on the other hand, once you have it, you can harvest a much larger area per time unit without encountering the capacity problems that quickly emerge with the 'sickle technology'.

The characteristic difference in the total cost curves between 'sickle technology' and 'reaper technology' now leads — so price theory dictates inevitably — to a difference which is just as characteristic between the *average* total cost curves, that is: The relation between the total costs per *unit of product* and the production volume (graph C). And this difference was precisely the explanation for the delayed adoption of the harvesting machine. To clarify this, it is elucidating to take a closer look at graph C. Four things are here of vital importance:

1   In the first place, one should realize that within the framework of neoclassical price theory, average total costs in a situation of equilibrium (this means, among other things, that there is price competition on the market) equal the price of the product made. You can imagine that as follows: A producer must recover at least his total costs[42] per unit of product with his selling price. If he does not succeed in this, he will sustain losses, and in the long run he will go bankrupt. In that regard, the average total costs are some sort of minimum selling price for the producer. On the other hand, no producer can afford asking more for his product than *exactly* those average total costs per unit of product. If he asks more, he will price himself out of the market immediately: For, his competitors offer the same product at a lower price (namely: The average costs per unit of product!) and why would his buyers not collectively go over to the competition? In the latter, the total average costs are at the same time some sort of maximum selling price for the producer. Result: In equilibrium prices equal average costs per unit.

2   Both average costs curves ('sickle' and 'reaper') in graph C attain their minimum at a certain production volume. In harvesting with the sickle the cost minimum is attained with production volume OQ_s; for harvest-

ing with the reaper, this is OQ_r. Put in plain words: For both technologies there is an optimal production volume seen from the angle of cost minimization. With less production, the average costs will increase as a result of the undermanning of the production machinery; with more production, they will do so as a consequence of economic 'overheating' of the production process. Note: The cost minimum for the relatively capital-intensive 'reaper technology' is attained with a *larger* production volume than for the relatively labor-intensive 'sickle technology' ($OQ_r >$ OQ_s) and that is also entirely plausible: The relatively high fixed costs of the Reaper must be 'spread' over a larger number of units produced and sold, than is the case with the 'cheaper' sickle technology.

3   The cost minimum realized with an optimal production volume is lower with the capital-intensive 'reaper technology' in absolute terms than with the 'sickle technology' ($OK_r < OK_s$), in other words, as long as the quantity produced is large enough, it will be possible to produce with the Reaper at such low average costs as with the scythe or sickle cannot be attained under any circumstance.

4   The cost minimum for production with the harvesting machine is reached, as stated earlier, with a larger production than when harvesting with the scythe or sickle. This implies that that there is one specific production quantity (OQ_k in graph C) where from a perspective of average total costs, it does not matter whether one harvests with the sickle or the Reaper. If the production is smaller than OQ_k, harvesting with the sickle is from an economic point of view the most efficient production method; if the production is larger than OQ_k, the harvesting machine wins.

Paul David now could show that circumstances in the Midwest of the United States until 1850, were such that an average grain production per farm of more than OQ_k was totally not achievable. Among other things, as the result of the land-issue policy of the American government the average acreage of the farms was much too small, and in addition, the population size of the United States was not large enough to create a demand for grain to make mechanization lucrative.[43]

After 1850 the situation had changed completely: Population had grown at a fast pace and the demand for grain had increased accordingly. From censuses of that time David could deduce that the average grain farm in the Cornbelt was now characterized by a much bigger acreage.

Then there was another condition: The construction of the railway, right through the prairie, really started to get going by the middle of nineteenth century, and that was in that time an extremely risky and labor-intensive job, where high wages were paid. The result was that the wages of farm workers in the Midwest increased as soon as, in a manner of speaking, a railway appeared on the horizon.

Naturally, this had consequences for the position of the average total cost curve of the two agricultural production methods: Both increased by consequence, but the average cost curve for the labor-intensive production method (harvesting with scythe or sickle) increased much faster because of increasing wages, than the average cost curve for the 'reaper technology', for this involved much less labor per unit of harvested grain. You can work out for yourself what happens in graph C, if both curves move upward, supposed that the curve for the 'sickle technology' climbs faster than the 'reaper curve': Point Q_k shifts over the horizontal axis to the left, which implies that the minimum production volume at which it becomes efficient to switch over to the harvesting machine is diminishing!

By analyzing a great quantity of historical statistical data, Paul David now could show that the circumstances economically justified the large-scale use of McCormicks harvesting machine only around 1850. This meant that the grain growers of the Midwest, who had always been keen on innovation, in this instant as well had acted exactly as was to be expected of modern, rational farmers, and this solved the mystery of the delayed adoption of the Reaper.

David's study throughout the years produced a real tidal wave of research which tackled more or less similar problems (for example: Why had it taken so long for the sailing ship to be definitively ousted by the steamship?) in 'Davidian' manner, and often yielded a satisfactory answer as to why certain production methods had succeeded in certain circumstances, whereas in others they had failed. The most important implication of David's study was that the generally accepted idea that the most modern technology in any circumstances, is also the most efficient from an economic point of view, could be relegated to the realm of fiction. This idea has been of great importance for the discipline of development economics: The question why the export of modern Western technology to developing countries, in order to increase labor productivity over there, all too often turned out utterly and completely wrong, could be answered simply within the framework of David's explanation for the delayed adoption of the Reaper.

5.7 The *Reinterpretation* as milestone of the NEH

In the first ten years of its existence, the new economic history developed itself in an environment that can be labeled to a certain extent as *splendid isolation.* Undoubtedly there was feverish activity, but those activities were limited to a relatively small group of researchers who, almost without exception, were attached to the economic faculties of the topnotch American universities, and in addition, sometimes part-time attached to the National Bureau of Economic Research, and who among themselves were precisely informed of each other's works through conferences and workshops, where always the same group of researchers of a scarcely varying composition engaged in sharp debates with one another. In those initial years it very much seemed as if that which the cliometricians had in common with each other, was especially concentrated in the methods they applied to their research, but that the subjects they broached were outstanding in its diversity. That isolation in respect of what was happening elsewhere in economic history was, of course, deepened by the fact that articles with a cliometric bias initially were published only in economic journals. Only in the course of the 1970s, for example, the great majority of the articles in the most prominent economic history journal, the *Journal of Economic History,* become cliometric in nature.[44] The instant leap from 40% to over 70% cliometric articles in the *Journal* between the second half of the 1960s and the first half of the 1970s, is a clear signal that in the early seventies the comparatively isolated position of the new economic history had been in, ever since its emergence has suddenly come to an end.

The publication in 1971 of the first great comprehensive overview of the results the new economic history had achieved in the first ten years of its existence, played a key role in this. This book was *The Reinterpretation of American Economic History,* edited by Robert William Fogel and Stanley Engerman (Fogel & Engerman (Eds.),1971).

Reinterpretation may be considered as the first major milestone of cliometrics, however, not because the contents were entirely new: Apart from the extensive introductions by the two editors to the nine parts in which the book was subdivided, the thirty-six different essays of which the book consisted, for the greater part were reprints — indeed, some had been thoroughly revised — of earlier published studies.[45] For the seasoned participants in cliometric congresses of the 1960s the book in fact held no novelty. No, the importance of the book was not to be underestimated for a different reason.

Figure 5.9: Robert W. Fogel

Figure 5.10: Stanley L. Engerman

First of all, the contents of *Reinterpretation* instantly made clear that the new economic historians had more in common with one another than only the methods and techniques they applied in their research. Sure, at a glance, the first thing to strike the attention, was the tremendous diversity of subjects brought up in the book. Of course, extensive attention was lavished on the role of the railways in the American economic development process in the nineteenth century, and the economic aspects of the system of slavery in relation to the consequences of the Civil War for the economic divergence between the North and the South in the second half of the nineteenth and the first half of the twentieth century: Two subjects which had meanwhile grown into the standard hobbyhorses of cliometrics. But in addition, numerous other subjects were dealt with: The structural changes the American economy had gone through in the nineteenth century; technological changes in a large number of different sectors; the influence of education and training on economic development; the manner in which the American economic expansion had been financed; the extent to which changes in factors of supply and demand had stimulated the development in the iron industry, the economic impact of immigration and urbanization in the nineteenth century; and the role that the American government had played in the economic field in various periods.

That great variety of subjects could not conceal, however, that all essays had in fact been written from one and the same fundamental question:

How could the historically unprecedentedly fast economic development of the United States since the second half of the nineteenth century be explained? Or more precisely still: W*hich factors* had *to what extent* been responsible for that baffling development? Because precisely in that question was enclosed the essence of the new economic history.

Secondly, the thrust of the answer that was given in *Reinterpretation* to the question as to the why of the exceptionally fast American economic growth was essential to the proceeding of the debate about economic growth in the final quarter of the twentieth century, even though some readers will hardly be able to contain their disappointment in learning the answer. For the answer was, that despite the gigantic quantitative historical drudgery that lay at the roots of each of the chapters, there was actually no univocal answer to be given, but to all appearances, the standard replies which had been generally accepted for decades and decades in the economic history discipline could not stand the — quantitative — test of criticism.

To extract that conclusion, you had to read between the lines a little, for that matter: *Reinterpretation* was not in the least intended as a proud presentation of that which ten years of cliometrics had ultimately yielded, and for that reason an all too clear Socratic thrust (now we know precisely why we do not know) was of course absolutely forbidden. A few examples may elucidate matters in this respect, however.

5.8 Technology and mechanization: Often essential and ...sometimes not

In traditional economic history technological progress, which you see reflected in the Western world in the enormous increase in the stock of capital goods in the nineteenth and twentieth centuries, was invariably considered to be one of the crucial factors that, in the long run, increased productivity. Mechanization of production was traditionally seen as one of the most important and immediately apparent sources of modern economic growth. From various essays in *Reinterpretation* it now became clear that in a number of sectors of the American economy mechanization was indeed the most important factor by far for the increase in productivity, but that at the same time, in a number of other sectors mechanization had not been a negligible factor indeed, but as main reason for the increase of production it was largely overshadowed by other factors. In the agricultural sector, for example, and especially in grain farming, mechanization was a decisive factor in the increase of production in the long run[46], but in the sector of sea transport, the influence of mechanization on the increase of productivity had hardly been of any importance. Douglass North relegated the traditional explanation that the substitution in the course of the nineteenth century of the sailing ship by the steamship had played the pivotal role in this process to the realm of fiction and thus solved a puzzle for which traditional economic history in fact had never been able to give a conclusive explanation.[47] For, if the substitution of wind energy by steam power was so important for the decrease in average costs for transoceanic transport, how could it then be explained that sailing ships and steamboats had existed alongside each other for so long? The first steamers had come on the scene already by the middle of the nineteenth century, while the commercial exploitation of sailing ships only definitively ended after World War I. North's calculations showed that not the nature of the propulsion[48] was the decisive factor, but the cargo capacity in relation to the size of the crew. Large ships had always been more efficient than small ships, and in the course of the nineteenth century the rapid reduction in the average transport costs for transport by sea was owed mainly to two factors. First, there was the decrease of piracy on the seas. By consequence, the need to arm ocean-going vessels had gradually disappeared and the result of that, in turn, was that the effectively exploitable cargo space per ship could increase and the number of crewmembers could be reduced. Secondly, the drop in the costs of sea transport in the nineteenth century had especially been caused by the fact that in this period small ships were increasingly replaced by large ones. That increase in average tonnage had little or nothing to do with technological progress in the shipbuilding industry: Also in the middle of the nineteenth century, shipbuilders were already capable of constructing big ships. The crucial point here was the expansion of port facilities: By a greater concentration of commodities in the sea ports, the average waiting time of sea-going vessels in port awaiting new cargo had decreased dramatically and the more intensive capacity utilization that was the result of that, appeared to have been an essential factor in the drop of average transport costs.

A similar story can be told for the development of that which in the nineteenth century was one of the fastest growing branches of industry in the United States, namely the production of cotton fabrics. Cotton mills (and not until much later: Weaving mills) were the outstanding examples in the United Kingdom where for the first time experiments were conducted with mechanized production techniques. In England in 1787 already a number of those factories could be found, but the United States swiftly followed the English experiments. The first, hydropower-operated, commercially successful cotton mill in America was established on Rhode Island in 1790, while the first mechanized cotton weaving mill was set up in 1814. The modern production techniques spread over the United States during the first quarter of the nineteenth century, but after these far-reaching innovations in production technology, technological innovations in this sector developed much more slowly. The odd thing is, that the development of average labor productivity in the American cotton industry expanded enormously precisely after the period in which big technological breakthroughs had occurred[49]: Between 1833 and 1839, the average annual increase of labor productivity was a mere 7 percent, while in the years between 1855 and 1859 the increase was still at least 3 percent per year.[50] Careful econometric analysis by Paul David (1970) of numerical data that had previously been collected by Lance Davis and Louis Stettler (1966) showed that the decisive factor in the increase of labor productivity (over 60%) simply had been capital intensification and increase in scale, which means: Caused by the fact that every worker had to operate more machines and, as a result, more raw material could be processed per hour. A substantial part of the productivity increase (30% in the period 1833-1839 and 17% between 1855 and 1859) had to be attributed to what was called *learning-by-doing*, the phenomenon that the efficiency of production 'crawls upwards' in the course of time because all persons involved, little by little, become ever better adjusted to the new production technology. The study by David was one of the first examples showing that big technological breaks after their introduction often took surprisingly long before their effect on the productivity could reach its full impact on the economy.[51]

161

One of the few chapters from *Reinterpretation* that had not been published earlier elsewhere, was a study by Robert Brooke Zevin (1971) which also dealt with the American cotton industry in the nineteenth century. Again, it appeared that technological progress had not been the only (and perhaps not even the most important) factor that had brought about the exceptional growth in this sector. The importance of Zevin's contribution was, that he managed to make clear that changes on the demand side probably had been for over 50 percent responsible for the increase in American cotton fabrics production during the first half of the nineteenth century. Four factors were of decisive importance in this: The fact that the American government protected the domestic market against cotton imports from England by way of an import tariff[52]; the increase in the American population and the increase of urbanization[53]; the increase in the real income per head of the population and, finally, the substantial drop in transport costs that, apart from technological progress in the sector itself, brought about a considerable drop in the prices of cotton fabrics.

The contributions by Peter Temin in relation to the American technological development in the nineteenth century could appropriately be called Socratic. In his study regarding the choice between water-mill versus steam engine as a source of power, he managed (more or less analogous to the reasoning Paul David had set forth in respect of delayed adoption of the Reaper) in a convincing manner to make plausible that this choice was inspired by various cost configurations emanating from local geographic conditions. In other words: The simple application of standard neoclassical principles yields a logically sound explanation for the choice between one or the other technology. The odd thing, however, is that in doing so, he completely demolished a generally accepted explanation for the difference in technological development between England and the United States that had indeed fully been based on neoclassical insights.

In 1962 the English economic historian Habakkuk had published a renowned essay, in which the rapid technological development of the United States compared to England was explained from the relatively large scarcity of labor in America, which would have led to a growing real wage differential. The relatively high labor wages in the United States would have led, according to Habakkuk, to the development of an in comparison to England, high labor-saving technology. In his dissertation (Temin, 1966), a summary of which was included in *Reinterpretation*, Temin denied that indications of that nature were to be found in American technological development and with this he undermined, in essence, the standard neoclassical model. However, Fogel (1967) in the following year already, suggested in a methodological article that Temin himself had to make a number of highly specific assumptions to be able to refute Habakkuk and later research suggested that Habakkuk had indeed been right.[54]

In the area of American industrial expansion in the nineteenth century, both editors of *Reinterpretation*, Robert William Fogel and Stanley Engerman, made a contribution about the development of the American iron industry, in which, by making use in an admirably elegant manner of a number of doctrines from neoclassical theory, and despite an acute shortage of quantitative data, a detailed breakdown could be made according to factors of supply and demand, as a result of which this study became the classic example that in subsequent years was followed all over.

5.9   Monetary policy: Often essential and ...sometimes not

Another example in which the *communis opinio* in economic history appeared unable to withstand detailed quantitative research into the problem in question, concerned the explanation of the economic crisis that had affected the United States in the forties of the nineteenth century. Of old, the blame for this had been laid on the measures the American president, Andrew Jackson, had taken against the *Second Bank of the United States*, which in those years fulfilled the role of central bank. Jackson had in 1832 prematurely withdrawn a charter which had been granted to the *Second Bank* to serve as bank of the American government, and in the following year had spread the government funds over a large number of smaller banks. These in turn had considered such funds as an increase in their reserves and on that basis had proceeded to expand their extension of credit. This resulted in a disproportionate increase of the volume of money in society, as the traditional story went, resulting in: Inflation. This inflation was intensified because the increased room for credit was especially used by private persons to finance land purchases (remember that this was the period in which the American frontier moved westward at a high speed). It was the central government that sold the new land, in other words: The money paid by the new land owners, again landed in the coffers of the central government that subsequently placed this extra money in the local banks, which in turn proceeded to credit expansion, etc. In this manner a classic inflationary spiral would have been created that undoubtedly sooner or later would have led to a crisis and a subsequent recession.

The crisis came in 1837. The cause would have been that the government suddenly demanded payment in hard cash for the land purchases, for which it previously had accepted payment in the form of bank transfers. The subsequent run on the banks (*The Panic of 1837*) was followed by a recession in the forties.

Detailed quantitative research into the size and timing of price developments and flows of money and goods by Peter Temin showed that the traditional explanation for the crisis of the forties could not be right.[55] The inflation of the thirties and the subsequent crisis of the forties had not been the result at all of American monetary policy, but originated abroad, so it appeared.

Temin concluded that the credit expansion by the banks was not based on the fast growing government funds in the banks, but on a gigantic increase in the stock of precious metal in the United States. That increase resulted from a combination of two factors, namely the increased

163

export of American cotton to England as a result of a long-term favorable economic development on the British mainland and, strangely enough, a development that in the history books is known as the 'Opium Wars'. The Americans had always imported huge quantities of silver from South America, which they previously had used to pay their imports of oriental goods from China. The increased American cotton exports to England were paid by the British importers to the American exporters with bills of exchange, letters of credit in English pounds. Precisely in the same period, a dramatic increase occurred in the opium use in China, initiated by English traders. The Americans discovered that they could pay their trade deficit in China just as well with the letters of credit they had received from the English in payment of their cotton. Those very letters of credit appeared to be an appreciated means in China to pay the English opium traders. The result was that the silver stock in the United States, which previously had drained away to China, now remained in the United States and this caused a galloping inflation in the thirties. The increased price level in the United States, in any case, would have had to lead to a decline of American exports and an increase in exports, as a result of which the excess of precious metal would have drained away again, but ...reality was more obstinate. In that time, in Europe, American loans were in great demand as an investment opportunity, and the American trade deficit was thus for a long time compensated by capital imports from Europe. That was the reason, according to Temin, why the inflationary climate in the United States was so persistent. The sudden end in 1837 had also little if anything to do with the American economic development, but again was the result of developments in England. Halfway through 1836, the English cyclical revival came to an end, resulting in an instantly declining cotton price, and the English central Bank was suddenly faced with decreasing gold reserves. The Bank of England promptly took measures to restrict credit. Through the intensive economic contacts between England and the United States, those measures before long made themselves felt on the other side of the ocean as well. For the boom in the cotton exports had been financed from American claims on English importers and because of the credit restrictions that now were effective, as well as the decline in the cotton price, the English importers ran into serious problems. The American trust in fiduciary money disappeared like snow in summer, and there was a run on the banks. The public demanded *en masse* the exchange of notes into coins and in the shortest possible time the banks were forced to discontinue the exchange, with which the Panic of 1837 had become a fact.

Temin's new view of the boom in the thirties and the subsequent economic crisis of the forties remained relatively unaffected for a long time and within cliometrics, where debates showed a strong inclination to go on endlessly, it seemed to be a rather exceptional example of consensus. But after over thirty years even that exceptional status of Temin's view came to an end: Recently, Peter Rousseau (2002) published a study in which, on the basis of new quantitative data and new, advanced research methods, it is suggested most emphatically that the impact of American economic policy on the events had been much greater than Temin assumed. According to Rousseau, the foreign causes of the inflation had been correctly interpreted by Temin, but the crisis which had subsequently followed had indeed been aggravated by domestic monetary measures.

The theoretical point of departure of Peter Temin in his analysis of the American economy under the presidency of Andrew Jackson, had been taken from a monumental study by Milton Friedman and Anna Jacobson Schwartz (1963), *A Monetary History of the United States*. This book played a central role in Friedman's attack on the in the 1960s highly popular Keynesian view of the role of economic policy. Keynesians were usually of the opinion that in comparison to fiscal policy, monetary policy was of minor importance. In the event of an imminent deficit of demand, the government, so the Keynesian model taught, should encourage demand by means of additional government spending and/or tax relief, and in the event of an imminent excess of demand, it should act in a restraining manner by cutting down on government spending and/or increasing the tax burden. The followers of the Keynesian theory did not deny that such measures also had a monetary impact, but that impact was considered to be of minor importance. One of the spearheads of Friedman's attack on Keynesianism was that he wanted to show that there actually was an independent and quantitatively important influence from the monetary realm on the real realm and from that point of view *A Monetary History* had been written. Part of the book was devoted to a monetarist review of the causes of the crisis of 1930s in the United States. The generally accepted interpretation of those days had a clear Keynesian slant: The crisis was explained from imbalances in the real realm and the monetary policy followed played a marginal role in that view. Friedman set the cat among the Keynesian pigeons by showing that a panic reaction of the Federal Reserve System, had not created the crisis, indeed, but did make a decisive contribution to the deepening of the crisis, and finally its growing into the most serious and persistent crisis which had ever scourged the United States. From the new economic history Peter Temin (1976) took on the defense of the Keynesians with a book having the significant title: *Did Monetary Forces Cause the Great Depression?* That the answer to that question according to Temin had to be an emphatic 'no' was remark-

165

able, because within the new economic history the neoclassical body of thought was dominant and Friedman, to be sure, wanted to dethrone the Keynesian theory in favour of a neoclassical monetarist view. With this, the Temin-Friedman controversy is one of the few examples of a new economic historian reasoning from another theoretic angle than the standard neoclassical model.

There is a second reason why this debate is remarkable: It prevails until this day, without it being clear in which direction the definitive answer should be found to the question Friedman had posed in 1963.[56]

5.10 *Reinterpretation* as research agenda: Limited consensus

The great variety in subjects broached in *Reinterpretation* could easily lead to the conclusion that the consensus within cliometrics about the methods and techniques with which economic history research should be conducted is the decisive centripetal force within the movement, but that the new economic history at the same time, both as regards the choice of issues and the nature of the answers to those issues, is especially characterized by centrifugal forces. These conclusions are not completely wide of the truth, but still need to be nuanced for a considered opinion. If you place the book edited by Fogel and Engerman in a somewhat broader perspective, it is indeed possible to discern in *Reinterpretation* a number of clear lines concerning content as well. The importance of this is that those lines mainly have dominated the economic history research agenda the final quarter of the twentieth century.

In the first place, there is the delimitation of the perspective of time. Sure, a number of studies involved the previous colonial history of the United States, and sure, in a few chapters the perspective of time was carried into the twentieth century. But this does not alter the fact that the lion's share of *Reinterpretation* deals with American economic development in the nineteenth century. The emphasis on the nineteenth century can only be explained in part by pointing to the fact that for that period relatively much quantitative data can be found: This does indeed not apply to the preceding centuries, but it certainly holds true for the subsequent one. More important, in my opinion, is the point concerning content: The nineteenth century is the period in which the process of structural economic change was taking place from a pre-modern (and for a long time stagnating) economy to a modern economic system, that is characterized by economic growth in the long term, and precisely the explanation for that specific process of transition, forms the central issue of the new economic history.

In the second place, it is not all that difficult to understand that in answering that question only a few things are highlighted. It is in this context elucidating to differentiate between supply and demand factors that played a role in the production of goods and services.

To start with the latter: Here, research focuses on the role that in the process of economic growth was played by the growth of the population and the increase in the real income per capita, but especially: Market growth. As to the latter point, two things are of importance: Firstly, the geographic increase in scale (from local, via regional to international), whereby an essential function is assigned to the dramatic decline of transport costs, resulting in what is called the 'transport revolution' in the nineteenth century. Secondly: The spectacular market differentiation which is the result of the division of labor and specialization in the production process. The supply factors include in fact only two on which attention is focused: capital and technology.

The factor capital mainly involves the contribution to economic growth caused by the growth of the capital stock and the manner in which such growth is financed. In the explanation for the financing of the growth of the stock of capital goods, the development of the capital market is highlighted.

As regards technology, the essential question is how new methods and techniques promoted the efficiency of production, in other words, how new technology was introduced into society, and how it did spread throughout the entire system.

Without exaggeration, you can maintain that, formulated in this manner, the *Reinterpretation of American Economic History* has formulated the research agenda of economic history, in terms of methods and content, until deep into the nineties of the past century. In first instance, this of course held true for research in the United States, but (possible to a somewhat lesser degree) also for Europe: Precisely at the moment that *Reinterpretation* appeared, the new economic history gradually gained also a firm foothold at the other side of the ocean, and much of the European research done in the seventies and eighties was evidently inspired by the American example.[57] The inevitable result of this development was that, while the introduction of cliometrics in the United States in itself had brought about an intensification of scientific research in the field of economic history, its subsequent victory in European academics caused the number of cliometric studies again to increase explosively. And although in this new

167

avalanche as well an certain Socratic tendency may be detected, it cannot be denied either that gradually the contours showed of a certain measure of consensus where it concerned the explanation of the emergence of a modern economic system characterized by continuous economic growth in the long term. Indeed, the consensus was restricted, but it formed the starting point of a dramatic shift in perspective within the economic history that became clearly visible in the nineties and ultimately turned the entire new economic history inside out. If only for that reason, it is important to try to capture that consensus in a few words.

On four points the research findings seem to point in one direction. First, time and again, it appears that the economic growth has been a very gradual process. Growth rates can differ hugely year by year and in the development of any country there are always periods to be distinguished with a more rapid and a less rapid growth, but it is certainly not so that modern economic growth in any society has ever developed within a couple of years. If you want to speak of an instant change, you would have to take a rather broad perspective of time: Angus Maddison (1995; 1999; 2000) in a number of studies has made a bold attempt to make a (of course highly rough) estimate of the economic growth since the beginning of our era, and in that perspective there is indeed a sudden and historically unprecedented "growth explosion" in the entire western world that gets going somewhere in the nineteenth century. The dominant thought in traditional economic history that certain technological breakthroughs that have a profound effect on economic life (the steam engine, the internal-combustion engine, the development of electricity as fuel transporter, etc.) have been of decisive significance, is certainly not denied to this day, but it is emphatically pointed out that decades have to pass by before the impact of such technological breakthroughs begins to make itself felt in the economy as a whole.

Secondly, in modern economic history, more than before, people have come to realize that minimal differences in growth percentages between countries, in the long term may result in gigantic differences in levels of prosperity. France and Argentina had about the same real income per head of the population around 1900. Today the French real income per capita is roughly three times as high as that of Argentina. The reason? In France, economic growth per capita in the twentieth century averaged approximately 2.2 percent per year and in Argentina, around 1.1 percent.[58]

Thirdly, on account of the long-term research a shift in emphasis occurred as regards the role of the government in the economic process. In most handbooks about macroeconomics, extensive attention is given to the role of economic policy. Economic history research shows in the direction that the influence of fiscal and monetary policy measures in the short term is indeed great: Slight miscalculations can have big destabilizing effects in the short term. Nevertheless, it seems as if the long-term effects of economic policy are relatively minor, unless ... an unsound policy is continued for a long succession of years. During the crisis of the thirties, for example, a number of countries for a long time held to the gold standard, whereas a number of other countries at an early stage already switched to floating exchange rates. In retrospect, the first group has suffered longer and more severely under the crisis on account of following that course, but in the years after the Second World War the difference was in fact hardly noticeable any more. Countries where dozens of years at a stretch an economic policy is followed that continuously leads to high inflation (Argentina seems to be again an obvious example), thus effectively undermine the opportunities for economic growth. A second example concerns the influence of the tax burden, but here the consensus is considerably lower: An extremely high tax burden is considered by a number of writers, especially originating from the United States, as a brake on private economic initiative, and thus as a serious impediment to economic growth. Other — mainly European — researchers have pointed out that countries with a relatively high tax burden and an extensive system of social security provisions, such as the Scandinavian countries, in the twentieth century have not scored lower than countries where a milder fiscal climate and a more austere welfare plan were prevalent.

This latter links to a point about which there does exist — and this time full — unanimity: A large degree of social and political stability is an absolute precondition for economic growth and to the extent that the government plays an important role in this, its influence is essential. The example given is time and again the influence of the American Civil War on the economic development in the United States in the second half of the nineteenth century. Not only were the negative consequences of the Civil War still felt for dozens of years after the end of the conflict, but the Civil War also signified the turning point in regional economic development of the United States: It was the main reason why the South of the United States landed in a long-term economic stagnation process.

The last — and for the development of the economic history research perhaps the most important — point of consensus concerns the role of markets in economic growth processes. Everywhere in the western world where a successful economic development process manifested itself, this was always accompanied by the growth and differentiation of markets, and by an increase of market efficiency. It was that conclusion that evoked a number of fundamental questions that in the eighties and nineties became very prominent. Everyone understood that there was indeed a con-

169

spicuous connection (where economic growth manifested itself, there was also market development), but at the same time everyone also understood that economic growth and market development were not the same. Gradually a question became inevitable that the neoclassical theory could not answer, because it implicitly considered market development as a 'natural' process. That question was: Why do markets sometimes develop, but especially, *why they often do not?*

Notes

1   It is not my intention to give in this chapter a full summary of all economic history research that was conducted in the framework of the new economic history. That would transcend the framework of this chapter and, moreover, such summaries have been published earlier, from admirably brief (McCloskey, 1987) to surprisingly complete (Atack & Passell, 1994). What I do hope to achieve with this chapter is to make the reader, by a number of representative examples, familiar with the specific approach of economic history issues, and the way of thinking which is characteristic of cliometrics.

2   The words 'for free' are not placed between inverted commas for nothing: Education for society as a whole after 1870 did not become instantly 'free', of course. The difference is, that prior to that time, only the parents and caregivers of the children who received education, paid for it. After 1870 the overall education costs are 'spread' over all English taxpayers, that is to say, that childless couples and people whose children do not or no longer receive education as well, started to pay part of the costs for education. This note is an illustration of Milton Friedman's famous dictum 'There is no such thing as a free meal'.

3   We assume for the sake of clarity that part of the taxes paid by the family that *is spent on education* also falls under the category 'all other goods and services'. That is not completely correct, because the family does not have a free choice of spending for that part: It *has* to pay taxes, and whether it finds the government spending on education useful or not, has nothing to do with it. But mind you, the amount of taxes paid by the family itself for education is a fraction of the costs of such education: All English taxpayers pay part of these costs indeed! Finally, how can the family find itself in point D? That point is 'to the northeast' of budget line AE and so budget-wise beyond the financial possibilities of the family? No, owing to the 'free' education offered by the government, budget line AE no longer applies! The quantity of education OE_1 offered is 'free' for the family and it can therefore spend its entire budget OA on other goods and services. Hence, the family finds itself indeed in point D.

4   See chapter 2, paragraph 10, pp. 48-52, preceding.

5 True, the development of the PC as we know it, really takes of only in the 1980s, but in the 1970s the then usual mainframes became considerably faster, cheaper in use and especially more user friendly, owing to the development of so-called spreadsheets and statistical packages and the possibility of timesharing: Different users could suddenly 'simultaneously' communicate with one and the same computer. These three developments meant an incredible productivity increase in statistical analysis compared to the 'punch cards era'.

6 (Kooij, 1978: p. 204)

7 See, for example: (Ashton, 1948; Taylor (Ed.), 1958; Deane, 1965; Flinn, 1966; Cipolla (Ed.), 1973; Thompson, 1973).

8 See chapter 4, par. 4.4., p. 85ff.

9 The graphs only show the figures for the nineteenth century. So, in theory it could be possible that a sudden increase in production in the Netherlands would have taken place earlier, for example in the eighteenth century. Because we do not dispose of the annual production figures for that period, we cannot verify this directly. It seems extremely unlikely, however: Within the group of other West European countries the Netherlands has for ages been considered a 'latecomer' where it concerns economic modernization, and the first 'Industrial Revolution' invariably was deemed to have taken place only in the second half of the eighteenth century in England. The entire eighteenth century is, moreover, considered a period in which the Dutch economy stagnated for a long time or perhaps was even on the decline. To make it totally cluttered: There are strong indications (see for instance: Maddison, 1991: pp. 30-35) that in our legendary 'Golden Age' (the seventeenth, thus, roughly) there indeed was economic growth in the sense of a steady increase in the production per capita in the Republic of the Seven United Provinces and which then later, in the course of the 18th century, turned into stagnation. In so many words, this means that there already had been modern economic growth, far before the first 'Industrial Revolution' would have taken place. It may be clear that these findings seriously undermine the term 'Industrial Revolution' as defined by us in the main text ('In the (...) sense of an instant structural transformation within the economic process with a clearly historically perceptible starting point...').

10 It seems as if here we come across a paradox: The term 'Industrial Revolution' originates from the first half of the nineteenth century (see p. 126 of this chapter) and so was for the first time used by more or less contemporary observers. Is it possible that all those contemporary observers, each and every one of them, had made such absolutely incorrect assessment of the pace of the economic change that, as it were, was right in front of them? The answer is of course: No, in the second half of the eighteenth and the first half of the nineteenth century, from a historical point of view, indeed there have been

super-fast changes in the field of the production of goods and services. The point is, however, that such changes occurred only in a few places and for that matter only in a few sectors of the economy. Evidently, those exceptional cases caught the attention of contemporaries, but precisely because of the fact that they were exceptional, their influence on the national growth figures is not or hardly to be found. It often took decades before such modernization processes had 'filtered through' to all sectors of the national economy. During that process they gradually lost their exceptional character, as a result of which they received less attention from contemporaries. But only when the entire economy gradually became modernized, the influence of the modernization became clearly noticeable in the national growth figures.

11 The standard version of the traditional viewpoint is to be found in (Dickerson, 1963).

12 The graphic analysis of Thomas' approach, as represented in Figure 5.5, is borrowed from one of the later participants in the debate, Peter McClelland (1969).

13 See p. 121, preceding. The principal critique from cliometic quarters came from Roger Ransom (1968), Peter McClelland (1969; 1973), Joseph Reid (1970; 1978), Frank Broeze (1973) and Gary Walton (1971; Shepard & Walton, 1976). In addition, criticism was also passed by other authors who strongly denounced the entire quantitative analytical approach in itself, as appears from the title of a study by David Loschky (1973): 'Studies of the Navigation Acts: New Economic Non-History'.

14 The matter of the colonies' profitability for the mother country was later once again scrutinized, concentrating on the relation between England and its colonies in the Caribbean. For this, see for example: (Thomas, 1968; Coelho, 1973).

15 See: (Davis & Huttenback, 1982; 1986).

16 For an overview, see: (Brookfield, 1975).

17 The economic history standard work of that time about this subject is (Wallerstein, 1974; 1980), that in respect of ideas is indebted to the work of the economist Johan Galtung (1971), one of the founders of the *dependencia* theories.

18 Cuba was generally regarded the classic example of how a former colony should extricate itself from western imperialism and that explains the virtually unquestioning adoration for the Castro regime within these circles and the idolatry for Castro's co-revolutionary, Ernesto 'Che' Guevara, who following the success of the Cuban revolution tried, usually in vain, to launch similar processes in other South American and African countries.

19 Note: This period was not chosen at random. It purposefully encompassed the years in which according to everyone British imperialism would have been at its peak.

20 According to the two authors, this held the explanation for the strikingly high investment percentage in education and other social goals that had been realized in the period by those areas.

21 (Davis & Huttenback, 1982: p. 119). A similar analysis of the financial relations between the Netherlands and its colonies has never been done, as far as I know. I would not be surprised if this would yield similar results, which might well seriously undermine the still popular myth about the Dutch wealth as a result of its colonial possessions. The latter is suggested if only by the fact of the famous patriotic dictum in the period of the Indonesian independence "Indië verloren, rampspoed geboren" ('Dutch East Indies lost, misfortune born') that nothing had ever been noticed in reality.

22 This paragraph is in part based on (Drukker, 1999).

23 (Weiss, 2001).

24 Compare: chapter 4, par. 4.5, p. 87ff, preceding.

25 See: (Weiss, 2001: p.1).

26 See: chapter 4, par. 4.5, p. 87, preceding.

27 Fogel and Engerman showed that the exceptional demographic parameters which Conrad and Meyer had distilled from the figures and which they had interpreted as proof of this phenomenon, could also be deduced from the demographic data of only white women.

28 The paradoxical thing was furthermore that the two authors — by American standards, that is — from a political point of few belonged to the far left, while the conclusions of their research as it were, demanded to be misused in support of rabidly right-wing political movements. The latter explains the sometimes peculiarly long-winded wordings in which they formulated their most important conclusions. What to think of, for instance, the following passage: *'...During the past decade we frequently presented papers to scholarly conferences (...) on various aspects of our research into the economics of slavery. Sometimes (...) one of our colleagues would come up to us and, with a nervous smile, ask: "What are you guys trying to do? Sell slavery?" We answered: "No. And even if we were, you wouldn't buy it. No one would buy it." We have attacked the traditional interpretation of the economics of slavery not in order to resurrect a defunct system, but in order to correct the perversion of the history of blacks - in order to strike down the view that black Americans were without culture, without achievement, and without development for their first 250 years on American soil..."* (Fogel and Engerman, 1974 (Vol.2): p.258).

29 See for example: (Passel 1974; David & Temin, 1974; 1979; Cannarella &Tomaske, 1975; Gutman, 1975; 1975a; Haskell, 1975; Sutch, 1975; Vedder, 1975; Walton, 1975; Wright, 1975; David, Gutman, Sutch & Wright, 1976; Margo & Steckel, 1982; Steckel, 1986; 1986a; Kolchin, 1992).

30 (Fogel & Engerman, 1977; Fogel & Engerman, 1980; Fogel,1989; Fogel & Engerman, 1992; Fogel, Galantine, Manning & Cardell, 1992).

173

31 All this, clearly emerged from anthropometric history research into slaves, which was especially initiated by two students of Fogel, Robert Margo and Richard Steckel (Margo & Steckel, 1982, Steckel, 1986a; 1986b).

32 See, for instance: (Vedder, 1975).

33 Significant in this connection is the research Robert Whaples (1995) published and in which he attempted, by way of an extensive survey among members of the *Economic History Association*, to discover about what subjects there was consensus within American economic history. Four positions had been directly borrowed from *Time on the Cross*. Three of the four (about efficiency and economic viability of the system of slavery) seemed to be subscribed by the large majority of the interviewees. And even the most controversial position, namely the one concerning the favorable material living conditions of slaves, appeared to have been rejected by but a small majority (58%) of the historians and by a *minority* (42%) of the economists.

34 Compare: Chapter 3, in particular par. 3.6 and 3.7, p. 63ff, preceding.

35 For the work of Le Roy Ladurie about the reconstruction of fluctuations in the standard of living on the basis of data on the height of conscripts, see: (Le Roy Ladurie, Bernageau & Pasquet, 1969; Le Roy Ladurie & Bernageau, 1970).

36 Here, it intentionally reads social and economic history, while elsewhere in this book I continuously refer to 'economic history' as a separate historical branch of study, in addition to social history. The reason is that the *standard-of-living debate* especially is a discussion that plays an important role in *both* specialties.

37 Fluctuations in the average body height reflect changes in the material circumstances in which a population has lived, but because men at an average are taller than women and children, and attain their adult height only by the twentieth year of their life, for this purpose the average body height should be used of a homogenous group in terms of age and sex, such as, for example, the physical records for military service.

38 The most important results of anthropometric history are summarized in: (Komlos (Ed.), 1994; Komlos (Ed.), 1995; Steckel & Floud (Eds.), 1997; Komlos & Baten (Eds.), 1998: Komlos & Cuff (Eds.), 1998).

39 Named for John Komlos, one of the pioneers in the field of anthropometric history and one of the first to attempt to formulate a coherent explanation for the 'early modernization paradox'. See: (Komlos, 1996; 1996a).

40 Here, I have simplified David's analysis, that is, 'translated' it in terms that are also understandable to the readers, whose knowledge of price theory does not go beyond the level of college prep economics 1. This 'translation' is in part borrowed from (Drukker, 1987).

41 In Graphs A and B the variable costs are drawn 'on top of' the fixed costs, so that in fact the fixed costs and the total (fixed plus variable) costs are depicted by the graphs.

42 The total costs include a minimal compensation for 'entrepreneurial efforts'.

43 Strong support for the correctness of David's analysis was the fact that in the period prior to 1850 among the small amount of Reapers sold, a strikingly large percentage was not purchased by one farmer, but by a number of farmers jointly.

44 Robert Whaples (1991) has conducted extensive research into the nature of the articles published by the *Journal* in the period 1941 (the year of its foundation) until 1990. It shows that the percentage of studies with a cliometric slant in the sixties gradually increased from over 15% between 1961 and 1965 to over 40% between 1966 and 1970. In the subsequent five years, that percentage suddenly leaps to 73% and afterwards gradually increases to over 80% in the years between 1986 and 1990. As this is concerned, the *Journal of Economic History* may be considered a smart representative from the midfield: The also American *Explorations in Economic History* converted a little earlier than the *Journal* to the new economic history, while the *Economic History Review* that is published in England, to this day only sporadically includes articles that as regards method may be reckoned to the new economic history. In general it holds true, as I have earlier argued, that the victory of the new economic history in Europe came about much later than in the United States and there also reached a less dominant position within the economic history discipline than in the United States.

45 Except for the introductions to the various parts that were written especially for this book, *Reinterpretation* consisted of at least 85% of studies which had earlier been published elsewhere. Among the few chapters that were published for the first time, there is also one general article about the economic aspect of American slavery (Fogel & Engerman, 1971) that in fact does not contain any new research findings, but recapitulates earlier studies in this field.

46 See: (Parker, 1971a; the famous study of the delayed adoption of the Reaper by Paul David (1966) also fits into this picture. David's 'Mechanization of Reaping the Antebellum Midwest' appeared also as a reprint in *The Reinterpretation of American Economic History*, for that matter.

47 (North, 1968, reprinted in : Fogel & Engerman (Eds.), 1971: pp. 163-174).

48 Knick Harley (1971) published an analysis of the economic backgrounds for the gradual replacement of sailing ships by steamers in the second half of the nineteenth century.

49 A clear summary of the debate is to be found in (Prevant Lee & Passell, 1979: p. 83 ff).

50 Remember that such a rapid increase of the average labor productivity is considerably higher than that of most industrial sectors today!

51 Within that sense, David's research from 1970 was a run-up towards his later publications in which the so-called productivity paradox is central. See for example: (David, 1990).

52 The role of pricing in the development of the cotton industry runs as a thread through the discussion about the development of the American cotton industry. That is understandable considering the fact that the matter of the import tariff was one of the essential points at issue between the industrialized North and the agrarian South in the Civil War. The Northerners were generally in favour of an import tariff for the protection of the fledgling American textile industries against the cheaper British imports (a classic example of the *infant industry protection argument* that also played a role in the debate between the German neoclassical economists and the followers of the Historical School). The Southerners strongly opposed an import tariff because they feared that the English would react with an import embargo on American cotton, which would take a heavy toll on the American plantation economy. Because this discussion is indeed especially concentrated on the effects of specific economic policies measures and only marginally has to do with the issue of long-term economic development, I will not dwell on it in this context. It is striking, though, that the majority of the new economic historians who have interspersed themselves in the debate, is convinced that the import tariff, in any case in the first half of the nineteenth century, offered the fledgling American industry effective protection, so that despite the fact that neoclassical *angehauchte* economics (and those include the large majority of new economic historians from those years) generally nourished a deep distrust of import restriction measures, because these actually frustrated a free market operation.

53 The increase of urbanization would have given an additional boost, according to Zevin, to the demand for mechanically produced cotton fabrics, since the possibilities for weaving and making clothes at home were few in the city.

54 See for example: (Abramovitz & David, 2001).

55 Temin had published his critique on the standard explanation and his alternative interpretation of the causes of the crisis two years before the publication of *Reinterpretation* already in book form (Temin, 1969). Further study by Hugh Rockoff (1971) into this matter, which was first published in *Reinterpretation*, confirmed Temin's analysis on the whole.

56 In his 'Where is there Consensus among American Economic Historians?', Robert Whaples (1995) concludes that the Friedman-Temin controversy belongs to the classic examples in which also in the long term no consensus seems to develop. See also: (Whaples, 1997). The fierce debate continues to the present day unabatedly. The latest goals: Ritschl & Woitek (2000) show with highly advanced econometric tests that Temin was right, but the co-author of Milton Friedman from 1963, Anna Jacobson Schwartz still insists (with a little help from some younger friends) that the monetarist view is the only correct one (Bordo, Choudri & Schwartz, 1995).

57 See chapter 4, par. 4.10, p. 106ff.

58 The example is borrowed from (Colander & Gamber, 2002: p. 124).

6 Black holes in the neoclassical universe

6.1 Kuznets *cum suis*: Empirical studies of economic growth

In the previous chapter a number of highly diverging studies were reviewed. Of course, in essence, they one by one started from the same approach, which is characteristic of cliometrics: The explicit application of
— almost always neoclassical — economic theory to historical issues and
to assess as accurately as possible how large certain variables have actually
been, c.q. how great the influence of certain factors has probably been on
a certain development. In addition they had two more things in common:
Usually they thoroughly swept the floor with the views that previously
were generally accepted, often without replacing them with a new, fully
crystallized explanation. That is what I called 'Socratic' economic history:
Knowing that you do not know and, especially, why you don't know. In
the second place, all those studies concerned questions which one way or
the other dealt with processes of economic development.
Nevertheless, the multiplicity of the subjects broached on in the above,
could unjustly have created the impression that cliometrics possibly in
terms of methods was characterized by unity, but that the historical issues
concentrated on were a rather disconnected mishmash: English education
legislation in the nineteenth century; economic aspects of mercantilism and
imperialism; the material living conditions of slaves; Marxist *Verelendung;* the
destabilizing effects of a reckless monetary policy, etc..
It is high time to undo that impression: If in the foregoing I especially
wanted to show that the tree of the new economic history in less than
a quarter of a century had branched out surprisingly vast, then now the
moment has arrived to return to the trunk and the roots.

Those roots were formed by the intensive cooperation that in the second
half of the twentieth century arose between economists and economic
historians, and that was directed towards finding a fundamental explanation for the phenomenon of economic growth. That quest followed

two paths: The first approach consisted of the systematic[1] collection of as many quantitative data as possible about the course of economic growth in as many a country as possible over as long a period as possible, and the comparative analysis of such data. The second approach was of an economic theoretical nature: The development of a formal theory about economic growth.

The first approach was from the very beginning dominated by two monumental studies. In the United States it was the work of Simon Kuznets[2], whose *Modern Economic Growth: Rate, Structure and Spread* was published in 1966. This book was a more or less crushing summary of several very extensive preliminary studies that had been published in the preceding years in the journal *Economic Development and Cultural Change*, and that in turn were the result of a gigantic comparative research of which Kuznets had launched the program as early as 1949.

Two years prior to Kuznets' study, *British Economic Growth 1688-1959: Trends and Structure* by Phyllis Deane and W.A. Cole (1964) was published, the first study in which the economic modernization process of England since the so-called Industrial Revolution had been quantitatively mapped.

Both books, which may be considered as the double fundament of all contemporary empirical studies of economic growth[3], had a common approach: The quantitative reconstruction of economic growth in the long term had been put in the framework of the system of national accounts. The difference between the two was that Kuznets' study formed a comparative study between a large number of widely divergent countries, in terms of history and cultural development: The analysis was not restricted to the countries that, as it were, formed a classic example of modern western economic development, such as for example England, the United States, France and Germany, but Russia and Japan as well formed part of it. Deane and Cole had restricted themselves to the economic development of England, but on the other hand, they had taken the perspective of time even more broadly than Kuznets.

The great importance of *British Economic Growth* and *Modern Economic Growth* for economic history did not remain limited to the, for that time, revolutionary approach: Both studies unsettled, each in its field, the then generally accepted view on the phenomenon of economic growth. From the figures of Deane & Cole it appeared, actually for the first time, that the so-called First Industrial Revolution in England had transpired much more slowly and gradually than had generally been thought. Deane &

Cole did find some growth acceleration for the years in which the Revolution was considered to have taken place, namely for the forties and the eighties and nineties of the eighteenth century, so that, with some trouble, you could still insist that the concept of Industrial Revolution did not *completely* vanish from sight, but their most important conclusion was nevertheless that the measure to which growth would have accelerated in those years had been much smaller than everyone had thought. And what's more, a masterly example of the irony of history has left nothing of even that one conclusion. The tremendous importance of Deane & Cole's work was their for that time revolutionary approach: Their book formed the basis for an entire generation of economic historians (Charles Feinstein, Nick Crafts and Knick Harley are the major representatives) who completed, refined and revised the figures of Deane & Cole on the basis of other data, and it emerged that the growth of the national product had occurred even more gradually than even Deane & Cole had thought possible.[4]

Except for the fact that the pace of economic modernization in England had been more gradual than previously assumed, the existing view on the structural change the English economy had undergone during the process of economic modernization was hardly undermined by their results. The emphasis lies on the change in the sectoral employment structure in an early stage of the change process (decline in the agricultural sector; increase in the industrial — and later still — the services sector, which forms an indication for an increase of the average labor productivity in the farming and stockbreeding sector, prior to and during the industrial expansion. That story also played a prominent role in the traditional explanations: A so-called 'Agricultural Revolution' would have preceded the 'Industrial', in order to prevent the latter from being prematurely smothered in a Malthusian crisis (food shortage) and/or a shortage of labor in the expanding industrial sector. Deane & Cole furthermore assigned a decisive role to heavy industry (mining and iron industries), to the textile industry and to the revolutionary changes in transport, and also in that, their story did not depart from the then prevailing view. The same goes for the dominant role they assigned to international trade as a 'growth engine' in the second half of the nineteenth century. In short, the fundamental review their book induced was about the *pace* at which economic change took place, but not so much about the *nature* of that process of change.

With regard to the latter the comparative study by Kuznets was a smooth addition. The traditional view on economic growth had been strongly influenced by the outstanding 'original example': England. The idea was that modern economic growth could ultimately only take place if a pioneering role would be fulfilled by heavy industry. That other countries, for example in the non-western world, had not achieved prosperity, was subsequently explained by pointing out the fact that those countries in structural respect differed so much from the English example, that the conditions for modern economic growth were absent 'by nature', and that they were for that reason doomed to poverty, unless one way or the other a process of 'industrialization' could be brought also about there.

Development economics in the 1960s was entirely imbued with this sort of thought, and the study by Deane & Cole evidently brought no change in that: For them as well, industrialization was the keyword in explaining the English modernization process. The economic development programs from that time were manifestly founded on that one train of thought: Basically they consisted of capital and technology transfers. If developing countries could dispose of investment capital to a sufficient extent and if they would have available the technology to 'embody' such investments in modern machinery, than industrialization would ensue 'automatically', and with that, economic growth and prosperity would prevail in the end.

180

It is hard to deny that the traditional view of economic development was torn between two alternatives and thus contained paradoxical elements. On the one hand it emphasized that every country had a unique history, which was determinant of the opportunities for economic modernization. On the other hand the belief was, that economic modernization would only 'spontaneously' realize itself through the English example of industrialization. The paradoxical thing was, that also in the western world numerous countries did achieve great prosperity, without any large-scaled industrialization, such as Australia, New Zealand, Canada, Denmark and Austria, or where there had been some degree of industrialization, but where industrialization had always lagged behind the development of the services sector, such as the Netherlands.[6]

The consequence of this was that countries that in their history came closest to the English example, had the most chance of modern economic growth. The more a country deviated from the English example, the smaller the chance that a process of economic development would spontaneously manifest itself there. For that reason, so they thought, those countries that deviated most from the English development (read: developing countries) should be brought by means of an 'artifice' (read: international capital transfers and technology transfers) in a situation that would come as close as possible to the starting point of England, to prevent a widening of the income gap between rich and poor countries, which was regarded as a threat to economic and political stability in global respect in the long term.

Kuznets' *Modern Economic Growth* invalidates the traditional view on two basic points. Firstly, Kuznets showed that the structural transformation process entailed by economic modernization in all countries studied by him, bore some rather striking similarities in spite of the huge differences that existed between those countries. Secondly, his study made clear that economic modernization did not have to go hand in hand with the development of heavy industry as driving force, as the English example had suggested.

The two essential factors that generated modern economic growth were, according to Kuznets, the same in all countries: The application of technology based on modern science in all sectors of the economy, and the growth of the stock of capital goods per worker, which as it were, formed the embodiment of the technological development in the means of production. Striking in this was, that the growth rate and the level of the stock of capital goods at a certain point in the development did indeed strongly vary from country to country.

The main conclusion of Kuznets' study was that the economic modernization process went accompanied by a process of structural social change that was more far-reaching than the modernization of the economy itself, but that did show the same pattern everywhere. Everywhere a — note: relative — decline in production in the agricultural sector in favor of a relative increase in both the secondary and the tertiary sectors could be noticed; a shift in the large majority (but not per se in all) of the economic activities from small-scaled, labor-intensive production units to large-scaled, capital-intensive enterprises, and a related change in the organizational structure from one-man businesses to large 'impersonal' concerns. In a later phase, the economic modernization in all countries studied by Kuznets went hand in hand with a more than proportional increase in international trade as part of the national product.

The scale enlargement in companies caused a relative increase in the percentage of skilled workers in relation to the percentage of semi- and unskilled laborers, and a shift from the rural areas to the city as the epicenter of production. A huge increase in the number of years and level of schooling, an unprecedented domestic migration, an increasing degree of urbanization, and a sizeable expansion of occupational mobility, formed the major social changes that were initiated by the economic modernization process.[7]

Kuznets time and again[8] stressed that the reverse side of the process of modern economic growth is not without danger, because the inevitable attendant structural social change, leads to the disruption of pre-modern social relations: For small farmers, craftsmen and unskilled workers, modernization often meant that the economic foundation was knocked off from under their existence. Domestically this could result in social destabilization that might nip the growth process in the bud[9], while from an international point of view, increasing imperialism and the danger of increasing tension among the rich countries should be considered as very real problems.

Easterlin (2001) points out that *Modern Economic Growth* only years after publication was seen as a milestone in modern economic history.[10] He explains this from the fact that Kuznets' approach during the long years of preliminary study prior to the publication of *Modern Economic Growth*, had been imitated so much, that the ultimate publication of his magnum opus left little surprises in the eyes of his followers.

Indeed, imitation of Kuznets has been so massive that in the years following the publication of *Modern Economic Growth*, there was hardly any one country to be found where, often on the basis of Kuznets' work, historical national accounts were not mapped by means of, for economic history, unusually large-scale research programs.

6.2 In the wake of Kuznets: Historical national accounts

In the Netherlands, the lead was taken by Jan Luiten van Zanden. Van Zanden in 1987 published an article in which Dutch economic growth in the nineteenth century is reconstructed on the basis of a number of random years, for which he had made a rudimentary assessment of national income, starting from a system of national accounts.[11] He was the first in that country. To be sure, before then a number of studies had already been published, that suggested that they had applied the same method [12], but in fact those could all be traced back to one source, an article from Teijl (1971) in which the national income — also for a number of random years — for the period 1850-1900 was directly estimated on the basis of the development of the capacity of the Dutch machinery, and the development of the government sector, without the assessments being framed into a system of national accounts. In retrospect this is precisely why Teijl deserves praise: For that time (practicing economic history in the Netherlands was still perfectly traditional at that time) his approach was unusually refreshing and modern, but that does not alter the fact that the quality of his assessment may still be best qualified as reasoned good guesses.

For that reason Griffiths & De Meere (1983) more than ten years later, concluded that the Dutch economic development in the nineteenth century from a quantitative viewpoint was still completely *terra incognita* and that, to put the country on the map, one had to go back to the basics, that is to say: Make a reconstruction on an annual basis of the real national income per capita, departing from the same systematics Kuznets and Deane & Cole had applied. The article by Van Zanden from 1987 was a first impetus to that end.

Figure 6.1 Jan Luiten van Zanden

In 1990 under supervision of Van Zanden a large-scale and long-term research subsidized by the *Nederlandse Organisatie voor Wetenschappelijk Onderzoek* (NOW) (Dutch Organization for Scientific Research), entitled: *Reconstruction of National Accounts of The Netherlands and the Analysis of the Development of the Dutch Economy in the Period 1800-1940.*[13] At the same time, from the economic faculty of the University of Groningen, Rainer Fremdling took the initiative to set up a similar research with as objective to estimate the size and growth of the Dutch capital stock over the same period. Both studies could be completed almost ten years later and had in the meantime yielded unprecedented production for the Netherlands in terms of articles, dissertations and other scientific publications.[14] These research projects saw to it that the Netherlands in less than ten years' time transformed from one of the worst documented western countries in the field of economic history, into one of the best documented.

However valuable Van Zanden's research may have been for Dutch economic history, the project was not unique internationally seen. In the wake of Kuznets, everywhere in the western world large-scaled research projects had been launched with the same objective: The reconstruction of national accounts over as long a period as possible.[15] A little later still, the same happened for a large number of other than western countries, while at the same time also a number of other economists, such as Angus Maddison[16] and the trio Irving Kravis, Allen Heston & Robert Summers[17], set themselves the task of making the historical national accounts that had emerged from innumerable countries, comparable to each other.[18]

From the analysis of the series from the historical national accounts and from the mutual comparisons of such analyses, to everyone's surprise (except, perhaps, that of Simon Kuznets, because he had established the striking uniformity in the economic development process on a number of points earlier already), no matter how different those countries were, the same pattern came up each time.

The uniformity found, ultimately resulted in a grave (some would prefer the word 'disastrous') undermining of the theoretical foundations on which the entire new economic history was built, namely neoclassical economic theory.

The above should especially *not* be interpreted in the sense that from the avalanche of cliometric research it gradually became apparent that neoclassical theory was *incorrect* in the sense that it was self-contradictory, but indeed in the sense that the more cliometric research being carried out, the clearer it became where the limitations of neoclassical theory were to be found, if it involved explaining the process of modern economic growth in its entirety. And such limitations in the long run appeared much greater than virtually any sincere new economic historian had first thought in his initial enthusiasm for the new approach.

This paradoxical development, namely that the application of neoclassical theory to explain the historical development process of economic growth, ultimately resulted in the fact that, precisely for that reason, the limitations of the same theory applied, gradually became clear, was the main reason for giving this book its probably somewhat cryptic title: The new economic history ultimately appeared to be a revolution that bit its own tail. How that went, I will try to explain below.

6.3 Extensive and intensive economic growth

To clarify what was the matter with the above-mentioned paradoxical development of the new economic history, we need to elaborate on the analysis of the growth process. As concrete example I will take my own country as a case study, and in doing so, I gratefully make use of the extensive quantitative economic history research conducted in the wake of the above-mentioned historical national accounts projects of Jan Luiten van Zanden, *cum suis*. The impression that may unwittingly emerge is that the conclusions that surfaced only hold true for the Dutch development. That impression I want to dismiss in advance: Of course, in the research into the Dutch economic development in the nineteenth and twentieth century a number of matters turned up, that solely concerned the specific Dutch situation. We are not concerned about that here. A number of general features of the growth process also surfaced, which appeared to hold true for other countries as well, and which together determined the above-mentioned uniformity of the western process of modern economic growth.
In other words, I take the Netherlands as a concrete example to demonstrate that what surfaced in the Dutch case, surfaced also elsewhere. And one of the first things we should dwell on, is the distinction between what is called 'extensive' and 'intensive' economic growth.[19]

To fix our thoughts: Let us ask ourselves what the direct causes are of the phenomenon 'economic growth'. In terms of a production function this is simple: Production is the result of the combined deployment of production factors (labor, land and capital) in the production process. The implication of this conclusion is, that if in the course of time, the deployment of production factors (inputs) in the production process increases, in normal circumstances the production (output), as a result of the increased inputs, will also increase even if the *nature* of the production process — basically that is the technology in the widest sense of the word, that is used in the production — does not change. Economic growth that results from an increase in inputs, *without the technology applied changing*, is called: *Extensive* economic growth.
To illustrate: The impoldering of the *Noordoost-polder* in 1942 augmented the Dutch agricultural acreage by close to 500 km², and with the planned colonization after the Second World War, the area was 'filled' with numerous agricultural enterprises (additional inputs in the form of labor and capital goods). Even if in the same period the technology of Dutch agriculture had not changed (*quod non*, for that matter), the agricultural production of our country would have risen, solely and exclusively as the

result of the additional production originating from the new polder: A classic example of *extensive* economic growth.

Intensive economic growth is then, *mutatis mutandis*, the growth of the production resulting from technological change in the broadest sense of the word.

Naturally, in our thoughts, we can substitute the case study of the *Noordoost-polder* for the *entire* Dutch economy: Year by year, both the stock of capital, and the input of labor[21] with which overall Dutch production[22] is realized, change.

The conclusion that in the long run the three variables that we are now discussing have increased considerably, and that this likewise applies to all other countries where a process of modern economic growth has manifested itself, is stating the obvious.[23] But supposing that we want to ascertain *to what extent* this increased production in the long run has been the result of the increased input of land, the increased deployment of labor and the increase in the stock of capital goods. At first, this seems a Gordian knot that is second to none, but precisely because of this type of problems, neo-classical economic theory is a strong aid.

6.4 The production function as the 'dissecting knife' for economic growth

The starting point of this neoclassical dénouement is a production function, that is a mathematical equation describing the relation between 'inputs' and 'output'.[24] The form most used in cliometrics is as follows:

$$Q = \beta_0 . L^{\beta 1} . K^{\beta 2} . G^{\beta 3}$$

in which the various mathematical symbols represent the following:

Q = the production in a certain year, in practice: the real gross domestic product;

L = the deployment of labor with which that production was realized

K = the stock of capital with which that production was realized

G = the quantity deployed of the production factor land;

and in which finally β_0, β_1, β_2 and β_3 represent the so-called 'parameters' of the production function, that is to say, the specific variables that in numerical terms describe the relation how a given size of the various 'inputs' (L, K and G) leads to a certain amount of 'output' (Q). For reasons of theoretical consistency, which we will not dwell upon here so as not to make things more complex, the parameters β_1, β_2 and β_3 need each be smaller than 1, and together sum 1 (thus: $\beta_1 + \beta_2 + \beta_3 = 1$).

That the above represented production function at first looks rather inhospitable and needlessly complicated with all those exponents, is the result of the fact that precisely that specification embodies all sorts of elegant mathematical properties that make it into a very strong analytical instrument in the framework of a neoclassical economic model. What the properties exactly are, does not matter so much for our story, and so we will skip this (probably to the relief of a great number of our readers). Essential to our story, however, is that you can unleash a mathematical trick[25] on the above-reflected 'archetype' that immediately makes its character much less inhospitable. For you can show that the 'archetype' reflected above transforms in a simple linear form when you do not write the 'inputs' and the 'output' in absolute variables, but in relative changes (in practice: Yearly change in percentages). So, if you are prepared to make about four new definitions, namely:

$$Q^*_t = \frac{Q_t - Q_{t-1}}{Q_{t-1}} \cdot 100\ \%$$

$$K^*_t = \frac{K_t - K_{t-1}}{K_{t-1}} \cdot 100\ \%$$

$$L^*_t = \frac{L_t - L_{t-1}}{L_{t-1}} \cdot 100\ \%$$

$$G^*_t = \frac{G_t - G_{t-1}}{G_{t-1}} \cdot 100\ \%$$

(in which the subscript t stands for a random year) so that Q^*_t, K^*_t, L^*_t and G^*_t now all of a sudden represent the *yearly change in percentages* of Q, K, L and G in year t in relation to the previous year, than it may be mathematically shown that the original production function may be rewritten in linear form, namely:

$$Q^*_t = \beta_0 + \beta_1 . L^*_t + \beta_2 . K^*_t + \beta_3 . G^*_t$$

and that looks a lot less forbidding already.

A second simplification that in the practice of research often is carried through is the manner in which the production factor 'land' (G_t) is considered. In neoclassical price theory G plays an essential role: From — among other things — the production function is theoretically deducted how the various production factor prices are formed (wage for labor, interest for capital, etc.) and for that reason G features in the production function in order to explain the land rent (lease). In empirical research, however, operationalization of G is problematic. In the first place, G (different from L and K) is interpreted differently in different studies: Sometimes it relates to the volume of raw and auxiliary materials deployed in production[26]; sometimes it concerns fallow land that is brought under cultivation for production purposes[27]. Both interpretations are debatable in the light of growth research. Raw and auxiliary materials may rather be considered a *precondition for*, than *a cause of* economic growth (a car will not go faster by putting *more* gasoline in the tank, but if it has *no* gasoline in the tank it will not move at all). Fallow land or pristine nature in itself does not contribute to national production; only when the land is brought into cultivation, it will contribute to production. The "bringing into cultivation" implies, however, that investments are made before the land is productive and thus the production factor 'land' in an operational sense is virtually not to be distinguished from other production means produced by men, that is to say: Part of the stock of capital.

In the practice of the quantitative empirical research into economic growth, the production factor 'land' (G) is therefore usually considered to be part of the stock of capital goods (K)[28], which again yields a simplification of our production function:

$$Q^*_t = \beta_o + \beta_1.L^*_t + \beta_2.K^*_t$$

Perhaps the above gave some readers the uncomfortable feeling of 'what do I need this for?' or in other words, 'what could possibly be the use of all those mathematical economic exercises in the light of the distinction between intensive and extensive economic growth?' (because that was what we were discussing).

It seems expedient, if only for that reason, to answer that question quickly: The above-described production function forms an analytical instrument to unravel on the one hand to *what extent more* output was the result of *more* capital goods, and *more* labor (together: the extensive component of economic growth) and, on the other hand, the result of all other factors together (that is, the intensive component of economic growth).

Owing to the unsurpassed historical national accounts project, we dispose of annual figures of Dutch production, of deployment of labor, and of the size of the stock of capital for (almost) the entire nineteenth and twentieth centuries. By transforming those series into yearly percentage changes, we in fact have annual series for the three variables our production function is about: Q*, L* and K*. By applying to those series a simple strategy, which is known as 'multiple linear regression analysis', we obtain estimates of the numerical values of the parameters β_0, β_1 and β_2 of the production function, which together in a quantitative manner describe in what manner production growth, capital increase and increase in deployment of labor in the long term have been connected to one another.

To understand the use of this sort of cliometric exercises well, we should, by way of interlude, go more deeply into the method of multiple linear regression. This is easiest on the basis of a three-dimensional graph we could imagine on a large scale as a corner in an unfurnished room (Figure 6.2). The angular point on the floor is the intersection of three axes: Two horizontal (along the skirting) on which respectively L* and K* are marked, and one vertical, on which Q* is marked.

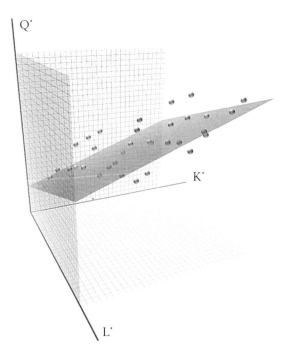

Figure 6.2 Multiple linear regression model of the production function

If we have at our disposal the annual series for the three variables, we can now for each year determine a point in space which represents the combination of the values scored for that year of Q*, L* and K*. We could represent such a point in the corner of our room by hanging a ping-pong ball on a thread exactly in that point in space. Okay, it is indeed a whole exercise, but if we do this for every observation of the annual series we have, gradually there will emerge a whole cloud of ping-pong balls in space.

The technique of multiple linear regression, does in fact nothing else but applying a flat plane through that cloud of ping-pong balls, in such a manner that the total distance of all ping-pong balls to the plane is minimized. In everyday language: The regression plane (in the drawing depicted as some kind of ceiling system crookedly rising in the room) intersects the ping-pong-ball cloud precisely in half. The beauty of it all is that the regression plane can also be represented in terms of a mathematical relationship and ...that mathematical relationship is exactly identical to our last version of the production function, with the crucial difference that the parameters β_0, β_1 and β_2 now have precisely the numerical values that determine the position of the plane in the space. In other words, the regression plane is the graphic representation of the relationship existing between Q*, L* and K* and the production function that is filled in with numerical function is the mathematical equivalent of that relationship.[30]

To show the meaning of the different parameters in the production function, imagine that we draw two lines on the walls of the corner of our room (precisely where the regression plane intersects the walls) and subsequently we tear down the whole. We will cut the walls loose along the vertical axis (Q*) and then we will cut the walls loose from the base.

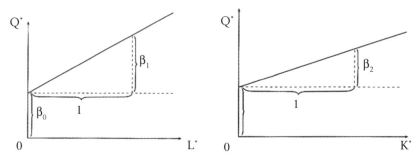

Figure 6.3 Multiple linear regression model: Partial relationships

The two walls that are left, are depicted in figure 6.3, and suddenly we see the economic significance of the various parameters: In the plane Q*L* we see that the intersecting line of the regression plane with the wall, meets the wall at an angle of which β_1 is the tangent. All this means that on average the growth of production (Q*) will increase by β_1 percent if the deployment of labor increases by 1% and the stock of capital goods remains the same.

In addition, we see that the intersecting line between the regression plane and the plane Q*L* meets the vertical axis (Q*) at the height β_0, which means that the growth of the production in a certain year will average β_0 percent, *if the growth of the deployment of labor as well as the growth of the stock of capital in that same year are both nil.*

The same story applies *mutatis mutandis* to the relationship between K* and Q* in the plane (Q*K*): the production increases in a given year on average with β_2 percent if the growth of the stock of capital in that year increases by 1% and the deployment of labor remains the same. And of course it also goes here, that the average annual production increase in a certain year still is β_0 percent, even if there has been no change in the stock of capital goods, or in the deployment of labor, in that year.

It will meanwhile not have escaped the reader that through the theoretical exercises in the above, we have neatly cut the Gordian knot that was the reason for those exercises. The question was whether we could unravel to what extent economic growth was caused by the two determinant extensive factors, increase in stock of capital (including: land) and increase of labor input. The last version of our production function represents this neatly:

$$Q^*_t = \beta_0 + \beta_1.L^*_t + \beta_2.K^*_t$$

An increase by 1% in labor input will result in an increase by β_1 percent of the production, and an increase by 1% in the stock of capital will lead to a growth in production of β_2 percent. Finally, the production function shows another 'autonomous' component (β_0) which is some kind of collecting bin of *all factors, other than capital increase and increase in deployment of labor,* which influence production growth.

Well then: Enough theory. What this all evolves around is of course: How big were those parameters β_0, β_1 and β_2 in reality? And the answer to that question was rather disconcerting to the confirmed followers of neoclassical economic theory.

6.5 The first black hole: The Abramovitz residual

To answer that last question, I have summarized, in first instance, the results of a multiple linear regression analysis of the Dutch figures for the period 1808-1913 in Table 6.1. Let us see what that gives.

Table 6.1 Results of multiple linear regression of production function, on the basis of Dutch figures, 1808-1913

Variables & Parameters	Q*	β_0	β_1	L*	β_2	K*
Average annual growth in percentages (Variables) & estimated values (Parameters)	1.8%	0.4	0.52	0.87%	0.41	2.31%

Sources: Time series from (Smits, Horlings & Van Zanden, 2000). Analysis: Own computations

From Table 6.1 it may be deduced that the average annual increase in production was 1.8%, that the labor input for that same period increased by 0.87% on average per year, while the stock of capital increased an average 2.31% per year. Table 6.1 also reflects the numerical values for the three parameters of the production function: β_0, β_1 and β_2 appear to be 0.4, 0.52 and 0.41 respectively.[31]

Table 6.2 Relative contributions to the production increase in the Netherlands, due to increase in labor input, capital increase and autonomous component, 1808 - 1913

1	Different contributions to production increase:	$Q^* = \beta_0 + (\beta_1 \cdot L^*) + (\beta_2 \cdot K^*)$ $1.8\% = 0.4 + (0.52 \cdot 0.87\%) + (0.41 \cdot 2.31\%)$
2	Calculated:	$1.8\% = 0.4\% + 0.45\% + 0.95\%$
3	Different contributions to production increase in percentages:	$Q^* = \beta_0 + \beta_1 \cdot L^* + \beta_2 \cdot K^*$ $100\% = 22\% + 25\% + 53\%$

Sources: Table 6.1

What does this mean now for the explanation of Dutch economic growth in the nineteenth century? For this we should do some arithmetical work, but, otherwise than with the regression analysis, a calculator will suffice (see: Table 6.2).

In row (1) of Table 6.2 the average growth percentages of Q*, L* and K* are simply linked to the values found for the parameters β_0, β_1 and β_2 .

In row (2) the sum from the first row is actually calculated. This shows that the average production increase of 1.8% is composed of a growth contribution of 0.45% caused by the increase of labor input for the period examined, while the growth contribution as a result of the capital increase amounts to 0.95%. Finally there is still another 'autonomous' contribution (our 'collecting bin' of other growth factors) of 0.4%.

In row (3) is computed how large the relative contributions of each of the 'growth factors' has been. This is dead simple: The total average growth of 1.8% is put at 100 percent, and subsequently it is studied how big the contributions of the various factors have been in terms of percentages. The growth contribution from the increase in labor input of labor then appears to have amounted to (0.45/1.8). 100% = 25 percent; the relative contribution resulting from the growth in the stock of capital comes down to (0.95/1.8). 100% = 53%, while the autonomous component accounts for (0.4/1.8).100% = 22%.

With this, the neoclassical explanation for economic growth caves in considerably. For, what do those percentages mean? They indicate that the neoclassical theory in the present case of the Netherlands in the nineteenth century cannot explain more than 78% (that is the sum of the contributions from the capital increase and the increase in labor input) of the economic growth realized in that period. Almost a quarter (22%) of the increase of the production is caused by the autonomous component (β_o), that is to say by all factors, different from the increase in capital and labor, *which obviously are indeed of influence on economic growth, but which are not explained by the variables in the model.* And a theory with which in respect of almost a quarter of the phenomenon to be explained, one cannot say much more than: 'Well... I haven't the faintest idea. It obviously appeared out of thin air", one can conveniently persist that— to put it mildly — it has its constraints.

Had it stayed at that, one could always insist that one had been able to explain the economic growth *for the larger part* (78% is not to be sneezed at, isn't it?). Alas, that conclusion as well is unsettled, if we see a bit further than our nose.

We may thereby fall back on a great number of different studies carried out in this framework by young Dutch economic historians who, apart from the trio Jan Luiten van Zanden, Jan Pieter Smits and Edwin Horlings, one way or the other were involved in the project 'Dutch Historical National Accounts', such as, among others, Ronald Albers, Bart van Ark, Arthur van Riel and Peter Groote.[32]

What we have computed in row (3) of Table 6.2 for the period 1808-1913, namely the relative contributions of the various growth factors, we can expand, evidently, to the twentieth century, if only to see whether the 'hole' in our neoclassical explanation (the autonomous growth component) was that large only in the nineteenth century: Possibly it will not be so bad for the twentieth century and that would give us a good reason not to put the neoclassical theory out for the garbage men immediately, as an instrument to explain economic growth.

Such an exercise was conducted by Ronald Albers. Albers (1999) expanded the period of research from 1815 to 1996 inclusive and, in addition, made a subdivision according to sub-periods, subdivided according to the major business cycles over the period in its entirety. Table 6.3 represents the results. For those who prefer graphs, Figure 6.4 represents a summary of the same results.

Table 6.3 Average annual growth of production and relative contributions from labor input, capital increase and autonomous component in percentages over sub-periods, The Netherlands, 1815-1996

Sub-period	Average annual production growth	Relative contribution L*	Relative contribution K*	Relative contribution β_o
1815-1854	2,06%	25,6%	26,9%	47,4%
1854-1896	1,76%	24,5%	68,7%	6,8 %
1896-1913	2,52%	24,6%	63,1%	12.3%
1913-1921	2,64%	-14,9%	19,4%	95,6%
1921-1938	2,36%	22,6%	50,3%	27,1%
1938-1950	2,41%	65,0%	9,5%	25,5%
1950-1973	4,76%	5,68%	36,6%	57,7%
1973-1996	2,28%	-6,1%	33,8 %	72,4%

Source: (Albers 1999: p. 11), supplemented by own computations on the basis of (Horlings, Smits & Van Zanden, 2000).

It is, I think, no exaggeration to conclude that those results are disastrous for neoclassical theory as an explanatory model for economic growth. The autonomous growth component of 22% we have found for the period 1808-1913 does not seem exceptionally high at all, if we expand that period and subdivide it into sub-periods. On the contrary: As it appears from Table 6.3, in the entire nineteenth and twentieth centuries there

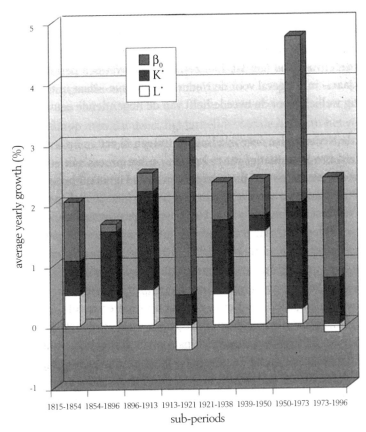

Figure 6.4 Contributions of L*, K* and β_0 to production growth, 1815-1996.
Source: Tabel 6.3

have been only two periods (1854-1896 and 1896-1913) in which the growth of the stock of capital and the increase in labor input together have brought about over 75% of the economic growth. In all other periods, the contribution of the autonomous component is more than 25%. Moreover, to our dismay we have to conclude that in a crucial period of Dutch economic development (namely, 1913 - 1921, when the production growth substantially accelerated) the autonomous component accounted for over 95% of the growth, while in the last two sub-periods the relative contribution of β_0 is more than 50% respectively 70%!

The conclusion is clear: Insofar as neoclassical theory tries to explain economic growth from the increase in labor and capital inputs (and that is precisely what it does), it appears to fail for a period of close to 200 years

— in any case for the case of the Netherlands — possibly with the exception of the second half of the nineteenth century.

I take the Dutch development to expound on the manner in which an attempt was made to get a quantitative grip on the process of economic growth, and what the results were of such attempts. It is high time to put the specific Dutch development in a wider perspective and that can be done in a surprisingly simple manner. The crucial point is that in quantitative research on economic growth *for other modern western countries, the findings have been similar.* Of course, the growth percentages differed considerably from one country to another in the different sub-periods, but one thing was indisputable: In the long run the autonomous component β_0 played an important - not to say dominant - role and what's more, it much seems as if this role becomes only more important as we approach the present date (this pattern as well can be found in the Dutch figures: The relative contribution of β_0 on average is a little over 20% until 1913 inclusive; in the period from 1913 to 1996 this is more than 50%).

This finding, namely that the neoclassical theory so to speak at its best could explain a small part of the economic growth, and that the major part evidently had to be explained on the basis of other factors, was considered so crucial that the autonomous component β_0 in the literature got its own name. Because β_0 can be interpreted — in the above I already called it some sort of collecting bin — as a residual of economic growth (albeit of considerable dimensions) when the contributions of labor and capital inputs have been processed, in honor of the American economic historian Moses Abramovitz, who was the first to track that residual, it is called 'the Abramovitz residual'. [33]

6.6 Making growth endogenous: Technology and human capital

The disconcerting conclusion that the standard neoclassical model in practice was a rather poor instrument for explaining the process of economic growth in the long term, resulted in wide attempts, after the discovery of the Abramovitz residual, to furbish up what I have described as the 'first black hole in the neoclassical universe[34]', in other words, to adjust the standard model in such a manner that the Abramovitz residual would be reduced to acceptable (that is to say: As small as possible) dimensions.

The manner in which this was done is rather obvious: For in the above, one factor had remained completely out of the picture, of which almost everyone who had ever given his opinion about economic growth (from David Ricardo to Simon Kuznets, inclusive, so to speak) had argued that it probably played a decisive role in the growth process: Technological development in the broadest sense of the word.

Indeed, neoclassical economic theory is basically a theory that explains the working of markets and within that framework, technological change cannot be explained: The phenomenon appears out of the blue as it were, in other words, within neoclassical theory it is considered an exogenous variable.

If one wanted to reduce the size of the Abramovitz residual, the appropriate way would be to integrate, one way or another, the rather intangible phenomenon of technological changes into the theory, or in other words, to 'endogenize' it.

In the course of time it appeared that the conversion of the theory in this sense was feasible, but also that the test of the endogenous theory of growth by historical quantitative data, proved to be an empirical minefield of the first order. How the theory was adjusted, is simple to tell, however.

In economic terms, the main effect of technological progress is that the productive *quality* of the production factors labor and capital increases, with the result that productivity, that is to say, the efficiency with which those production factors are deployed in production, increases. In terms of our production function: Technological progress leads to an increase in the course of time in the quantity of 'output' per unit of 'input' in the whole economy. The overall productivity increase is reflected in the positive value of β_0 that we found in our estimate of the production function for the Netherlands for the period 1808-1913 (Table 6.2) and in the — also positive — values we found in the production functions estimated by Albers over the sub-periods between 1815 and 1996 (Table 6.3). This also elucidates the second name that β_0 was given in the neoclassical theory: Besides 'the Abramovitz residual' it is also called 'total factor productivity' (TFP). If technological progress is one of the dominant factors that in the long run cause the increase of total factor productivity, then it becomes understandable why in our estimates of the production function the Abramovitz residual is so alarmingly big: This is because the standard neoclassical model completely ignores technological progress!

But, mind you, let us not rejoice too soon: The positive values of β_0 that we have found up to now *do not only and solely* reflect the technical progress realized: If that were only true. We said it earlier: β_0 is a collecting bin of *all* factors which cause production to grow, save for those two that in the production function serve as variables (namely L* and K*) and technological progress is only one (and probably: Quite a dominant) element from that collecting bin. To use an example that is not completely plucked out of the air for the nineteenth century: The additional agricultural production that is the result of a number of good harvest years in a row resulting from exceptionally fair weather conditions, is also reflected in β_o and that nice weather has nothing to do, obviously, with technological progress. Or, as Moses Abramovitz himself said: *'The residual is a measure of our ignorance'*, and the central question is then of course whether we can filter the measure *in which technological development influenced the growth* through that 'collecting bin of our ignorance', some way or other.

In the new economic history, despite the, at first glance, rather intangible nature of the concept of 'technological change' (it is everywhere and nowhere, so to speak), brave attempts have been made to get a better grip on it quantitatively.

The reasoning was approximately as follows: You can imagine that technological progress for an important part is 'embodied' in the stock of capital goods and in the quality of the production factor labor.

As regards the first: There are but few people who will doubt that the 'machinery' of the Republic of the Seven United Netherlands (think, for instance, of means of transport moved forward by pack and draught animals; ovens fired with timber, coal or peat; wind and water mills, sailing ships, etc.) generated less 'output' per unit of 'input' — hence: Was characterized by a lower TFP — than the 'machinery' of our country in the middle of the nineteenth century, with the advent of the steam engine, and that the nineteenth-century machinery in turn would be defeated by the twentieth-century one.[36]

A second point we have to keep in mind if we wish to integrate technological progress some way or other into our model, is that the composition of the stock of capital goods may indeed change year by year, but that such change usually[37] transpires very gradually: Every year old capital goods are scrapped and dismantled (or sold for whatever reason abroad) and via investments every year new ones are added. It is clear that the most recent technology is only embodied in the newest capital goods, and that capital goods as they grow older, also embody an earlier technology. In this way we can imagine the entire stock of capital goods at a given moment as being built up of various 'vintages', for which every vintage embodies a certain level of productivity, and for which the most recent vintage is characterized by the highest productivity, while productivity gradually diminishes as the vintage in question gets older. If we would be able now to make estimates of the pace at which the various vintages disappear from the production process and the new vintages are added to the stock of capital goods and we would also be able to infer from quantitative historic material how high the production levels of the various vintages have been, then on the basis of these data we could possibly adjust our production functions in such a manner that in the explanation of economic growth it would allow for the thus reconstructed gradual change in the average productive quality of the stock of capital goods which is caused by the technology it embodies.

The exact same story can be told for labor: Because of technological progress the quality of the production factor labor has increased throughout the years: In our modern western world people on average are physically taller, stronger and healthier than in the past; they grow considerably older and moreover: Their level of education has increased substantially. The economic implication of this is, that on average they have become potentially more productive from generation to generation. In this respect you can also reason that such quality improvements very gradually manifest itself because the composition of the labor force slowly changes year by year: A number of workers dies, retires, becomes unemployed or departs abroad, while every year the labor force is replenished by 'fresh' school-leavers, re-entrants to the labor market and immigrants who start to work in this country. Here as well you can insist that the latest 'technology' (and the one that most promotes productivity) on average is embodied in the most recent 'vintages' of laborers, even if one in this context must not in first instance think of 'engineering technology' in any sense (bolts and nuts), but especially of medical technology, education technology and of course, the increased knowledge in general. And again, if we could assess the rate at which the qualitative composition of the labor force changes, and we could moreover obtain an indication of the various 'levels of productivity' of the different 'vintages' of laborers, in principle we could then adjust our production function in respect of the quality change in the labor input throughout time.

199

It looks nice, but we said it already: The test of this endogenous growth theory in practice appeared to be a minefield of the first order, and up to now we have not succeeded in filtering in the manner described above, the 'pure' technological progress embodied in the stock of capital and the labor input from the Abramovitz residual. This does not mean, however, that no results have been achieved at all, and the good news is, that those results all point in the same direction.

Let us, to begin with, again take the Netherlands as case study. And again, we gratefully make use of the earlier mentioned study by Ronald Albers into the causes of the Dutch production growth over the period 1815-1996. Albers adjusted the standard production function by adding a production factor, H^* (H stands for Human Capital) which represents the quality improvement of the labor input.

$$Q^*_t = \beta_o + \beta_1.L^*_t + \beta_2.K^*_t + \beta_3.H^*$$

The problem of how to measure a quality improvement like that quantitatively, was solved by him simply and effectively by supposing that the quality improvement is reflected by the increase in the average number of years of education[38] in the population, while also taking into account the fact that the percentage of graduates of higher vocational education and university graduates has increased considerably throughout the years. For that reason he computed a *weighted* average of the number of years of education, in which a higher education got a higher weight.

The revised results of Albers' research are summarized in Table 6.4 and Figure 6.5. The following matters immediately strike the eye:

1. The relative contribution of K^* has not changed in relation to Table 6.3. This is logical, because Albers only tried to break down the contribution of L^* in a quantitative and a qualitative component (H^*).
2. The Abramovitz residual (β_o) had clearly diminished in Table 6.4, compared with Table 6.3 and the reason is evident: The relative contribution of H^* is large (in all sub-periods, save 1938-1950, larger than the quantitative contribution of L^*) and seems to grow more important over the course of time.
3. It is still not the case that we are able to push back the residual to a negligible quantity: Only in the second half of the nineteenth century (1854-1913) and between 1921 and 1938 it is less than 10%. In the other periods it is still close to 20 to well over 30%, with an enormous peak in the sub-period 1913-1921 of more than 65 percent.

This last point, namely that the residual in most sub-periods is still of a substantial size, is a bit in the line of expectation. Albers attempted to break down the contribution of labor input in a quantitative and a qualitative component, but he did not do so for the contribution from capital. In other words, the size of the residual would probably further decrease if we would be able to do the same for the contribution from the capital growth as Albers did for the contribution from labor. Unfortunately, such

Table 6.4 Average annual growth in percentages of the production and relative contributions from increase in labor input, capital increase, and the contribution from the quality improvement (H*) of labor (human capital) and the autonomous component, sub-periods, The Netherlands, 1815-1996

Period	Average annual production growth	Relative contribution from L*	Relative contribution from K*	Relative contribution from H*	Relative contribution from β_0
1815-1854	2.06 %	12.9 %	26.9 %	28.8 %	31.4 %
1854-1896	1.76 %	13.8 %	68.7 %	22.8 %	-5.4 %
1896-1913	2.52 %	14.2 %	63.1 %	18.4 %	4.3 %
1913-1921	2.64 %	-8.2 %	19.4 %	22.3 %	66.5 %
1921-1938	2.36 %	11.7 %	50.3 %	30.4 %	7.6 %
1938-1950	2.41 %	31.5 %	9.5 %	28.7 %	30.3 %
1950-1973	4.76 %	2.7 %	36.6 %	20.8 %	39.8 %
1973-1996	2.28 %	-2.5 %	33.8 %	46.1 %	22.8 %

Source: (Albers,1999: p.12), supplemented with own calculations on the basis of (Horlings, Smits & Van Zanden, 2000).

an exercise, based on the exact same method, does not yet exist, as far as I know, in Dutch economic history literature.

Nevertheless, we can be a bit more specific about the role of technological progress, insofar as this is embodied in the stock of capital goods, on the basis of a number of different studies by Bart van Ark, Herman de Jong and Jan Pieter Smits.[39] A tricky detail in this, is formed by the fact that those last studies are based on a theoretical point of departure that departs just a little from the method Albers used, so that the Albers' results concerning human capital on the one side, and the results of Van Ark, De Jong and Smits concerning the role of the technological progress embodied in the stock of capital goods, are a bit difficult to interrelate. In the current state of affairs, you can — as far as Dutch development is concerned — spot the quality aspects either of the one (human capital) or of the other (fixed capital), but not of both at the same time. Fortunately, many international comparative studies have been done according to more or less the same method, in which both aspects are given a chance, but in these, the emphasis usually is on the big western economies such as France, England, Germany and the United States.[40]

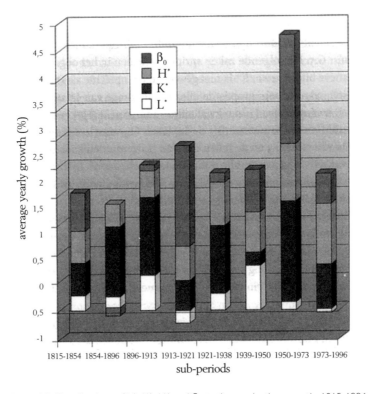

Figure 6.5 Contributions of L*, K*, H* and β_o to the production growth, 1815-1996
Source: Table 6.4

Let us first look at what research into the Dutch economic development in the long term has yielded, and subsequently place the results against the background of international comparative studies.

To that end, we first have to consider the method used. The tricky thing is that one author often tackles the issue just a little differently than the other (the *analysis* of the growth problems is internationally less standardized than the quantitative *description* of growth via the method of national accounts), but that does not alter the fact that it is possible to give a global description of the manner in which the different researchers address the problem. Slightly simplified it boils down to the following.

The point of departure is again the concept 'production function', but in this instance this production function is mathematically doctored in advance to focus as sharply as possible on the central point — economic growth. This latter happens by altering the production function in such a manner that the independent variable (or, the variable you are trying to explain) becomes average labor productivity, that is to say, the total production in a certain year, divided by the total quantity of labor with which production in that year has been realized[41]. And the number of employed (in fact the labor force, corrected for unemployment) is multiplied by the number of hours worked on average in that year (here a correction is also made for part-time jobs). The result is the total production per man-hour and that variable is interpreted as the driving force of the growth process: By reconstructing the average labor productivity of a country for a long sequence of successive years, we obtain an accurate quantitative image of the development of the growth potential over the course of time. With an international comparison at a certain point in time, it holds true that the country with the highest average labor productivity is considered to be technologically the most advanced country at that moment. In the terminology of Maddison: *...In analyzing long-run development, it is important to distinguish between the 'lead' country, which operates nearest to the technical frontier, and 'follower' countries, which have a lower level of productivity...*[42]

The average labor productivity in essence is determined by two other variables, the capital intensity of the production process and a residual item that is called the Total Factor Productivity (hereinafter simply: TFP). The capital intensity is in quantitative sense empirically determined by dividing the production volume by the size of the capital stock: The capital output ratio.

203

The reformulation of the production function in this manner (for which capital intensity is explicitly included as an explaining variable) is a direct consequence of the fact that in the first theoretical growth models of neoclassical tailoring, like that of Solow (1956) and Swan (1956), the growth of the capital stock (and, as a consequence, the growth of the capital intensity of the production process) was originally considered as 'main driving force' of economic growth. For a good understanding of the rest of our story, it is of importance to realize that the capital intensity positively influences average labor productivity indeed, but that there is also something at work, what is called: Decreasing marginal productivity, that is to say that the *additional* increase in labor productivity that is the result of a step-by-step increase in capital intensity, decreases in the long run. In ordinary speech: By putting more machines at a laborer's disposal, his production per hour will increase, but *if the nature of the production process does not change meanwhile*, the additional production per hour that is the result of all those extra machines will finally diminish and in the end even become nil: No one is capable of operating an innumerable number of machines all at once. Or, for those who wish to imagine it more concretely: Give a group of ten excavation workers whose task it is to move a mound of sand, and who together have four spades and four wheelbarrows at their disposal, every day one spade and one wheel-barrow extra. You will see that the total production (quantity of sand moved per day) will increase day by day, but that this daily increase will diminish in the long run, and by the time that our brave excavation team has 10 spades and 10 wheelbarrows at its disposal, you will to your dis-appointment have to conclude that the production is not increasing at all any more, even when you provide one gross of spades and a dozen of wheelbarrows.

The fact that decreasing marginal productivity is mathematically in-grained in these early neoclassical growth models, implies that these mod-els predict in the long run a 'stationary state' of the economy, as long as nothing else happens but a gradual increase in the capital output ratio: Logically at some time there will be a moment when a further increase of the capital intensity will no longer have any effect on the average labor productivity.

In that sense, the neoclassical theorists are directly indebted to their intel-lectual forefathers. In classical economic theory existed consensus, from Adam Smith to David Ricardo, that economic growth was indeed imag-inable, but... also that it would always be a temporary phenomenon and that in the long run the 'stationary state' (*steady state* in their terminol-ogy) would recur.

However, the classical economists lived and wrote in the second half of the eighteenth and the first half of the nineteenth centuries: They were standing right in front of the 'First Industrial Revolution', and so witnessed a historically unparalleled process of social change. No wonder then that they were of the opinion that it was a temporary matter, and that in the long run society would return to its old, familiar pattern. The neoclassi-cal growth theorists lived and wrote in the second half of the twentieth century and they knew better: Since the phenomenon that was called the 'First Industrial Revolution', the economy in the western world had never returned to a *steady state*. Of course, there had been periods in which the average labor productivity had increased faster than in other periods, and in addition there were examples of countries where an initially promising process of growth in the long run was smothered in economic stagnation and decline (recently, Zimbabwe is a good example, but certainly not the only one), but as regards the modern western countries in general, the growth of average labor productivity in the long term showed no signs to near nil, and any theory that stubbornly held on to this, naturally, was doomed to fail beforehand if it concerned an explanation for modern economic growth.

If one thing was clear, it would be the growth of the following: The rescue of the theory was in the second factor that was presented in the neoclassical growth model as explanatory factor for the growth of average labor productivity: The mysterious TFP.

Readers of this book will realize that the TFP is a dead ringer for the earlier mentioned 'Abramovitz residual'. Both are a residual item, that is, the quantitative equivalent of a collecting bin of all factors that determine economic growth, after you have filtered from it the influence of the factors that according to the theory are decisive (inputs of production factors in the former specification we used; *capital output ratio* in the Solow specification). No wonder that new economic historians and growth theorists saw it as their main, common task to solve the mystery of total factor productivity. For, who could answer the question as to what factors determined TFP, for a major part had also answered the question of what is the cause of economic growth.

On the basis of the earlier mentioned research by Van Ark, De Jong and Smits, it is possible to obtain a global picture of the development of the average labor productivity over the past two hundred years in our 'example country' (The Netherlands), and the extent to which the increase of capital intensity and of total factor productivity have influenced the growth of average labor productivity (see Table 6.5 and Figure 6.6).

205

From the figures in first instance an exceptionally varying and crumbled picture emerges, so that it becomes complicated to draw unequivocal conclusions, but with a bit of good will, we may conclude the following:

1   Between 1820 and 1973 the average labor productivity in every sub-period increases, except for the years between 1929 and 1947 in which the growth of labor productivity is negative. This latter should not surprise us: These are exactly the years in which the largest economic crisis took place that has ever afflicted the western world, followed by five years of world war: Not exactly the circumstances in which you would expect a spectacular productivity growth. The gradual increase in labor productivity over the course of the last two centuries does not seem to be, however, a law of the Medes and Persians: In the last two sub-periods, the growth is considerably lower than in the preceding period.

2   The relative contribution of capital intensification continuously increases between 1820 and 1913. In the course of the twentieth century it gradually diminishes, however, even though here as well a period of exception is found: 1947-1973.

Table 6.5 Average annual growth, in percentages, of average labor productivity and the relative contribution from capital intensification and 'crude' factor productivity, sub-periods, The Netherlands, 1820-2000.

Period	Average annual growth of labor productivity	Relative contribution from capital intensification	Relative contribution from 'crude' TFP
1820-1850	1.1 %	0 %	100 %
1850-1870	0.9 %	11 %	89 %
1870-1890	1.5 %	20 %	80 %
1890-1913	1.1 %	36 %	64 %
1913-1929	3.2 %	28 %	72 %
1929-1947	-0.6 %	17 %	83 %
1947-1973	4.6 %	39 %	61 %
1973-1995	1.7 %	6 %	94 %
1995-2000	1.0 %	-50 %	150 %

Source: (Van Ark & Smits, 2001: Table 4, p. 12), supplemented with own calculations.

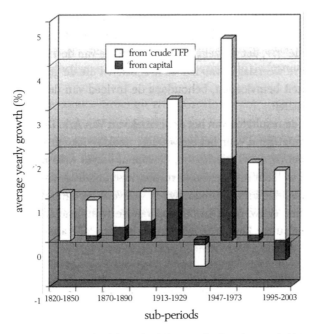

Figure 6.6 Average labor productivity and relative contributions from capital intensification and 'crude' total factor productivity, The Netherlands, 1820-2000
Source: Table 6.5

3   The contribution of the total factor productivity is in every sub-period considerably larger than the contribution from capital intensification. In itself, this should be no surprise: We have to do here with the so-called 'crude' TFP, that means that the contribution of the TFP in Table 6.5 is the quantitative reflection *of all other factors* influencing the average labor productivity, save the influence of the increased capital intensity.

4   In this form, the results of the research by Van Ark, De Jong and Smits are simply crushing for the simple neoclassical growth model: Indeed, the main conclusion has to be that the capital output ratio has made an observable and probably not fully negligible contribution to the increase in average labor productivity, and that this certainly holds true for the nineteenth century. Throughout the twentieth century, however, it seems as if the relative contribution from capital intensification is growing ever smaller, and 'all other factors' (crude TFP) have apparently had an ever greater influence.

The weighty question is of course: What were those other factors? At this moment we have not been able to draw any conclusion other than that the influence of TFP is considerable, and seems to be ever growing in the course of time, but that which we called the 'mystery' of the TFP in the above, we still have not been able to figure out.

To shed a little more light on this, we may regard pioneering international comparative research by Nick Crafts (1997) that Crafts in turn based on earlier research by Angus Maddison (1991; 1996). The essence of this research is to correct, in a comparison between France, Germany, England and the United States, the crude factor productivity, as it appears from the existing data of Van Ark, De Jong and Smits, for all possible factors that possibly determined the TFP. The residual factor, which remains, is called the *'refined total factor productivity'*. The misery, however, is that in the Crafts/Maddison research the variables are just a little differently related than Van Ark, De Jong and Smits do, and that the research does not concern the nineteenth century, but is restricted to three sub-periods between 1913 and 1992. This does not allow for a proper direct comparison to the Dutch development. All the same, the results are an important step in the unraveling of the 'TFP mystery'.

Maddison and Crafts simply took as dependent variables the average annual growth of the Real Gross Domestic Product (RGDP) (in that respect they applied the same method as Albers). The growth in production is determined by the contribution of the input of production factors (total

Figure 6.7 Nick Crafts

Figure 6.8 Angus Maddison

factor inputs, in the formula: TFI) and by a residual item, the meanwhile familiar 'uncorrected' or crude total factor productivity (in the formula: CTFP), so:

Growth RGDP = Growth from TFI + Growth from CTFP

The growth as a result of the increased inputs of production factors is subdivided according to: Increase in capital - whereby they immediately distinguish between fixed capital (machinery, in the formula: FC), human capital (rise in the productive quality of labor, in the formula: HC) and a residual item 'other inputs' (in the formula: OI), so:

Growth from TFI = Growth from FC + Growth from HC + Growth from OI

The crude factor productivity is subsequently corrected for that which in the growth theory is known as 'disembodied technical progress'. This is a (in my opinion somewhat ill-chosen[43]) collective term for all factors which one way or the other do influence total productivity, but which on account of their nature for one reason or another are not 'embodied' in the stock of fixed capital goods or in the stock of human capital.

In this context you have to think of efficiency improvements which may arise, without the technology changing, but simply and solely through an expansion of the market (the so-called 'scale effects' or *economies of scale*).[44] It may be clear that also an increase in international trade can bring about a similar effect.[45]

In addition, there is another, not unimportant productivity-enhancing factor that in principle applies to all countries, save for the country which has the highest average labor productivity: the *lead country* in Maddison's terminology. The technologically most advanced country is having a more difficult time than all other countries in one respect: It operates on the frontier of the technologically feasible, and thus, to create new possibilities for a productivity increase, it has to develop such new technology itself with all ensuing costs and risks: *Trial and error* is the keyword here, for which the term 'error' cannot ever be excluded beforehand. The *follower countries* have it easier in principle: To a certain level they borrow, buy or 'steal' the newest technology from the lead country, and adopt and adapt it to their own specific circumstances. This potential productivity benefit (which of course is not 'embodied' in anything, but simply emanates from the fact that not all countries in the world at the same time operate on the technological frontier) is called the *catch-up* effect.

Finally, another productivity-increasing effect is distinguished, which is the result of gradual shifts in the economic structure of a country. When the agricultural sector of an economy is characterized by a lower average labor productivity than the industrial sector, the whole economy will undergo an increase in the average labor productivity, if on balance more people will withdraw from the agricultural sector and take up work in the industrial sector.[46] This latter factor is known as the *structural effect*.

Crafts and Maddison thus tried to find out the 'TFP mystery', to 'crack' the uncorrected CFTP by finding out to what extent non-embodied effects play a role, and the residual item that results after this exercise, is called the corrected TFP (in formula: RTFP, which stands for *refined total factor productivity*), so:

Growth of Crude Total Factor Productivity (CTFP)
MINUS Growth from foreign trade
MINUS Growth from catch-up
MINUS Growth from structural effects
MINUS Growth from market expansion
EQUALS **Growth of Refined Total Factor Productivity (RFTP)**

In Table 6.6 I have summarized the results of the Crafts-Maddison study and to keep it orderly, I have averaged their results for France, Germany, England and the United States.

Table 6.6 Average annual growth, in percentages, of Real Gross Domestic Product (RGDP) and relative contributions to RGDP-growth from increase of Total Factor Inputs (TFI), Crude Total Factor Productivity (CTFP) and Refined Total Factor Productivity (RFTP), sub-periods, averaged over France, Germany, England and the United States, 1913 - 1992.

Period	1913 - 1950		1950 - 1970		1970 - 1992	
Growth	Average annual growth	Relative contribution from	Average annual growth	Relative contribution from	Average annual growth	Relative contribution from
of RGDP	**1.63 %**	**100 %**	**4.47 %**	**100 %**	**2.14 %**	**100 %**
from TFI	**0.99 %**	**67 %**	**2.18 %**	**49 %**	**1.39 %**	**65 %**
from FC	0.69 %	42 %	1.62 %	36 %	1.01 %	47 %
from HC	0.36 %	22 %	0.30 %	7 %	0.42 %	20 %
from OI	-0.06 %	- 3 %	0.26 %	6 %	-0.04 %	-2 %
from CTFP	**0.64 %**	**39 %**	**2.29 %**	**51 %**	**0.75 %**	**35 %**
from foreign trade	-0.01 %	-0 %	0.32 %	7 %	0.11 %	5 %
from catch-up effect	0.00%	0 %	0.29 %	6 %	0.20 %	9 %
from structural change	0.12%	7 %	0.23 %	5 %	0.01 %	0 %
from scale effect	0.05%	3 %	0.14 %	3 %	0.04 %	2 %
from RTFP	**0.48%**	**29 %**	**1.31 %**	**28 %**	**0.39 %**	**18 %**

Source: (Crafts, 1997, based on Maddison, 1991; 1996), supplemented with own calculations. In some cases percentages do not add up to 100 on account of rounding.

Let us try to oversee the battlefield:

1 The contributions of total factor inputs (including the quality improvement embodied in humans and machines) and of the crude total factor productivity to RGDP-growth fight for the first place from period to period: In the sub-periods 1913-1950 and 1973-1992 the winner is the contribution from TFI (61% and 65% respectively); in the intermediate period it is the contribution from the CTFP which is in the lead (51%). So we have to conclude that the influence of the CTFP on the production growth is substantial, but strongly varies from period to period.

2 The contribution of CFTP to RGDP-growth can indeed be substantially reduced by taking into account the 'non-embodied' productivity-promoting effects, such as foreign trade, the catch-up effect, economies of scale and the structural effect, but here as well it goes that the rela-

tive influence of those different effects strongly varies from period to period.

3   Once we have tried to include all imaginable influences on economic growth in our explanation. we are still left with a substantial part of RGDP-growth that we cannot explain: The growth contribution from the refined total factor productivity in the three periods distinguished is 29%, 28%, and 18% respectively. Apparently there is still a considerable part of production growth that seems to come 'like pennies from heaven', or to paraphrase the legendary words of Moses Abramovitz: Given the size of the RTFP we still do *not* know for a considerable part where economic growth comes from!

Readers who are blessed with a vivid historical imagination will be a bit surprised probably, because with all calculations it would seem as if the outstanding productivity-promoting process, that is technological change, has hardly been incorporated in the various contributions. Where can the dramatic change that was brought about in the nineteenth century by the introduction of the steam engine and the development of the railways be found in the numbers? Where is the internal-combustion engine, the introduction of electricity as an energy transporter and the gigantic development of the chemical industry in the twentieth century? Where do we find in the numbers the influence of the computer and the ICT revolution in the final quarter of the past century? Of course, to a certain extent the effects of those revolutionary technological revolutions are integrated in the numbers by taking into account the quality improvement in the stock of physical and human capital goods, but it strongly seems as if the undoubtedly large contribution of the most important technical breakthroughs have been largely obscured in the RTFP: No wonder that this RTFP (remember: '...A measure of our ignorance...') is still as large as it is, if you systematically leave out of the picture the supposed principal factor.

211

This criticism adds up to a certain extent: The only thing you can bring forward in defense of this sort of empirical growth research is, that the method from the very beginning was directed towards filtering out all other factors, *save that rather intangible technological progress*, and that, supposing this has succeeded for the greater part in the Crafts-Maddison analysis, you see the influence of those huge technological breakthroughs reflected, as it were, in the substantial contribution of the RTFP, but that it still is not clear *in what manner* those technological revolutions have encouraged economic growth.

To find out, Paul David decided to visit the lion in his den. In a number of case studies he tried to ascertain precisely what effect the big technological breakthroughs had had on average labor productivity. His results in first instance appeared to be highly preposterous and were also perpendicular to what the neoclassical theory predicted.[57] David's research findings were so paradoxical that since then within the new economic history about three new terms emerged that to the present day in the literature continue to wander about: 'Productivity paradox', 'QWERTY-economics' and 'path dependency'.

6.7 The second black hole: Paul David and the productivity paradox

The reason for David's research was a loose remark from growth theorist Robert Solow who, as a result of the phenomenon that the economic growth since the beginning of the 1970s in a large part of the western world[48] had considerably slackened while at exactly the same time the advance of computerization started, in 1987 had once written: 'Everywhere I look, I see computers, but in the growth figures they are conspicuous by their absence'.[49] Solow of course pointed out an anomaly: In 1987 it was perfectly clear that the computerization of society and the subsequent ICT revolution was a technological revolution of the first order and on the basis of that, one would have expected an acceleration rather than a slackening of economic growth.

The point of departure of David's study is a global historical division of the history of the western world in ages in which one particular technology prevails, the so-called *technology regimes*. The characteristic distinction between such ages is determined by a term he calls *general-purpose technology*. By this he means that in history every now and then technical breakthroughs occur that completely turn the nature of technological events in society upside down, because they truly penetrate all facets of society: Afterwards, so to speak, nothing is like it once was. It is not that the various technology regimes perfectly link up: It is quite well possible that one still has important effects, whereas the onset of the next is already noticeable. Also, there is no regularity at all to be discerned: 'Technical mega breakthroughs' appear 'out of thin air' at random, even if it is not that every country has a similar chance of such 'mega breakthrough' happening: In countries where generation after generation relatively a lot of attention and money is given to research and its possible applications in daily life (the so-called *Research & Development (R&D) expenses*) the chance of a mega breakthrough occurring is greater than in countries where such R&D expenses are smaller.

In this way, since the so-called Industrial Revolution, three technology regimes may be distinguished in the western world: [50]

1 The age of the steam engine and the development of complex constructions in iron and steel (roughly speaking the second half of the eighteenth century until the beginning of the twentieth);

2 The age of the internal-combustion engine, the electric motor, the development of electricity as an energy transporter and the revolution in the chemical industry (roughly since the final quarter of the nineteenth century until the present day);

3 The age of digitalization and automation, computers and ICT technology (roughly since the final quarter of the twentieth century also to the present day).

For all three 'regimes' it is true that there was a period in which scientific technological insights did exist already, but were hardly applied on a significant scale (the so-called *pre-paradigm phase* in the words of David). For the 'steam/iron/steel age' this was until the end of the eighteenth century approximately; for the internal-combustion engine/electric engine/chemistry age, approximately until 1890, while for the computer/ICT age this is a bit difficult to determine since at this moment we still do not know what future productivity developments computerization and the development of ICT technology will bring. In such a 'pre-paradigm phase' naturally there are no noteworthy effects of the macro breakthrough on economic growth to be expected.

This is different for what in analogy with David's terminology would be called the 'paradigmatic phase': The time when the new general-purpose technology has definitely won the fight with the preceding technology regime. The absurdity of David's results was that he did not find an acceleration of economic growth in the paradigmatic phase, but rather an amazing delay that, moreover, seemed to be concentrated in the sector (that is, the industrial) that would have profited obviously from the new technology. The delay in growth that occurred in the western world when computers and ICT pervaded society on all sides, appeared to be no odd historical exception, but it had happened also at the time of the technological macro breakthrough at the beginning of the twentieth century and presumable also in the wake of the 'First Industrial Revolution"!

In David's own words: '...*At (the) time the leading industrial countries were experiencing the early phases of their transition from an industrial regime based on steam, to the one that was being built up around electricity; (...) in the United States, as well in Great Britain, the decades surrounding the turn of the century were marked by greatly retarded rates of industrial productivity...*[51] This peculiar anomaly has since been known in economic history as the 'productivity paradox'.

However absurd it may look at first sight, a rough and ready explanation for the productivity paradox is not too difficult to give: With common sense you come a long way. For what is really happening? The introduction of the new general-purpose technology (remember: it encroaches on *all* levels of society) requires a huge operation: The entire stock of capital goods, including a great part of the infrastructure, has to be rebuilt. In addition, the new general purpose technology will in first instance show growing pains which may be remedied only by a nearly indefinite series of in itself minuscule improvements. Moreover, initially no one will have any experience with the operation of the system: The consequence is that not only the stock of fixed capital will have to be rebuilt, but likewise the stock of human capital! Finally: Precisely because the new technology on its introduction still suffers all sorts of teething problems, it is probable that both technologies (new ànd old) will be used alongside each other for a good length of time, where the old technology functions as some sort of back-up system, in case the new technology fails.[52]

One of the most learned and productive new economic historians of the second generation, Joel Mokyr, wrote, elaborating on the work by Paul David and others, in the nineties of the previous century a — stunningly large — number of studies[53] in which the social results (and especially their timing) of scientific and technological breakthroughs were empirically examined. Time and again it appeared from his research that it can take incredibly long[54] before a breakthrough in scientific knowledge ultimately translates into a macro breakthrough in the technological field, and that it again can take a very long time before that macro breakthrough via an infinite series of 'micro breakthroughs' has definitely nestled in all tiers of society.

The historically unavoidable evidence of the existence of such thing as a productivity paradox could explain a lot of things that otherwise had remained relatively puzzling. When on all sides efforts were made to quantitatively reconstruct economic growth in the long run, had not one of the main surprises been that from the account of contemporaries during the so-called 'Industrial Revolution' it again and again appeared that they had been stunned by the pace at which they saw their familiar society change right before their own eyes, while the quantitative reconstruction of economic growth time after time suggested that such change had occurred most gradually? The explanation for the productivity paradox fitted in great in that picture: Contemporary observers understandably were stunned about the technological macro breakthroughs they encountered in their lifetime in their immediate environment, but the effect of such macro breakthroughs in the growth figures was an extremely gradual and slow process: This became crystal clear from the research that intended to solve the mystery of the productivity paradox.

The research, geared towards the unraveling of the productivity paradox, was for a second reason, apart from the fact that previously absurd developments suddenly became understandable, of crucial importance for the development of economic history. It meant again an undermining of neo-classical economic theory as the central explanatory model for economic growth. The point is that neoclassical growth models had invariably predicted (naturally under the known set of in practice extremely unrealistic neoclassical assumptions) that in the long run the development levels of different countries would converge. The underlying central idea was that the technologically most advanced country encounters more difficulties in introducing new productivity-improving technologies than the so-called follower countries, because the lead country must find out everything for itself via trial and error, while the follower counties through the so-called spillover effect (the technologically leading country is not able to prevent that the highly sophisticated technology it has developed, drains away to other countries) can simply copy such advanced techniques, after having adapted them to their specific circumstances.[55] Moreover, if no new technology breakthroughs occurred, so the theory stated, any technology regime would in the long run land in a course of diminishing returns, while for the follower countries, shortly after the introduction of the new technology, a course of constant or even increasing returns could be, at least temporarily, among the possibilities. The consequence of this reasoning was that the production levels of all competing countries would in the end 'automatically' grow towards each other.

Extensive empirical research into the topicality of the convergence hypothesis on balance had produced an extremely fragmented and conflicting picture: Yes, in some periods there had indeed been convergence, but the convergence for the time being limited itself to the modern western countries only. When you included the growth figures of non-western countries (more specifically: Latin American countries, former communist countries in Eastern Europe and the 'classical' developing countries in Asia and Africa), nothing remained of the convergence and it would

rather seem that there had been *divergence* between the Western countries on the one hand and the rest of the world on the other.[56]
In addition, even in a comparison that restricted itself to the western countries, periods were found in which convergence could not be shown. In short, what neoclassical theory predicted — and mind you: That prediction contained crucial elements for the development to be expected in the future in the field of income distribution between rich and poor countries, and that is *'alles sal reg kom'* (all will be well) as long as you allow the market to freely do its beneficial work! — could in fact hardly be shown in the historical data material and not at all, when it concerned the convergence in the productivity development between rich and poor countries.

The explanation of the productivity paradox could now to an important extent contribute to answer the question why convergence in practice seemed to materialize very arduously and even seemed conspicuous by its absence when it concerned a comparison between poor and rich countries: The interfering and time-consuming social transformation process that is necessary to change from one technology regime to the other, forms a serious impediment for a smooth convergence and the impediment of course has greater weight as the country in question from a technological point of view is farther from the level of the most advanced country of the moment.[57]

6.8 The third black hole: 'QWERTY' and path dependency

The point that technological change apparently forms a crucial factor in the explanation for economic growth in the long term, and that this factor could only be arduously incorporated in the standard neoclassical model, was weakening with a vengeance of what for almost half a century had been the theoretical gospel for the major part of the new economic history. An avalanche of cliometric research had also proven beyond a shadow of a doubt that one of the main social implications of the neoclassical growth theory, that is global convergence, in practice went considerably more difficult and not as smoothly as the theory had supposed, and there where the social implications were most dire (particularly in relation to the income distribution between rich and poor countries) it did not seem to occur at all.
To top it all, the new economic history in its explanation for the productivity paradox had also managed to present a number of plausible reasons for why convergence did not at all manifest itself globally. Had it stayed

at that, probably it would have been possible for the proud cliometricians (remember: The new economic history had meanwhile become the authoritative paradigm in economic history worldwide) to bravely continue, after some modifications and adjustments to the violated neoclassical model), on the course once taken. But no, for the staunch followers of the neoclassical gospel in economic history, the misery had not gone by as yet. The cause was again a study from Paul David[59] and again a historical case study into the manner in which technology in the past had developed itself, but contrary to his research into the productivity paradox, where the social impact of gigantic technological revolutions was unraveled, it now concerned something that at first glance seemed no more than a minimal detail in comparison: The evolution of a keyboard of a typewriter. But however insignificant the subject may seem, for neoclassical theory as the foundation of the explanation for economic growth in the long run, the effects were, if possible, even more disastrous.

David's point of departure was again stunningly simple. Almost all modern keyboards, those of computers as well, have the same layout, the so-called 'QWERTY keyboard', which means that the letters are positioned at set places on the keyboard and that you can recognize that specific layout because the first six letters at the upper left side form the unpronounceable nonsensical word QWERTY. (Figure 6,9) There is a historical reason for this. The letters have been positioned in such a manner that in writing a random English text on a mechanical typewriter in which the type bars are mounted on steel levers, you have the least chance of the levers *jamming* during typing, that is to say that they get entangled because the one lever is still busy retreating while the other is already under way to the inked ribbon that makes the impression of the letter on paper.[60] The jamming of the levers of a mechanical typewriter was invariably the main check on typing speed, and given the fact that typing speed was the dominant criterion for economic acceptance of the typewriter, the QWERTY keyboard was soon considered a standard solution that guaranteed an efficiency optimum in this, as a result of which all manufacturers world-wide without delay copied the QWERTY configuration from one another.

In the course of the technological evolution of what I for the moment will call 'text-producing machines' gradually the mechanical *raison d'être* for QWERTY disappeared. With electrically operated typewriters the speed at which the type bars moved had become so high after a short time that the danger of jamming only sporadically presented itself to the quickest typists and in addition, in a fairly simple manner a mechanism could be built in by which jamming could be avoided completely without the

217

maximum number of touches per minute falling under the level of even the most nimble-fingered users. With the introduction of other letter supports, such as a 'golf ball' carrying all characters (an IBM invention) or a wheel on which the characters had been positioned in a daisy-like pattern (a Japanese invention) the need for a QWERTY layout to prevent jamming no longer existed. The advent of the PC and the accompanying development of word processing programs finally opened the possibility of an in principle completely free arrangement of the keyboard.[61]

Simultaneously with the technical evolution outlined above, in the course of time, on the basis of an avalanche of linguistic, cognitive and ergonomic research, other keyboard arrangements had been developed that totally eclipsed the familiar QWERTY layout and it did not involve marginal difference either: Configurations had been designed whereby the average typing speed of trained users[62] was dozens of percents higher than the maximum speed that could be reached on the QWERTY keyboard.

To illustrate: In The Netherlands, for instance, in the seventies (mind you: that is exactly the time when electronic word processing machines became a common phenomenon!), a revolutionary keyboard that went by the name of 'Velotype' was introduced. (Figure 6,10) The revolutionary thing about it was that it did not produce one letter per stroke, as was the norm, but it opened the possibility to record an entire *syllable* with one stroke. Experienced typists, after an intensive training in working with the exotic keyboard. achieved a typing speed with the 'Velotype' that was spectacularly higher than with a QWERTY keyboard. The 'Velotype' had a fleeting career in politics: Parliamentary stenographers in the Upper and Lower Chambers for a number of years used a keyboard similar to the 'Velotype', and so were able to record in writing a verbatim report of a parliamentary debate at the speed of speech, including interruptions, paroxysms of rage, etc., synchronous and virtually impeccable. Meanwhile, the 'Velotype' has been completely forgotten and added to the collection of curiosities of innovations that 'did not make it'.[63]

The fundamental question Paul David tried to answer in his essay about that which he called "QWERTY economics' was why, that evidently superior technology of all those alternative keyboard configurations that had been developed in the course of time, had never left behind the experimental phase and in practice one by one ingloriously went down whenever they had to compete against the — viewed from the viewpoint of productivity — inferior, but overwhelmingly present QWERTY standard. Neoclassical theory was completely unusable in this case, because it would have predicted the exact opposite: Competition would have ensured that the

Figure 6.9 QWERTY keyboard

219

Figure 6.10 Velotype keyboard

QWERTY keyboard would have gone under to any other configuration that could attain a higher typing speed.

The only reasonable answer David could think of was that technological development was not (as supposed by neoclassical theory) solely determined by the own criterion of the highest productivity within a given set of circumstances, where in those circumstances less productive technologies would mercilessly be competed out of the market, but that apparently there was something as 'path dependency', that is to say that the course of historical development is also decisive for the survival of a certain technology. The invincibility of the QWERTY keyboard could indeed be explained only from the simple fact that *for years on end it had been the only worldwide norm in that field* and had for that reason succeeded to become so deeply rooted in society that it had become impossible, so the speak, to get rid of. In other words, technological development apparently was a process that showed a likeness to evolution in a biological sense. Biological evolution seemed to be determined by two mechanisms: On the one hand a selection mechanism was constantly active (*survival of the fittest*), but on the other hand the question *why at a certain time precisely that specific life form had survived in terms of evolution*, could only be answered by involving *the evolutionary history of that specific life form itself* in the explanation. He who deems this to be a confusing complicated line of thought, may perhaps benefit from the following example: The theory of biological evolution can excellently make plausible why the human being has evolved out of primates. The keyword is of course 'natural selection'. But in answering the question why *precisely that specific form* of homo sapiens, as we know it now, has evolved out of the anthropoid apes, *the specific evolutionary history of homo sapiens itself* is a fundamental part of that explanation. Or, to formulate it even more absurd: If mankind had evolved from the giraffe and not out of the anthropoid ape, he would have looked differently now.

If the history of the QWERTY keyboard (which can effortlessly be expanded with numerous similar examples) suggested that technological development indeed showed a likeness to a biological process of evolution, it would also immediately be clear why neoclassical theory was completely unsuited as explanatory model for technological change. For, neoclassical theory does dispose of a counterpart of the biological concept 'natural selection' (that is: Competition), but the idea that the history of a development process itself is also decisive in the result of that process at a given moment, cannot be put into neoclassical terms.

Neoclassical theory is basically an a-historical theory: Historical differences are defined away, as it were. That is precisely the main reason why the new economic historians initially considered it such an appealing analytical instrument for historical development processes: One universal model with which in principle all processes of economic development could be explained, for that was the original thought behind the cliometric revolution, wasn't it?

But if technological development basically was an evolutionary process and technological development was a dominant factor in the explanation of economic growth in the long term (and in fact there was no one who doubted that), then, of course, it was an illusion to think that only within a neoclassical framework a conclusive explanation for long-term economic development processes could be found, simply because the evolutionary character ('path dependency') of technological change could not be fitted into the neoclassical framework. Paul David summarized the situation in exactly two words: 'History matters', and that was in fact the kiss of death for neoclassical theory as universal explanatory model for economic history.

6.9 The fourth black hole: Operation of market forces versus market development

The conclusion that technological development has an evolutionary character should, for that matter, *not* be interpreted emphatically in the sense that it shows that neoclassical theory is unfit to answer *all* questions of economic growth. I wrote that David's QWERTY essay was the kiss of death for neoclassical theory as universal explanatory model, but of course that does not mean that there are no questions to which the neoclassical explanation can be applied successfully. Let us try to find out something more about which questions can and which cannot be answered within the framework of neoclassical theory. To that end we will first have to go a bit more deeply into the nature of that theory itself.

Neoclassical economic theory basically is a theory that explains how markets operate. In other words, the neoclassical model is an excellent instrument if you want to explain how the allocation problem in an economy is solved through the operation of market forces, and it also has a number of very strong arguments in store as to why especially the operation of market forces (to be true, under a whole range of very strict conditions that in reality shall never be completely fulfilled, but which in various situations can indeed be approximated to a greater or lesser extent) leads to optimal allocation. With optimal allocation is meant: That solution of the allocation problem that in the given circumstances generates the highest possible welfare for the country in question.[64]

The wave of comparative quantitative economic history research that became possible because of the fact that gradually more historical national accounts of countries came at the disposal of researchers, yielded in any case one irrefutable conclusion: Wherever and whenever the process of modern economic growth took place, it had gone accompanied by a structural transformation of the entire economic system, again and again characterized by ever increasing labor division and specialization: A phenomenon that, please note, already in 1776 was pointed out by Adam Smith as the essence of productivity increase!
Increasing labor division and specialization, supposes a related growth and refinement of the market system, and that as well was patently confirmed by comparative economic history research: Where modern economic

growth in the western world — compared to the non-western world - had resulted in unprecedented high levels of welfare, this had always been accompanied by a historically unprecedented expansion of the markets that were active within the system, and in addition, of an unbelievable increase of the efficiency with which those markets operated.[65]

The resounding victory of the new economic history within the economic history discipline was largely attributable to the fact that the cliometricians had been able to explain the success story of economic modernization in the western world elegantly and clearly on the basis of a theory that in essence explained how markets operated, and precisely because the operation of market forces had stood at the basis of that successful modernization, this explanation was very convincing. But that victory at the same time disclosed the Achilles heel of the same theory. The fundamental characteristic of countries where no economic modernization process according to western model had occurred, or where that process in time had turned into stagnation and decline, was that there had been *no* market developing, or that an initial market development process for one reason or other had been nipped in the bud, and that was a phenomenon neoclassical theory had no answer to. Within the neoclassical framework, market development would always 'by nature' occur. In those cases where history had taught otherwise (and you only had to look a bit further than the end of your modern western nose to discover that this had been rule rather than exception in the history of mankind) neoclassical theory was stuck for an answer.

If you wanted to answer the question why it was that in a large number of countries no economic modernization had occurred (or where such modernization process at a certain time had degenerated into economic stagnation and decline), then the point it was all about was of course, why market development had taken place in some situations, but not in others. That question was put already at the beginning of the seventies by one of the cliometricians of the first hour, Douglass Cecil North. His final answer fundamentally changed the nature of the new economic history: Again the neoclassical theory had to concede ground and make way for other insights. North's influence extended far beyond the actual domain of economic history: His work was the reason for a completely new approach within economics that knows a growing number of practitioners and which has been given the name of 'neo-institutionalism'.[66]

Essential for our story is that North's insights to an important extent have contributed to traditional economic history, which had once been so humiliatingly jeered by the new economic historians during their grab for power, suddenly being rehabilitated for the greater part.

6.10 The revolution that bit its own tail: *Encore...!* Institutions

Douglass North attacked the pressing problem for which neoclassical theory had no answer: Why in some situations apparently no market development had occurred, while in others it had, by first thoroughly tampering with a number of fundamental assumptions of the neoclassical paradigm. In a neoclassical world, he reasoned, all economic transactions are supposed to take place in a social vacuum (that is what I described in the previous paragraph as the a-historical character of neoclassical theory). In addition, the neoclassicists suppose that all costs made in production can be reduced to costs that are directly related to the conversion of production factors in products: The theory, for example, assumes that with market transactions, the cost of collecting transaction-relevant information are nil, and that accession to the market is also completely free (that means: Free of charge) to all parties. These assumptions are in conflict with the real world: In reality, market parties have to make an effort (and thus incur costs: The expression 'time is money' is indeed true in economic theory) to obtain transaction-relevant information and moreover, such information is generally far from perfect. The accession to the market is not completely free in reality, and therefore in practice it always involves costs (in time and/or money). Both supplying and demanding parties are constantly running risks during the transaction process: They can be robbed; they may be misled by other market parties; their merchandise may be lost by force of nature, etc.. These are all costs that cannot be directly related to the physical conversion of production factors into products, but that do nevertheless indeed exist. North sums them up under the denominator 'transaction costs' and concluded that in the neoclassical model it is assumed that all those transaction costs are nil, while in reality this is not in the least so: *'The neoclassical world is a supposedly frictionless world, which means that transaction costs are zero. In the real world. they are never.'*

The fundamental point of North's[67] reasoning is now that the social environment within which the economic process is evolving, is decisive for the level of the transaction costs. The social environment (*the man-made environment*) he sums up as the whole of 'institutions' that exists within that society: That is for instance the prevailing system of ownership rights and the manner in which such rights are socially maintained. but also the

manner in which the provision and processing of information is organized.[68] Not only the entire prevailing system of written and unwritten
laws is included and the manner in which that system is preserved, but
also the norms and values of society, the social ideology, yes, even the
'culture' prevailing in that society.[69] And that is precisely where the shoe
starts to pinch in North's definition of the *institutional context*: You know
where you have to start when you try to describe what the institutional
context is all about, but it is far more trickier to determine where exactly
you have to stop. In other words, it is rather difficult to describe precisely
what does *not* belong to the *institutional context*.

Nevertheless, it is possible to elucidate with a single example what North
means by his hypothesis that the institutional context determines the
level of transaction costs. Let me start with an impious example. Why
are there so few whisky parlors in Saudi Arabia? According to Douglass
North's view the answer would be: Not because there are no *potential*
suppliers of alcoholic beverages, and even less because there would be no
potential consumers. The real reason is that the institutional structure of
Saudi Arabia is such that no-one in his right senses would think of opening a liquor store in that country: The transaction costs are simply pro-
hibitively high, because the law prohibits the sale of alcoholic beverages
and because the law is also enforced in a rather rigorous manner. Exactly
the same reasoning can be applied to numerous other examples: Why are
XTC pills cheaper in Amsterdam than in New York? Answer: Differences
in transaction costs resulting from a different institutional structure. Why
is cocaine in Bogotá cheaper than in Amsterdam? Answer: For precisely
the same reason why XTC is cheaper in Amsterdam than in New York.

These examples may be somewhat more impious and absurd, but they
do make clear precisely what it is all about: The social context can be of
such a nature that there is no market development, simply because the
transaction costs are so high that no one will take the risk to start market
transactions of some scale, while the single reckless fool who does, before
long will be ruined as a result of his own risky behavior, thus establishing
a wise lesson for the large majority that preferred to wait a while longer
to see which way the wind blows.

When you are prepared to look in this way to the differences between
— economically successful — modern western countries and countries
that did not achieve economic development, you have to come to the
conclusion that the modern western countries apparently succeeded to
build up an institutional structure in the course of their history that was
characterized by relatively low transaction costs, whereas underdeveloped countries apparently have not been able to do so. The most fun-

damental question after the why of economic growth that emerges now, could not be but dual: Firstly, what are the determining characteristics of an institutional structure that generates low transaction costs? And, in line with that: By what mysterious mechanism would institutional change be directed? Indeed, if you could answer this last question, you might have a possible explanation why in some countries (in the long to very long term) things went well economically, and why it went bad in other countries.

A global answer could in principle be given to the first question, albeit that the precise relation between institutional structure and the level of the transaction costs requires further substantiation.

The global answer emanated directly from the manner in which North attacked neoclassical theory: It assumes a total frictionless operation of markets, as a result of which (in theory, that is) the transaction costs are zero. The economic success in the long run of the modern western countries could be explained already now (even though it was more or less in the form of evidence from the absurd) from the fact that the institutional structure of those countries in the course of centuries had evolved in such a manner that they had approached the neoclassical ideal of a frictionless operation of market forces ever more closely. Of course, that does not yet answer the question *why* they did manage in the west and elsewhere they did not.

225

These two crucial questions to the present day are central in neo-institutionalism. In answering the second question, the study seems to go into the same direction as that in which Paul David sought for the mechanisms that drive technological change: Institutional change, just as technological change[70], would be a process that showed a strong resemblance to a process of evolution in a biological sense. In the above I already pointed out that the inevitable implication of that thought is that with this, the specific history of the institutional process of change will form part of the answer to the question why that specific institutional context at a given moment looks the way it does.[71].

It will hardly be a surprise where the neo-institutionalists sought to join in for their quest for the previous history of processes of institutional change: That was naturally in the traditional economic history that, indeed, of old had placed precisely that question at the heart of the discipline. Did I not write at the beginning of this book what the new economic history on its emergence reproached traditional economic history: '...That economic history was not concerned with the *analysis and the explanation of the economic process* but fully focused on the *description of the social environment* in which that process occurred and the manner in which that environment changed in the course of time...?'[72]

Half a century later, the second generation of new economic historians had come to the discovery that precisely that description of the social environment, and the manner in which that environment changed in time, formed an integral and indispensable part of the explanation for the process of economic development in the long run. The snake could not bit its own tail with any more precision.

Indeed, the editors Bart van Ark, Simon Kuipers and Gerard Kuper of a recent standard work about the relationship between productivity. technology and economic growth put the finger on the sore spot, when they write in their introduction: '...It appears (...) that catching up has been a key force in improving the productivity performance, but *it also appears that catching up has not been automatic and that in many cases convergence has not gone all the way.* The role of "ultimate" sources of growth features dominantly in the explanations for this. *Many of the papers have dealt with institutions but, at an even deeper level, there may also be a role for differences in culture, mentality and preferences of people that affect the institutional arrangements in different countries...*'[73]

Paul David said it more succinctly: 'History matters.' 'Even good, old economic history', one would be inclined to add.

Notes

1 That is to say: Within the framework of a system of national accounts. See chapter 4. par. 4.4. p. 85ff.
2 Kuznets received the Nobel Prize for economics in 1971.
3 See for instance: Easterlin (2001) for Kuznets and Harley (2001) for Deane & Cole.
4 See for instance: (Feinstein. 1972; Lindert & Williamson. 1982; Harley, 1982; Crafts, 1983; 1985; Crafts & Harley, 2000).
5 There existed disagreement in development economics about the question whether developing countries during a certain 'initial period' needed to protect their borders through trade barriers against 'cheap' imports from the western world. Some economists argue, by analogy with the *infant industry protection argument* of the advocates of the German *Zollverein* in the nineteenth century, that temporary protection against western competition was necessary to have the industrialization get off the ground. Some neoclassical diehards among the development economists pointed out, however, that

relatively low wages in developing countries in any case yielded a competitive advantage as to the western world and that temporary protection in the long run would prove detrimental: For, the competition mechanism is eliminated through this and that is precisely the obvious essential condition for an internationally viable industrial sector in the long run.

6   Traditional economic history generally had great difficulty with the explanation of welfare development in those countries that differed strongly from the English example. This appears, for instance, from the terminology in which the development of such countries is disposed of in the volume *Industrial Revolutions and After* of the authoritative *Cambridge Economic History* from 1965, discussing '...pre-*industrial* levels of economic organization...' in those countries or where their level of prosperity is simply labeled 'paradoxical' (borrowed from: Easterlin, 2001; italicized by me. jwd).

7   This summary of *Modern Economic Growth* is partly based on (Easterlin. 2001).

8   See for example his address at the acceptance of the Nobel Prize for economics in 1971 (Kuznets, 1971).

9   The classic example of an economic modernization process being smothered by social destabilization is, of course, Iran, where the economic modernization program initiated aroused so much resistance among population groups who felt threatened in their traditional existence, that a reactionary revolution of Muslim fundamentalists put an end to the regime of the shah (and at the same time, naturally, also to the process of modernization). It seems as if at least the same tendencies are noticeable in Indonesia at this moment.

10 In a number of recessions (for example: Blitz (1968) and Williamson (1968) Kuznets was even explicitly reproached for a lack of adequate theoretical foundations. This was in itself not undeserved, but things were slightly different, however: Kuznets believed that the economic theory of those days could contribute next to nothing to an explanation for the phenomenon of economic development and that was not wholly unjust: Compare: Chapter 4, par. 4.2, p. 81ff. ...above. Or, in his own words: '...*Much economic writing and theorizing (...) (is) geared to the current conditions and oversimplified to the point of yielding a determinate answer. (...) Such theories (...) tend to claim validity far beyond the limits that would be revealed by an empirical test...*' (Quoted by: Easterlin, 2001: p.87)

11 (Van Zanden, 1987)

12 For instance: (Van Stuijvenberg & De Vrijer, 1980). An overview of earlier estimates of the Dutch economic growth in the nineteenth century is to be found in (De Vries, 1984).

13 Three years earlier the Central Bureau of Statistics, through investigations conducted by Den Bakker, Huitker & Van Bochove (1987). had published revised national accounts for the period 1921-1939. The study by Van Zanden

was purposefully embedded in the same methodology the CBS had used, so that the joint results in the end would yield an uninterrupted series of mutually comparable annual figures for the Dutch national income and — by way of an investigation headed by Fremdling — of the size of the Dutch stock of capital goods over a period of 200 years. In fact. this result was achieved in 2000.

14 For instance: (Smits, 1990; Groote, 1991; Callewaert, 1992; Horlings, 1993; Vermaas, 1993; Knibbe, 1993; Albers & Groote, 1994; Burger, 1994; Horlings, Smits & Van Zanden, 1994; Van der Voort, 1994; Groote, 1995; Horlings, 1995; Horlings & Smits. 1995; Smits, 1995; Vermaas, 1995; Horlings & Van Zanden, 1996; Albers & Groote, 1996; Groote en Albers, 1996; Burger, 1996; Clemens, Groote & Albers, 1996; Horlings & Smits, 1996; Verstegen, 1996; Albers, 1998; Smits, 1998l 1999; Smits, De Jong & Van Ark, 1999; De Jong & Van Ark, 1999; Albers, 1999; Jansen, 2000; Smits, 2000; Smits, Horlings & Van Zanden, 2000; Van Riel & Van Zanden, 2000; Van Ark & Smits, 2001). The numerical data produced by this enormous amount of research was summarized in (Smits, Horlings & Van Zanden. 2000).

15 See Chapter 4, par. 4.4, p. 85ff., above.

16 (Maddison, 1982; 1989; 1991; 2001).

17 (Kravis, Heston & Summers, 1982; Heston & Lipsey (Eds.), 1999; Summers & Heston, 1991).

18 The point is that historical national accounts are generally quoted in the currency of the country itself or, in case of real figures, in the value of such currency in a certain year. The historical national accounts of the Netherlands, for instance, are expressed in guilders and the real figures in guilders of 1913. For comparison with other countries one or other common unit would be required, for instance US dollars in 1960. Direct conversion via the exchange rate yields biased results, because the exchange rate of a country for any reason may be overvalued or undervalued in relation to the real purchasing power ratio among the currencies. First, in some way. the purchasing power parity of the currencies must be determined. Slightly simplified, generally this is done by calculating for one and the same bundle of goods what it costs in one country. expressed in the currency of that country and what that same bundle costs in another country, expressed in the currency of that other country. Subsequently, the national figures can only be converted into a common unit via the calculated purchasing power parity between the two currencies. In fact, you would have to determine the purchasing power parity for every year separately. But, fortunately, a few ingenious tricks have been invented which keep this quantitative drudgery just manageable.

19 The distinction between 'extensive' and 'intensive' economic growth was introduced by Douglass North (North, 1961: p.7 ff.).

20 The growth of the stock of capital goods is usually calculated from historical statistical material with the aid of the *perpetual inventory method*. This method is basically founded on the idea that the size of the stock of capital goods in real terms (that is: Corrected for changes in the price level) at the beginning of each year in the course of that year changes in a positive sense owing to the additions to the stock of capital goods (investments) and in a negative sense, because of demolition, sale of capital goods abroad and destruction (for instance, by war or natural disasters). By correcting the stock of capital goods year by year for the changes that have manifested themselves throughout that year, it becomes possible to construct a time series that reflects the change in size of the stock of capital goods. A succinct and very clear exposition of how this functions exactly in practice may be found in (Groote, 1995).

21 The labor input may be operationalized for every year by calculating the average number of working hours worked in that year per worker, multiplied by the number of workers in total.

22 In practice, RGDP is usually chosen as operational approach.

23 He who does not believe this, is referred to one of the comparative quantitative studies of Maddison (1982; 1991; 2001): One of the rock-solid conclusions that emerges from those studies is that modern economic growth everywhere has gone accompanied by a huge growth of the stock of capital goods and the input of labor.

24 Over the course of time dozens, of different mathematical specifications of production functions have been developed that all describe a different supposed relation between 'inputs' and 'outputs'. In cliometrics, however, there is one, which constantly recurs in literature, the so-called Cobb-Douglass production function). Here as well we depart from a Cobb-Douglass specification. This form of the function was for the first time specified in 1928 in an article in a journal entitled 'A Theory of Production' that was written by two economists, Cobb and Douglass respectively (Cobb & Douglass, 1928). The article has been one of the cornerstones of neoclassical theory for years.

25 For the undaunted devotees: It concerns the so-called 'Taylor's theorem'.

26 See for instance: (Fogel & Engerman, 1971).

27 See for instance: (Parker, 1971).

28 In the dissertation of Peter Groote (1995), for example, in which capital formation in the infrastructure of our country is quantitatively reconstructed over the period 1800-1913, land reclamation (impoldering and the like) plays a central role of course. The extra territory that is so added to the Dutch national economy does not end up in the books as land reclamation, but as addition to the Dutch stock of capital goods.

29 In Figure 6.4 only points for positive values of Q*, K* and L* have been drawn to keep it orderly. In reality, the cloud of points could also extend to 'beyond the corner of the chamber'.

229

30 It may be clear that the closer the cloud of points encloses the plane, the better the plane reflects the relation between the variables. You can imagine that it is conceivable that the cloud of points hangs in the room as some sort of gigantic sloppy sphere. That simply means little or no relationship can be detected between the variables and that you could draw any plane through it. In statistics, the extent to which the cloud of points connects to the plane is analyzed by a technique that is the twin brother of the regression analysis: Correlation analysis.

31 In the above, I pointed out that the theory requires the sum of both parameters β_1 and β_2 together must equal 1. Naturally, practice appears to be more obstinate: From the table it appears that they come a long way together (0.52 + 0.41 = 0.93). but exactly 1, no, they do not add up to that. The reason is that the figures at the very best form an approximation for the relations supposed in the theory, but that they never exactly represent such theoretical relations.

32 In fact, this group in its entirety formed the first general full-blast Dutch cliometricians.

33 Theorists consider that too much honor for an economic historian. The same residual they call the Solow residual, named after their own hero, growth theorist Robert Solow. In addition, there is a third author, John Kendrick, who can reasonably boast to have discovered the 'residual'. The first publications in which the residual is mentioned are (Abramovitz, 1956; Kendrik 1956; 1961; Solow; 1957; 1961).

34 In fact, the expression 'reverse black hole' would be more appropriate: Indeed. 'black holes' in the universe are objects in space whose gravitation is so big that no form of energy whatsoever can escape from them. The 'black holes' in the universe of the neoclassical theory are characterized by exactly the reverse phenomenon: Energy (economic growth) is constantly escaping from the 'black hole', seemingly without an apparent reason.

35 Also the term 'new growth theory' is sometimes used as synonym.

36 Note: Here, it expressly does *not* state that the most recent technology *in all circumstances* is the most efficient. It only states that with the most recent technology in very special and very specific circumstances levels of production may be obtained that in no circumstance can be obtained with 'older' technologies. He. who does not understand this. may perhaps once more read the wise lessons of Paul David concerning the late adoption of the Reaper. (See Chapter 5, par. 5.6 p. 150ff.

37 It says here 'usually' because wars and major natural disasters (earthquakes, for example) may cause abrupt changes in the stock of capital goods.

38 Albers tried another alternative, by approximating the quality of labor input, through the total spending on education. This yielded statistically unsatisfactory and historically absurd results. This is in the line of expectations, because,

of course, there is no direct relation between spending and quality improvement. The weighted average of the number of years of education is a more direct operationalization and correspondingly works better.

39 (Smits, De Jong & Van Ark, 1999; Van Ark & Smits. 2001).

40 For example: (Crafts, 1997; Maddison, 1991; 1996; 2001).

41 In practice: Again the real gross domestic product per man-hour or another closely connected other definition, such as the real national product per man-hour.

42 (Maddison, 1991: p. 30).

43 As indeed appears from the continuation of the text, those factors sometimes have something to do with technology, but sometimes nothing at all. The expression 'disembodied productivity' is a flag that, in my opinion, better covers the load, but this term has never become established.

44 This seems more mysterious than it is: The person prepared to return to the Paul David's solution to the 'mystery of the Reaper' (chapter 5.6, p. 150ff., and turns back the pages to Graph C in Figure 5.8 (p. 153) will immediately see what is meant. Supposing that the production size at a given moment is at Q_k and slowly moves in the direction of Q_r. During the entire course, the 'reaper technology' is the most efficient, but while on that course. the company is confronted with declining average costs, until the point Q_t is reached: In other words, the company can produce ever more efficient as long as the course is traversed, not because the production technology changes, but because the existing technology as it were only reaches its true 'efficiency maximum' at production volume OQ_r. The same line of thought can be applied to the production technology of an entire country.

45 The classical study by Phyllis Dane and W.A. Cole (1967) (see this chapter, p. 177ff) had already emphasized how crucial the role of the growing international trade had been for the English economic development in the second half of the nineteenth century.

46 This structural effect formed the hinge function in Paul David's explanation for the at first glance paradoxical phenomenon that the real national income per head of the population in the North American economy between 1809 and 1840 apparently had increased, without there having been a notable technological change (David, 1967). For a clear summary of the debate on the matter, see: (Lee & Passell, 1979: pp. 52-62).

47 (David, 1986; 1990).

48 That is, in Europe and the United States, Japan and a number of other South Eastern Asian states (Taiwan, South Korea, Hong Kong and Singapore, among others) achieved saliently high growth rates in the seventies: There, the blow was dealt later, so to speak.

49 (Solow, 1987: p.36).

50 David in (David, 1990) focuses on the latter two technology regimes. From more detailed investigation (for instance: Crafts, 1985) it may be inferred that the phenomenon of the productivity paradox also manifested itself in England during the so-called 'First Industrial Revolution'.

51 (David, 1990: p. 355).

52 A nice historical illustration of this point is the forecast of ICT adepts from the beginning of the eighties of the past century that the ICT revolution over time would lead to a situation in which paper as data carrier would disappear (the ideal of the so-called paperless office). Anyone who in any form is employed in the services sector knows that this forecast has not come true to this day: If anything, the mass of paperwork has increased as a result of the highly efficient manner in which computers can produce printed paper. Of course, it has meanwhile become possible for every household to fully process its entire financial administration electronically, in principle, and to store all information digitally only. Have the familiar paper bank and giro statements disappeared by consequence? No, they have not.

53 (Mokyr, 1994; 1994a; 1997; 1998; 1998b; 1998c; 2000; 2000a).

54 Mokyr made it plausible that the technology of the so-called 'First Industrial Revolution' in England was based on scientific insights which, would you believe, emerged in the seventeenth century! (See: Mokyr, 2000a).

55 Compare: This chapter, p. 209 ff., above.

56 Compare: Chapter 1, pp. 36-37, notes 15 until 20 inclusive, above.

57 One can differ of opinion on this in all reasonableness: Within the neoclassical paradigm you could reason that a country that is far removed from the technologically most advanced country (say, to take a concrete example, Afghanistan or Somalia versus the United States) in principle has an easy time of it to adapt the latest technology: In a manner of speech, you virtually can start 'with a clean slate', whereas in those countries that from a technological point of view are closer to the United States the 'old technology' is embodied in gigantic machinery that you would first have to dismantle or, if possible, to convert to make it suitable for the new technology. Something like this was the message that one of the illustrious forefathers of the new economic history, Alexander Gerschenkron, put forward in his famous collection of essays *Economic Backwardness in Historical Perspective* (Gerschenkron, 1962a). In the Dutch non-specialist literature about technological change that idea is known as the 'dialectics of progress'. Even highly respectable economic historians sometimes resort to it. So, without too much difficulty, you can maintain that one of the central arguments of Jan de Vries (1981) in his *Barges and Capitalism: Passenger Transportation in the Dutch Economy, 1632-1839* in his explanation for the delayed construction of a network of railways in the Netherlands is the surprisingly high efficiency of the then already existing technology for passenger transport: Towing barges and stage-coaches. The current state of

affairs with respect to the 'dialectics of progress' can be summarized more or less as follows: Yes, there are indeed random historical developments to be found in which the initial 'backwardness' seemed to promote a relatively quick adoption of new technologies. These are exceptions, however. The successful adoption of new technologies is in general seriously hindered (or rather promoted) by institutional factors or — still more intangible — 'culture'. Countries that in the past have lagged behind technologically for a long time are generally also characterized by a 'backward' institutional structure or, according to some respectable authors, even a 'backward' culture. Those two factors often seem a very obstinate hindrance for a successful functioning of the mechanism that underlies the 'dialectics of progress'. You can underpin the same with proof from the absurd: If the 'dialectics of progress' would be a generally occurring phenomenon with technology transfers, you would expect that precisely between the poorest developing countries and the rich western countries convergence would have to occur. What you see is precisely the opposite. For a more detailed discussion of the relation between economic development on the one side and 'institutions' and 'culture' on the other, see par. 10 of this chapter, following, and chapter 7.

58 The development of the standard neoclassical growth model of the second half of the fifties of the previous century into the endogenous growth theory of the seventies and later, which we have discussed in the above, from a cliometric point of view may be regarded as a succession of frantic efforts to adjust the theory to historical anomalies (that is, not to be reconciled with the standard model) that had come above table by the cliomectric research itself.

59 (David, 1986).

60 There are a number of alternative explanations for the 'QWERTY configuration'. An explanation which I found to be one of the most original, is that an inexperienced typist with a QWERTY keyboard could produce the principal sample word that would have been used tons of times at demonstrations on the introduction of the typewriter - that is: *typewriter* - with the greatest speed because all letters that you need are located close to one another on the top row of letters. This explanation is cherished by a small minority of technology historians. It does not substantially affect the validity of Paul David's arguments.

61 It is illustrative of the stubbornness with which QWERTY has managed to maintain its position that most common users of a PC do not even know that every contemporary word processing program has the possibility to change the layout of the keyboard completely to one's own liking, let alone that they would want to avail themselves of the opportunity!

62 That men can run faster than women on average is generally known, but that women can type faster on average is much less well-known. It is a mystery to me why we seem to find that of less importance.

63 'Velotype' keyboards have meanwhile become much sought-after collector's items, and that says a lot about their limited and short-lived success.

64 To someone who is not familiar with the principles of welfare economics on neoclassical foundation, this claim of neoclassical theory will seem almost magic and on the grounds thereof will not be very credible. Still this is not the case: Again, and this time italicized, to focus attention on the constraints of the theory: *Under very strict conditions that can never be fully met in practice* neoclassical theory demonstrates that a completely free operation of market forces may result in a solution to the allocation problem that is characterized by the quality that no actor in the system can augment his welfare *without in doing so affecting the welfare of one or more other actors*. This quality is called 'Pareto optimality'. named for the Italian-Swiss economist Vilfredo Federico Damaso Pareto (1848 - 1923) who was the first to formulate the welfare optimum in this manner.

65 The efficiency of a market may be measured at the speed and accuracy with which market parties are informed of transaction-relevant data and the speed and reliability with which transactions are settled, all this, of course, against the costs of such exchange of information and goods and services. To turn back to the '*very strict conditions* (of neoclassical theory) *which can never be fully met in practice*' (see: note 64 to this chapter, above): One of those 'very strict conditions' is that such information exchange on the market is perfect (that is to say: All market parties at all times dispose of all transaction-relevant information) and also 'free'. The latter once again clearly illustrates that in practice the conditions of neoclassical theory can never be *fully* met.

66 In 1993 Douglass North, together with another new economic historian of the first hour, Robert William Fogel, was awarded the Nobel Prize for this contribution to the development of economics.

67 North's thoughts about the role of institutions in economic development processes have gradually evolved until they crystallized in (North, 1990). In the book he published in 1971 together with Lance Davis, it can be clearly seen that the authors arrive via an in essence strictly neoclassical line of thought at the conclusion that institutional change shall always run towards increasing efficiency. This point of view was later abandoned: It was indeed possible that this happened; only the history of the modern western countries taught that. It was, however, certainly not a law of the Medes and Persians: This was taught by the economic history of a great many countries in the non-western world. The evolution in North's own thought can be followed well in subsequently: (North, 1971; Davis & North, 1971; North, 1977; 1978; 1984; North & Weingast, 1989; North, 1990).

68 These are precisely the two things that go through the vanishing point in the neoclassical model!

69 It is telling in this context that Peter Temin in 1997 published an article under the challenging title 'Is it Kosher to Talk about Culture?' (Temin, 1997). Within the neoclassical paradigm it was of course highly 'un-kosher' to connect culture to economic growth. The answer in Temin's article, however, was an unequivocal 'yes', which was the writing on the wall that economic history was busy to gradually extricate itself from the embrace of neoclassical theory that in that time apparently started to become suffocating.

70 Remember that the institutional context and the technology prevailing in a certain society overlap in any case in part (probably even for a major part): This is so because both concepts have in common that it is tricky to delineate them exactly. It is, however, completely clear that, for instance, the manner in which a society provides itself information and processes that information forms part of the institutional context, and it may be likewise clear that the manner in which the society does so, is heavily dominated by technological factors.

71 Compare: Par. 6.8 of this chapter, pp. 216 ff , above.

72 Chapter 2, par. 2.10, p. 48 ff, above.

73 (Van Ark, Kuipers & Kuper (Eds.), 2000: p. 13, italicized by me, jwd)

7 À la recherche de l'histoire économique perdue

7.1 The different lines brought together

It is time to bring together the different lines that have been set out in the foregoing and to see to what extent we are now capable of giving an answer to the two questions we put forward at the beginning. We have seen that the economic history in the second half of the nineteenth century evolved as an independent discipline as a result of the methodological conflict (the *Methodenstreit*) within economics resulting in the isolation of economic history from economic theory in the first half of the twentieth century. The traditional economic history endeavoured, through comparative historical research, to explain processes of economic development by emphasizing the factors that promoted or impeded a development process in the long run. Because it was generally thought that those factors were dominated by social aspects (the manner in which people worked together and the manner in which such cooperative relations developed over time) there existed within traditional economic history a close connection with social history. So it is understandable why, precisely in the period when traditional economic history reigned supreme, economic and social history were interwoven to the extent that they were usually bracketed together: Socio-economic history, for which the underlying thought was that both constituent parts, insofar as it concerned specialist monographs were to be *distinguished* from each other, indeed, but not *separated* where it concerned the explanation for economic development processes that were considered to be determined significantly by the nature of the cooperative arrangements in society, and hence by factors that basically were of a social nature.

In this period theoretical economics took the exact opposite road. The writers of the classical school, which dominated economics until the second half of the nineteenth century, following the founding father of classical economics, Adam Smith, had always devoted an important place to social circumstances in their explanation for economic development, which was clearly illustrated if only by the in that time current designation of the discipline of economics: *Political economy*. The strict formalization of the theory in mathematical terms that was the predominant characteristic of the neoclassical school implied that economic theory was rigorously stripped of any social 'setting'. Political economy as a general designation of the discipline disappeared and was replaced by bare 'Economics'. In the course of the twentieth century, the neoclassical paradigm began to dominate economic theory and, as a consequence of the obvious a-historical character of neoclassical theory, economic history was marginalized within economic faculties.

In the same period, within general history, as practised within the faculties of arts, an increasing interest in economic and social history gradually emerged. This was especially the merit of the *École des Annales*. In the opinion of the *Annales* historians the essence of the historical discipline consisted of describing and analysing social development processes of the past.

To adequately map such processes, their approach awarded a central role to statistics, whereas they believed that they could thus explain the developments mapped by means of applying concepts and theories borrowed from other disciplines, such as economics, sociology, demographics and anthropology as 'explanatory instruments' to the historical developments that formed the object of their studies.

The strong international influence of the *Annales* after the Second World War resulted in the discipline of history, as it was traditionally studied in the faculties of arts, acquiring more affinity for the socio-economic approach, with the result that history in general grew ever more 'socio-economic'. In other words, in the same period in which theoretical economics and socio-economic history became increasingly cut off from each other, general and socio-economic history grew closer together, in the sense that within general history gradually more space became available for model-wise approaches that previously had exclusively belonged to the domain of socio-economic history. And the latter undoubtedly was to be attributed largely to the *École des Annales*.

The fundamental problem that the *Annales* adherents constantly came across was the choice of the model used to attempt the explanation of certain historical development processes. Statistics is a great tool to reconstruct the development of specific variables over the course of time, but it is not that such reconstruction in itself provides unmistakable indications of the manner in which the variables have influenced one another. The latter offers an explanation for the phenomenon that I described as 'the problematic quest for "primal structures"' that characterizes much of the work in the *Annales* tradition and resulted in that even the most prominent representatives of the *Annales* sometimes took recourse to hermetically closed theories that pretended to be able to formulate the 'general development laws of history', such as Marxism, or that they in revised versions of earlier published studies suddenly appeared to have switched from the one to the other basic explanatory model, without it later becoming clear what the reason had been for the paradigm shift.

And again, precisely in the years in which the *École des Annales* commenced its triumphal progress within the faculties of arts, for the first time a group of young American economic historians made its mark: They sincerely believed — in any case in the confident and sometimes overconfident initial phase of the new economic history — that they for the most part could answer the question the *Annales* adherents struggled with, the quest for the universally applicable historical development model. For the most part, because they did not pretend to have found a general historical development model, but indeed a model that was universally applicable to *economic* development processes. These new economic historians from the very beginning, had their home base *not* in the faculties of arts, but in economic faculties, and the surprising thing was that they thought they had found the solution in that which for traditional economic historians was no more or less than the lion's den: the neoclassical equilibrium model, in other words, the showpiece of theoretical economics that was stripped of any historical context.

239

That exactly was the crux: Because neoclassical theory had purposefully been stripped of all social context and thus had an outspoken *a-historical* character, precisely that characteristic offered the possibility to make it applicable in principle to *all* economic development processes. In addition, new economic history had a shaft left in its quiver: Where the *Annales* historians always had had the greatest difficulty to connect the statistical data in an unambiguous manner to an explanatory model, new economic historians solved these problems in a superior manner by way of the introduction of econometric testing procedures in their research. This meant that accurate empirical control possibilities arose in relation to the question whether and if yes, to what extent the relationships assumed in the explanatory model between the variables that constituted the model, were supported by the patterns that were perceptible in statistical data.

It would have been only natural, in view of their partiality for a model-wise analysis of historical development processes and their emphasis on

the historical statistical reconstruction of the variables that had constituted the processes, if it had come to an immediate intensive exchange between the *École des Annales* and the new economic history. That did not
happen, however, and the main reason for this was a 'language problem',
that had a restraining influence in various manners. Firstly, new economic
history alienated itself from the traditional economic history because of
the fact that its researchers availed themselves of the highest specialized
technical lingo of modern mathematical economics and econometrics, a
language that was often insufficiently understood by the majority of traditional economic historians. Secondly, international university exchange
in the 1960s was less than today. Furthermore, the fact that the *Annales*
historians published in French generally was no problem for the dissemi-
nation of their ideas in the faculties of arts of other European countries,
but that did not hold true for the economic faculties in the United States.
Only when, after many years, the major studies of authoritative *Annales*
historians were translated into English, the body of thought of the *Annales* became more widely known within new economic history.[1]
All this implies that traditional economic history and new economic history developed relatively cut off from each other during well over twenty
years (say, from the second half of the 1950s until far in the 1970s).
Traditional economic history profited within the walls of the faculties
of arts from the growing interest in socio-economic analysis of historical development processes within general history, which was the result
of the influence of the *École des Annales*, while new economic history,
relatively separate, within the American economic faculties blossomed
out, and from that position — in the United States, in any case - gradually
grew to dominate the economic history discipline.

This development was paradoxical. New economic history from the very
start was considered the obvious approach, able to close the gap that
had opened up following the *Methodenstreit* in economics between the
followers of the (inductive empirical) historical and the (deductive abstract) neoclassical school. It was not without a reason that Robert William Fogel in this context spoke of the *Re-unification* of economic theory
and economic history. But for this 'reunification' a steep price was paid
indeed: The reunification between economic history and economic theory
in that manner, originally implied again a divisive element, now within
the economic history discipline itself, more precisely between traditional
economic history and new economic history.
The surprising success of new economic history, although still limited
to the economic faculties of the American top universities, was mainly
occasioned by the fact that the leading American economists considered

the methods and techniques of new economic history as a fully-fledged branch of applied economics, whereas traditional economic history had always been denied this qualification. New economic historians spoke the same language as students of theoretical economics and followed the same methods of research. More than that, new economic history in the eyes of theoretical economics could render an important contribution to the question whether the explanation of modern economic growth forecasted by the neoclassical growth theory corresponded to what had apparently happened in reality over the course of history in the different countries of the western world. The result was that soon already close cooperation sprung up between the new economic historians and the empirical-research oriented economists. That cooperation significantly contributed to the resounding success of new economic history. Measured against the number of quantitative analytic publications in the leading scientific journals and on the basis of the fact that a majority of the chairs in economic history at top universities in the United States are held by new economic historians — meanwhile often second or even third generation already — this success in fact continues until this day.

Nevertheless, you can hardly deny that this success was not devoid of certain ambivalence. Of course, a great number of ideas and convictions that often had been considered inviolable for generations within traditional economic history were conclusively exposed by new economic history. It appeared that many of such convictions could not stand up to the double-edged sword of cliometrics. Some of the explanations for essential economic history issues within the traditional economic history, generally accepted for years, suddenly appeared to be a lot less convincing if you made the economic theoretical framework more explicit and that was the one point in which new economic history distinguished itself from the traditional approach. In other cases through new numerical data or a strict econometric analysis of existing numerical data it appeared that the influence of certain factors, which were traditionally considered of crucial importance, on the development process had been much smaller than previously had been believed. In retrospect the fact that many traditional explanations had become unsettled because additional quantitative data pointed in another direction was not so surprising: Because new economic history fairly soon developed into a hot topic, many ambitious young researchers felt attracted to economic history and the result was a true explosion of new research in the economic history field. The development of the modern PC and the ever more powerful and user-friendly software (statistics packages and spreadsheets) in the 1970s brought along an unbelievable increase of labor productivity where it concerned the reconstruction and the analysis of historical statistical data. A not

241

unimportant part of the capacity of new economic history to undermine a number of traditional insights simply emanated from the fact that the new economic historians disposed of infinitely more quantitative information than earlier generations of economic historians.

The surprising success of the new economic history was nevertheless also partially of a destructive nature. The dogmas that had been cherished by traditional economic history for years on end were demolished or at least unsettled, frequently without a broad consensus on the answer to the question 'tell us, how it is *really* then'. A striking characteristic of cliometrics is that debates often go on for years, yes, for decades, without it becoming convincingly clear which party actually is right. Must we draw the conclusion that the success of the cliometric revolution in the mild light of eternity showed a strong resemblance to the classic Pyrrhic victory? No, that would go too far, for there indeed was one point on which a wide consensus was reached, even if it had to be acknowledged that the idea had been generally accepted for many generations within traditional economic history as well and thus cannot be considered a brand-new insight that was the exclusive result of cliometrics. You can at best insist that where other dogmas from economic history sooner or later often succumbed on the cliometric test bank of theoretical explicitness and quantitative testing, the insight concerned here through the years has managed to hold its own virtually intact.

7.2 NEH and neoclassical theory: Market allocation and growth

It is not unimportant to conclude that this insight is supported by two pillars. Firstly, in the form of a generalization based on an overwhelming quantity of historical obviousness it may be considered as the one (but very fundamental) lesson taught by economic history, since the emergence of the Historical School approximately a century and half ago. Secondly, it is supported by what is considered the main result of the development of deductive-reductionist theories since the emergence of the neoclassical school: The so-called general equilibrium model.

In a nutshell the lesson is as follows: The historically seen exceptionally rapid economic growth that manifested itself in the countries of the western world since the second half of the eighteenth century has always gone accompanied by the growth, differentiation and perfectionism of markets as determining economic allocation mechanism. Economic growth, defined as a non-incidental increase in production per head of the population, is brought about by an increase in productivity, which is the phenomenon that economic systems appear to be able to generate more output per unit of input over the course of time. The question that is subsequently asked is of course what causes an increase in productivity in the long term.

The answer to that question was already formulated by Adam Smith in 1776 and meanwhile can hardly be labelled surprising. Surprising at the most is that his answer has withstood the ravages of time amazingly well. The three central concepts that bring about productivity growth are: specialization, division of labor and technological development. In *The Wealth of Nations* a strong emphasis is placed on the first two as productivity-promoting factors, while technological development within the meaning we ascribe to the concept (the systematic application of scientific knowledge for problem solving in everyday life) hardly plays a role. This should not come as a surprise: Modern technological development is a phenomenon that only began to manifest itself in the nineteenth century. Classical authors after Adam Smith (Ricardo, for instance) are more interested in technological development in the contemporary meaning of the word.

Specialization is understood to be the concentration of labor and capital within one company, while division of labor consists of the breaking-up of tasks required for the manufacture of a product (or a part) in partial tasks, which may take place within one company as well as among several companies. It may be clear that specialization, division of labor and technological development are inextricably bound up: division of labor is a precondition for specialization, while increasing specialization requires modification in the manner in which products are manufactured, which by definition implies a change in production technology.

243

Why do the interrelated processes of specialization, division of labor and technological development result in an increase of productivity? The answer to that question is so obvious (we so to speak see it happening all around us, every day) that you easily tend to overlook it. The point is that this results in a concentration of specialized knowledge and know-how that through the continuous training in the special skills required by the manufacture of that one specific product (or part thereof) tends to increase in the course of time. Any child knows the secret of top achievements in any human activities in which to a certain degree a quality criterion can be set (for instance, with sports or music): Talent, specialization and training. Venus Williams, given the nature of her highly specialized skills, will be able to run faster than most women, and she may even outrun most men, but, but still on the track she will lose out to any professional female athlete who is specialized in just that branch of athletics.

Maria João Pires will undoubtedly be able to manage surprisingly well on the organ or harpsichord for someone who has never specialized in these instruments, but give her a transverse flute and she would fumble worse even than a moderately talented pupil after one year at the local music school.

It is also like that with economic activities: The concentration of talent, in combination with specialization and training makes for productivity. Of course, there are differences as well between making music, practising a sport, and manufacturing goods and products.

The most conspicuous difference is the role of technological development: It may be clear that this role, although not entirely to be neglected as regards achievements in sports and playing music, is much more prominent in economic activities where productivity is the pivotal criterion. This in itself is correct, but in effect it does not undermine the position that specialization and training are essential conditions for an increase in productivity over time. The judgement as to which technological changes will probably be highly successful in a certain specialized production process requires two things: Knowledge of the technological possibilities available at a given moment, as well as specialized knowledge of the production process concerned.

Market allocation now plays a crucial role in this process. First of all, it is crystal clear that specialization is only possible when there exists already a market in one form or the other: Only a completely autarkic household, in which all products necessary for the survival of the members of that household are also actually manufactured within the household, can do without a market. As soon as there is only the beginning of specialization, any form of barter becomes necessary and that is, by definition, the most basic form of a market. In line with this, market differentiation is a condition for an increase in specialization and a necessary condition for the productivity increase resulting from increasing specialization.

Under a number of very specific conditions (but mind you, those conditions are essential!) an economic system based on market allocation shows properties that are of extraordinary importance to economic growth. The most important of these conditions are: All market parties are guided in their behaviour exclusively by stable and rational preference schemes; accession to the market is completely free for everyone; there are, both on the demand side and on the supply side, a large number of market parties that operate independently from each other; the goods traded at the markets are homogenous, that means that they are similar and of the same quality; all market parties dispose of all information that might be of relevance to their course of action on the market and can make a correct assessment of the possible economic consequences of their course of action for themselves.

Under these conditions (and that is the essence of the neoclassical model) market allocation will lead to a general equilibrium in the economic system. Translated into 'the language of ordinary people' this means that, in the first place, competition will cause production in all sectors to take place with the maximum attainable efficiency under existing technology and hence: The highest productivity. Furthermore, all goods and services produced end up there where they yield the greatest benefit for the users and moreover: Exogenous shocks cause such changes in the relative prices of products and production factors that the system in reaction to an exogenous shock always moves into the direction of a new equilibrium. Finally, it may be shown that the general equilibrium in this sense is Pareto optimal, which means that no singular subject can improve its economic position without at the same time damaging the position of another.

The neoclassical equilibrium model can be considered a formal scientific confirmation of the correctness of the adage of Adam Smith that economic allocation within a system of freely operating market forces does not lead to social chaos, but — within the existing possibilities of the prevailing technology and under a number of very specific conditions — indeed to as high as possible a production of goods and services at as low as possible prices, which, in accordance with certain well-defined criteria, are socially optimally divided over the economic subjects, whereas finally — as grand finale — it can also be made plausible that this system especially generates strong impulses to immediately test out in practice the technological innovation that under the given circumstances promises an even more efficient production.

245

7.3 Neoclassical theory as description of the western model of success

General equilibrium theory, as the above described model of neoclassical tailoring is called, in the course of the twentieth century grew into an almost unassailable paradigm within theoretical economics. Despite the fact that after the Second World War it was subjected to heavy criticism, more in particular from Keynesian and neo-Marxist quarters, where, oddly enough, the result of the theoretical debate in a number of essential cases was to the advantage of the critics of the neoclassical theory.[2]

That peculiar immunity becomes somewhat understandable, if you consider that the neoclassical diehards are especially to be found in American
universities and America in this period was becoming increasingly dominant in the international scientific debate.[3] This holds true for almost all
disciplines and certainly so for economics. The answer to the question
why the neoclassical equilibrium model gained such tremendous popularity precisely in the United States is obvious: If there was one country
in which the specific conditions of the general equilibrium model were
closely approximated in reality and where the economic development
process in the nineteenth and twentieth centuries had evolved along the
lines predicted by the neoclassical model, it would be North America.
And no one could deny that precisely the United States had been the
economic precursor in the western world during the entire twentieth
century. No wonder, that the neoclassical paradigm obtained a virtually
unassailable character over there indeed. American economists saw the
process of neoclassical development happen in front of their very eyes, so
to speak, and had to conclude as well that no other country had been able
to equal American economic growth in the long run.

In that light also, the essence of the new economic history (mind you:
initially also of American origin) had to be interpreted: The successful
process of economic development could be explained by showing that
such processes had evolved within a body of social preconditions that
bore strong resemblance to the conditions of the neoclassical model for
general equilibrium. Processes of economic stagnation and decline were
then, *mutatis mutandis*, explained by showing that the social preconditions within which such processes had evolved, did not match the neoclassical equilibrium conditions or had increasingly departed from them
over time.

With that approach, the economic success of western economies could be
explained satisfactorily in principle and viewed against that background,
the success of the new economic history is completely understandable.
But with that success, a gnawing doubt appeared. For it could not be
denied that the fast economic growth, that was characteristic of western
economic development, was an exception, seen from a global point of
view. And the conclusion that everywhere else, where there had been no
economic modernization after the western model, this had been the result of the fact that no social development process had taken place there
that increasingly approximated the conditions of the neoclassical model,
was of course a first rate bromide, which could moreover not be reconciled with the neoclassical world view. One of the pillars on which the entire equilibrium theory rested, was indeed the assumption that economic

subjects allowed themselves to be guided in their choices by rational considerations on the basis of stable preference schemes, for which they were in addition also considered to be able to make a correct assessment of the consequences of their behaviour. If that assumption was not in flagrant contradiction to the manner in which economic subjects behaved in reality, why had not an economic modernization process after western model come off the ground *everywhere* sooner or later? As economic subjects could correctly assess the consequences of their actions, who would *not* have opted for a course of action that would have yielded apparent prosperity, if only by following the western example? And still, this was precisely what happened time and again in the non-western world. Apparently, something serious was wrong with the neoclassical theory where it concerned explaining economic stagnation and decline.

7.4 Undermining from NEH (1): Douglass North and institutions

Three authors from the ranks of the new economic history — all three originally staunch followers of neoclassical theory — Douglass North, Paul David and Joel Mokyr, were the first to openly express their doubts about the usefulness of the neoclassical equilibrium model as universal explanatory model for economic change. Remarkable in this is, that it concerned no new club of youthful revolutionaries who rebel against that which meanwhile had become the economic-historical establishment. North is one of the Old Guard: He had already made his name as economist before the new economic history first made a name for itself and was one of the older participants in the first cliometric conferences at Purdue University that had heralded the birth of the new economic history. Paul David had attended those conferences as a research assistant of Moses Abramovitz at Stanford University and hence is typically a prominent representative of the first generation of new economic historians among whom also rank Fogel and Engerman, for example. Joel Mokyr, finally, studied economics and economic history in the years that the cliometric approach dominated within American economic history[4] and for that reason is to be considered as a 'second generation cliometrician'.

From the development in the writings of Douglass North the reasons can be clearly seen why at length he began to doubt the usefulness of neoclassical theory as a universal paradigm for economic history. His earliest studies in economic history can be characterized as often highly meritorious and often very important contributions to the re-interpretation of a wide variety of sub-problems from American economic history, which was the trademark of the new economic history.[5] Until far into the 1970s he operated strictly within the neoclassical framework. At the beginning of the seventies, however, a striking shift of emphasis in his work may be noticed: The partial studies make way for attempts to explain processes of structural economic change in the long to very long term, which often go so far back in time that quantitative data are very rare or even completely lacking, and the persuasiveness of the explanation is exclusively based on the internal logic of the explanatory model applied. The unifying element in those studies is formed by the fact that still a consistent attempt is made to explain the processes of structural change from a strictly neoclassical perspective: What it constantly comes down to in essence, is that the increase in population and the ensuing changes in the density of the population, cause such changes in the relative prices that, as a result, other economic organizational forms gain viability because within the changed (relative) price relations they lead to more efficient production. In this manner, it is made plausible why, what North calls, the 'First Economic Revolution' took place: The transition from a society of hunters and gatherers to one of the earliest forms of sedentary agriculture, approximately ten thousand years ago (North & Thomas, 1977). The rise and fall of feudalism is explained along the same lines (North & Thomas, 1971), the revival and loss of mercantilism and, finally, the emergence and development of western capitalism in the nineteenth and twentieth centuries (North & Thomas, 1973; North, 1981).[6]

248

In that same period North little by little begins to ease away from the standard neoclassical model and that is not incomprehensible given the subject he focuses on in those years: Typical of neoclassical theory is that it fully abstracts from the social environment in which the economic process is taking place, and what North in those years tries to do now in

Figure 7.1 Douglass C. North

his studies into the processes of structural change is *not* to explain the economic process itself, but *to explain the change in the social environment.* If you would want to stay strictly within the boundaries of neoclassical theory, it may be clear that such an approach looks suspiciously like exorcising the devil with Beelzebub.

The first steps to come out of this dilemma were a couple of essential additions to the neoclassical standard model: an expansion of the neoclassical theory with a theory about the role of institutions within the economic process and a theory about the influence of ideology in relation to the process of information processing. Both amplifications in first instance were probably not meant otherwise than to make complete the neoclassical theory in a number of traditionally weak spots, but ultimately, the introduction of those additions appeared to be of much greater significance: Within the development of North's thoughts, in the end they became the Trojan Horse for the neoclassical model. Let us see now how North's innocent additions ultimately proved fatal to the neoclassical model.
North's theory about institutions (described by him as *man-made environment*) departs from the conclusion that the social environment in which the economic process is taking place is of decisive influence on the outcome of the process. In a nutshell: An absolute condition for economic growth is an economically efficient social organizational system. The two issues involved are: First of all, the nature of the rights of ownership in the goods and services that are generally accepted in society, and the ways in which these ownership rights are enforced. Secondly: The manner in which the information supply is organized in society. Let us take a closer look at these two matters.

The current system of ownership rights and their enforcement is determining for the degree in which the individual economic initiatives are stimulated and finally, these initiatives are at the root of economic growth. A social organization in which the individuals can one way or the other pluck the fruits of their own efforts, is conducive to the individual initiative. Think, for example, of the difference between a feudal relationship for control over the proceeds of the land and a land lease relationship. If the larger proceeds that are the result of additional efforts made by a predial serf do not accrue to him and his family, but for reasons of the feudal provisions, go in full to his master, the serf in question will reduce his efforts to a minimum. Only when the greater proceeds as a result of his efforts, fully or at least in part accrue to him (as with a land lease relationship), the serf will be inclined to actually make the additional effort.

249

The implication of this line of thought (mind you: The point of departure still is strictly rationally thinking economic subjects, in other words: The reasoning still fits in within the preconditions of neoclassical theory) is that economically efficient social organization forms are characterized by the phenomenon that robbery and theft, extortion and fraud in economic transactions, arbitrary confiscation of the fruits of individual efforts by the government (that is inclusive of extremely high tax burdens) and forms of non-economic appropriation and shift[7] are efficiently and effectively combated. The more effective the combating, the lower the risk that any third party will take off with the fruits of the economic efforts of specific individuals or organizations and thus: The more individuals and organizations willing to undertake production and productivity-enhancing activities. And the more efficient the combating, the less inputs will be required for the enforcement of ownership rights and the more inputs can be deployed for the production of other goods and services.

The following thought experiment might be elucidating. Imagine a society where the Dutch saying 'God punishes immediately' must be taken quite literally: Everyone who in whatever manner 'cheats' in economic transactions will forthwith be zapped mercilessly by a short bolt of lightning away from the earthly world, and everyone will be well aware of this, indeed. Suppose that the same god also has the habit of telling his subjects in their dreams what exactly will be the different material effects of the whole range of economic actions they are contemplating and what the chances are of those different actions indeed having the success desired. Contrast that imaginary world to a society in which 'cheating' is *never* punished and in which no one has the slightest idea of the effects of his or her economic activities and what chances of succeeding such activities may have. Little imagination will be required to realize two things that are crucial in this context: Firstly, in the first type of society more individual economic initiatives will be displayed than in the second; secondly, the average total costs of every product marketed in both societies will be lower in the first type of society compared to the second, even if the relative prices of all production factors are equally high in both societies and the production technology in both societies is identical. The explanation for that difference in average costs is quite simple: It is not caused by a difference in *production* costs (the costs arising from the physical conversion of production factors into products) but by a difference in the *transaction* costs (the costs arising from the actual exchange of goods and services, that is to say, the costs that the parties involved in the exchange have to make to gain and process transaction-relevant information and to cover risks of premature frustration of such transactions caused by unforeseen circumstances).

In reality there is of course no supernatural power that immediately punishes any form of 'cheating' in economic transactions and in addition makes available, immediately and free of charge, to anyone and everyone, all information needed to make conscious economic decisions, but that does not alter the fact that in reality there do exist huge differences among societies as to what is considered 'cheating' and how 'cheating' is detected and punished.[8]

For as far as the 'economic rules of the game' are concerned (the description of the system of ownership rights) and the punishment for noncompliance with those rules of the game (the enforcement of ownership rights), an important role is reserved in reality for the government, with as a result, that an institutional addition to the neoclassical theory soon gets the nature of a theory about the role of the government in an economic system of market allocation. And that is precisely where the weakness is located: The neoclassical model in fact cannot do *without* a theory of the government, but at the same time is at considerable odds with itself as soon as this government is introduced into the model.

That an economic system that is in essence based on market allocation (as in neoclassical theory) ultimately cannot do without some form of government, unavoidably arises from the fact that apart from individual or private goods and services (rolls, bicycles and haircuts) there also are collective or public goods and services, that is to say, goods whose consumption, as an individual, one cannot avoid. A dyke that protects the country against floods, nolens volens also protects the possessions of inhabitants who would rather abandon their worldly goods to the waves, and the same goes, for example, for services geared towards keeping the peace and sovereignty: Anarchists and pacifists as well 'consume' perforce the services of policy and army, even though they probably would rather not, on the basis of their philosophy of life.

The question now is how collective goods will be produced in a system that is based on market allocation and this question is even trickier than it would seem at first glance. Elaborating on the example of the construction of a dyke, you would at first reason that all economic subjects (according to the neoclassical assumptions, all completely rational decisionmakers, who, moreover, dispose of complete information in respect of the economic consequences of their decisions) realize that cooperation here will lead to the most efficient solution and therefore unanimously decide that everyone will contribute pro rata to the construction and the maintenance of the dyke in question. But there are two snags here, which in literature are known as the *free-rider problem* and the *prisoners dilemma*. Both demand some explanation.

251

Precisely because no one can escape the protection of the dyke as soon as it is built, it is for every economic subject individually rational to *not* contribute to its payment: If everyone pays, except me, I will have free protection from the dyke, and he who pays for something he can obtain for free does not act rationally in the neoclassical meaning of the word. Now you can follow this reasoning through, by assuming that all economic subjects (rational as they are) foresee the free-rider problem and conclude that on the basis of free choice such cooperation probably will not work. On the basis of that, they decide again unanimously to establish an authority that can enforce payment for the construction and maintenance of collective property: The birth of government! In neoclassical literature this is sometimes worded in splendid euphemism: Government is the only body in society that by law can use force to eliminate the free-rider problem. This seems a simple and elegant solution to the problem but ...nothing is further from the truth. As soon as the 'monopoly on force' in society is transferred to the government, why would that government then restrict itself to enforcing payment from its subjects for the creation and the maintenance of collective property? All economic subjects in a neoclassical world are considered to be rational decision-makers, indeed, and among other things, this means that they will always opt for 'more' instead of 'less', if with the exact same effort they can obtain 'more'. If the government, now as the only authority in the system, is able to enforce payment by means of force, why does it not use that position of power to exploit its subjects to the bone to maximize its own revenues? In addition, the question as who ultimately decides what is collective and what is private property, is rather difficult to answer. If the answer to that question is left to the government, there is a good chance that the government will assign itself tasks (and enforces payment for this) that could have been produced more efficiently in the market sector. Consulting with subjects about such matters through democratic vote in first instance again seems to offer a way out, but who can force the government to carry out such democratic vote, if all means of coercion have been transferred to precisely that government? To make matters worse, even if the government would stick to its word, it can be proven beyond a shadow of a doubt that (via the so-called *voting paradox*, that is) such democratic vote can result in logically inconsistent solutions.[9]

The inevitable conclusion must be, that the snake again bites its own tail: No one will deny that an efficient economic organizational structure (that is an institutional structure which entails relatively low transaction costs) for two reasons is an essential condition for economic growth. In the first place, on account of the lower transaction costs, the total average costs are lower than in systems with a less efficient economic organization and for that reason more inputs can be deployed for the production of additional goods and services. In other words, with two economic systems that are perfectly identical to each other, except for the level of the transaction costs, in the system with the lowest transaction costs more production will be possible than in the other, simply because there are more inputs for production available. Secondly, in a relatively efficient economic environment individuals and organizations are stimulated more to undertake production and productivity-enhancing activities because they have a better chance to actually claim the fruits of their own efforts. No one shall deny either, that an economically efficient social organization is a classic example of 'collective property': Every economic subject within the system enjoys its advantages, in other words, no one can individually 'avoid' its consumption. The latter inescapably implies that a 'free-rider problem' is looming: For any individual it is more advantageous to enjoy the benefits of the system 'free of charge', than to pay for them, and the consequence of that is again that the government is the obvious authority to play a pivotal role in the creation and preservation of the system, namely, by making use of its position of power and so force its subjects to pay for the costs of maintaining the system. And that is precisely the point where the snake bites its own tail: Within the neoclassical model there is no reason why the government would fulfil this role. Suppose that the government, just as all other parties in a market economy, will maximize its revenues within the boundaries of the possible, then the consequence is that, availing itself of its 'monopoly on force', it will increase the tax burden to a maximum and the result is with unerring precision a socio-economic organizational form that is lethal to every form of individual economic initiative. Suppose that the government, as only party in a market economy, consciously *waives* its own self-interest, then you would promptly undermine one of the fundaments of the neoclassical model, which parts from the assumption that *all* economic subjects act from well-considered self-interest.

An issue that is closely connected to the free-rider problem is that which I earlier referred to as the prisoners dilemma, originating from game theory. The relation with the free-rider problem is, that here as well it is made clear that 'strategic cooperation on a voluntary basis' is a much trickier problem than the neoclassical theory supposes.
The prisoners dilemma basically consists of the following reasoning: Two thieves are suspected of jointly committing burglary and are interrogated separately from one another. Both thieves realize that if they both keep silent they will have to be released for lack of evidence, but also that if

253

they both confess, they will both be sentenced to two years' imprisonment. So far there is no problem for either of them, what the best strategy is: Silence. But suppose for a moment that if either of them spills the beans and the other does not, the squealing thief will be rewarded by the judge for his frankness with one year's remission (so: One year in prison instead of two), whereas the silent thief will be punished for his silence with an additional year (three years instead of two). Now suddenly there is no longer an unequivocal optimal strategy for either of the thieves: Silence is still the best, but only if *both* of them keep silent. If one confesses and the other does not, this will be favourable for the confessor (1 year less behind bars), but unfavourable for the silent one (1 year more). In short, whereas every one understands that keeping silent is still the best *overall* strategy, it does not apply to every thief individually. For the best individual strategy has become dependent upon the strategy opted for by the other: For A it is *only* best to keep silent, if B also keeps silent, and that is precisely what A does not know. Supposing that B confesses, it would indeed be better for A to confess as well. And A does indeed have a reason to confess if he does not know what B is doing: It also keeps open the possibility that B does not confess, which would be favourable for A compared to the result of both of them confessing. And the dreadful thing is that the prisoners dilemma is perfectly symmetrical: What goes for A, goes for B. In short, it is a difficult situation.

The implications of the issue of the prisoners dilemma are again undermining the fundaments of neoclassical theory, even if this possibly is not completely clear beforehand. It is all about the relationship between cooperation and information in an economic system. In a neoclassical world it is assumed that all transaction-relevant information for all economic subjects is available in full and free of charge. And although neoclassical theory in itself is not very explicit about cooperation[10] (it simply calls entities that take independent decisions in an economic system 'economic subjects', and further leaves aside whether those 'economic subjects' only concern isolated individuals or organizations in which individuals are working together), from the two suppositions of full, free information and rational decision-making based on consistent preferences, it may be deduced that economic subjects, according to neoclassical theory will always voluntarily proceed to cooperating if the cooperation results in more efficient economic solutions.[11] Again, in reality there is of course never full and free information for all and the interest of the issue of the prisoners dilemma is, that this proves beyond a shadow of a doubt that in circumstances of limited information, (in terms of the prisoners dilemma: A does not know what B is doing and vice versa) voluntary cooperation is no longer 'automatic', even if it is clear to all parties involved that coop-

eration (A and B decide to both keep silent) will unequivocally result in the best solution, and all parties involved on the basis of strictly rational grounds decide (less time behind bars is always preferred to more).
The issue of the free-rider problem and the inescapable fact that there exist collective goods in reality, makes it clear that neoclassical theory cannot exist without a theory of the government as a body able to enforce payment for the consumption of collective goods. To make it even more complicated: In the above we have deduced that the most important condition for the stimulation of economic development, according to North, is in a social organization characterized by relatively low transaction costs. The point is now, that if such an efficient economic organization does exist, it has all characteristics of collective property: All members of society enjoy its benefits, even those members who, for whatever reason, prefer not to share in the costs of the system. The prisoners dilemma and the likewise inescapable fact that in reality there never has been full and free information, has as a consequence that the assumption that is implicit in neoclassical theory, namely that government functions in a market economy arise 'automatically' because a strategic cooperation between individuals on a voluntary basis, does not work. It is for this reason that neoclassical theory in the view of North needs a second addition, namely in the area where political organization and ideology interlock, and that is precisely the point where neoclassical theory definitely loses ground, as far as North is concerned, as a universal explanatory model for economic development.[12]

255

Ideology may be considered as a more or less systematically coherent body of concepts and ideas about the manner in which the world is organized and with which man explains the reality surrounding him. Three conclusions are essential in this context: First, that several ideologies exist; furthermore, that the followers of a certain ideology are of the opinion that their interpretation of the world is the right one; and third, that an ideology always is a mixture of 'ontological judgements' ('how things are') and value judgements ('how things ought to be'). The result is that every society to a certain degree is characterized by ideological conflicts: Different ideologies strive for political power to realize their ideas about 'what it should be like' in society. This continuous ideological struggle, which in some instances is not particularly of a violent nature (the fight between the liberals and socialists in most West European countries nowadays, for example) and in other instances gives cause for extreme force (Muslims versus Hindus in some parts of Asia, for example), induces constantly changing balances of political power, the result of which is not to be predicted but which is indeed decisive of the institutional structure of a society (remember: *The man made environment*, in North's terminology). The question why in some societies an institutional structure has emerged that is conducive to economic development, and not in others, can now be answered in the sense that an efficient economic organization is the result of a long balance of power in favour of an ideology that places economically efficient institutions high on the political agenda. And because there is no reason at all to assume that ideologies that assign high priority to economically efficient organizational forms in the political arena have a greater chance of survival than ideologies that do not want to have anything to do with this, there is no reason either to assume that societies always set course for greater economic efficiency, as supposed by the convergence hypothesis that is based on neoclassical theory.

7.5 Undermining from NEH (2): Paul David and path dependency

The evolution in the works of Paul David shows a striking resemblance with that of North, albeit that he reached similar conclusions along completely different roads than North, namely that neoclassical theory could at best be viewed a special case of a theory about economic development, but not as a universal explanatory model. As research assistant of Moses Abramovitz, David stood at the cradle of the new economic history and his first publications fit perfectly in the research program that characterized the first years of cliometrics: He made a significant contribution to the explanation of economic growth in the United States in the first half of the nineteenth century (David, 1967), he engaged in a fierce debate

Figure 7.2 Paul David

with Fogel in reaction to the latter's *Railroads and American Economic Growth* (David, 1969), he participated in the debate about the role of tariff policy of the United States in relation to the development of the cotton industry (David, 1970) and he was one of the fiercest critics of *Time on the Cross* (David & Temin, 1974; 1979). It is striking that in his most famous study, published during the early years of cliometrics, 'The Mechanization of Reaping in the Antebellum Midwest' (David, 1966), the seeds can already be found of his later works, in which he definitively breaks with neoclassical theory as universal explanatory model of economic development.

David's explanation for the delayed adoption of the *Reaper*[13] in fact went along neoclassical lines and moreover, formed a logically sound and convincing story. Nevertheless, if you would think more deeply about the implications of his analysis, a number of unsolved questions remain, that in fact cannot be properly reconciled with the neoclassical body of thought. The essence of the explanation for the delay in the adoption of the mechanic harvester is, that the average acreage of farms in the Midwest of the United States was too small for an economically efficient use of the *Reaper*. But the question promptly arises why American farmers immediately following the introduction, had not proceeded, on a voluntary basis, to large-scale land consolidation to increase the average acreage size to a level at which the efficient deployment of the *Reaper* would become possible indeed. They would have forthwith done so, had they actually been rational calculating decision-makers who disposed of complete information.

The manner in which new technology is developed and the manner in which new technology is disseminated in the long run became the central theme of David's scientific work. But despite the fact that his empirical studies show a huge variety of subjects, there are two central themes to which he constantly returns: The phenomenon of the productivity paradox[14], or the phenomenon that huge technological breakthroughs do not immediately result in an increase in productivity, but rather to a reduction because for a longer period two technological regimes exist alongside each other and it often takes dozens of years before a mega-breakthrough has spread throughout the entire economic system. The second phenomenon David constantly encountered in his empirical studies, was the phenomenon of 'path dependency' in technological development, the phenomenon that the prehistory of technological development processes is co-decisive for the direction in which the technology further develops.[15] Both phenomena are clearly in conflict with neoclassical theory, in the sense that in the neoclassical world the most efficient technology avail-

257

able at a certain moment will (via the mechanism of competition) immediately replace the old — less efficient — technology, which is at odds, both with the empirically well documented phenomenon of the productivity paradox, and with the phenomenon of path dependency, implying that other factors (namely: The history of the technology itself) than only pure economic efficiency play a decisive role in the specific way a certain technology will develop. The result was that David exchanged his neoclassical background for an evolutionary approach to technological change, with the consequence that the specific historic character began to play a leading role in his vision on economic development.[16]

7.6 Undermining from NEH (3): Joel Mokyr and knowledge acquisition

And again a similar development in thought is to be found in Joel Mokyr. Mokyr, a Dutchman by birth, spent his teenage years and the first years of his university training in Israël, where he studied economics and history. From there he migrated to the United States, where he obtained his doctorate in 1975 at Yale. So, Mokyr studied in the United States precisely in the years that the new economic history blossomed tremendously, and for that reason was tried and tested in neoclassical theory, which emerges clearly in his early works. In one respect, Joel Mokyr was the odd one out, however:

Figure 7.3 Joel Mokyr

While most new economic historians focused on the economic history of the standard economic successes of western modernization (the United States and England), as one of the first cliometricians, he engaged in the study of economic development of two countries that in the nineteenth century characterized themselves by long-term economic stagnation: The Netherlands (Mokyr, 1975; 1976; 1980a) and Ireland (Mokyr, 1980a; 1980b; 1980c; 1985). The interesting thing is that Mokyr, reasoning from a strictly neoclassical perspective and despite meticulous, quantitative research, could actually not find any reasons within the neoclassical model itself for the stagnation, and as a result he finally ran into institutional factors that are deeply rooted in the history of both countries. With this Mokyr, departing from a neoclassical perspective, comes very near to North.

After a period in which he occupied himself with a wide variety of enomic history issues, in the long run he concentrated, just as Paul David, on issues of technological development. All this resulted in a new standard work in the field of technological history (Mokyr, 1990), in which two things occupy a central place: In the first place the conclusion that in successful processes of technological innovation, there always is a close relationship between the development in thought itself, as well as in the manner in which new ideas are applied in practice. Successful technological innovation is, in Mokyr's view, pre-eminently a process, in which there is a constant co-evolution between pure and applied science. Secondly, in this book, Mokyr proves that huge technological breakthroughs (*macro-inventions* in his terminology) are only used to the full after a very long time, via an infinite series of *micro-inventions* in practice, a view that links up closely to David's idea of the productivity paradox. In his latest book (Mokyr, 2002) he even goes one step further: In fact, the question is raised as to what is the origin of technological innovation proper. The answer to that question is: Technological innovation emanates from the emergence of new ideas, some of which finally result in successful applications in everyday life. The question how it is that during certain periods some societies are apparently extremely fruitful in causing new ideas to emerge while others are not, is answered *de facto* in a perspective borrowed from North: In the end, it is the ideological and institutional factors that are decisive. It may be clear that through this development in his ideas, Mokyr as well has since long abandoned the neoclassical path.

259

7.7 An alternative economic theory: Evolutionary economics

Exactly in that same period as in which in some new economic history circles doubts arose about neoclassical theory as a universal explanatory model for processes of structural economic change, also in economic theory proper criticisms were passed that in the long run severely undermined the neoclassical foundations. The two most important spokespersons in this were Richard Nelson and Sidney Winter. Their paths had crossed on several occasions, including in the time when both had temporarily abandoned their academic careers, to provide consultancy services for the government and the business community.[17] When they took up publishing under a joint name in the seventies (Nelson & Winter, 1973; 1974), Nelson had in the meantime become an authoritative expert in the field of industrial organization, specialized in long-term strategies for companies, while Sidney Winter had grown into a formidable critic of the prevailing neoclassical theory, which he had attacked in a critique on a famous article by Milton Friedman (1951) especially for the unrealistic character of the assumptions of the neoclassical standard model.[18]

In their criticism, Nelson and Winter started from the point that neoclassical theory by origin is a static theory, and that economic development is a dynamic process.[19] The consequence of this is that neoclassical theory by definition is not capable of giving a description of the process of economic change itself. It analyses under which conditions a market system is in equilibrium and at best can make plausible that an exogenous shock yields 'automatically' a new equilibrium. In fact, two situations of equilibrium are compared to one another (the so-called: 'Comparative static

Figure 7.4 Richard R. Nelson

Figure 7.5 Sidney G. Winter

analysis'), but within the preconditions of the neoclassical model, the new equilibrium is brought about *immediately* and the time path along which the adjustment has come about is ignored. In reality there is, of course, never a general equilibrium: The system is continuously subjected to exogenous shocks, and the implication from this, is that it is at best constantly on its way to a new equilibrium, but that this equilibrium is never attained in effect. But, if that is correct, the concept that is the central focus of neoclassical analysis, namely 'long-term general equilibrium', looses any form of real purport! Naturally, every theory abstracts from reality, but the point is, according to Nelson and Winter, that neoclassical theory abstracts from what is the most essential characteristic of processes of economic change: The manner in which the system adjusts over time to changes in the environment.

Why had economic theory ever set out on that fatal course? The answer, according to the two authors, is to be found in the circumstance that economics, in the course of its development, has seriously attempted to profile itself as a 'real', 'solid' discipline and thereby has conscientiously followed the example of the natural sciences.[20] The most conspicuous methodological similarity between those 'recognized' scientific disciplines, such as physics and astronomy, was in the fact that development of theories took place within the framework of strictly formal mathematical models and by following that example, theoretical economics, automatically as it were, came on the path of the static equilibrium analysis: Equilibrium analysis within a static model is par excellence suited for mathematical formalization, but dynamic processes in which an important role is also reserved for disequilibrium, are unusually stubborn, when it concerns putting them into mathematical terms.[21]

Following the publication in the seventies of a number of highly critical articles in respect of neoclassical theory, which in retrospect have to be considered as just as many preliminary studies[22], in 1982 appeared *An Evolutionary Theory of Economic Change* (Nelson & Winter, 1982a), the first economic theory study in book form from their hand that meant a definite break with neoclassical theory and furthermore, at least had the pretension to offer a fully fledged theoretic alternative: A radically different approach that was labelled 'evolutionary economics' by the two authors. Initially the book was given attention in journals in the field of marketing and management, but was virtually ignored by leading scientific journals in the field of general economics.[23] Only in the 1980s, the evolutionary approach of economic development got the wind in its sails: A rapidly growing number of followers justified in 1991 the founding of an own scientific periodical, the *Journal of Evolutionary Economics*.

261

Let us try to summarize the main points of criticism of neoclassical theory formulated by different evolutionary economists and see which alternatives they offer. The first point that strikes the eye is that the first evolutionary standard work, the book from 1982 by Nelson and Winter, in one specific aspect radically differs from the then prevailing theoretical works of neoclassical style: In the book by Nelson and Winter, as formulated by one critic, 'day-to-day reality returns to the full in economic theory'. Where neoclassical reference books usually are completely dominated by mathematical and economic exercises and references to the economic reality at best play a modest role here and there, in particular to illustrate a theoretically deduced position, *An Evolutionary Theory of Economic Change* is filled to the brim with empirical research into the manner in which organizations (especially companies) have *really* behaved in economic life. In other words, the evolutionary approach in any case differs from the neoclassical approach in one respect, in the sense that, unlike in the neoclassical line of thinking, there is no strictly deductive reasoning from a number of assumptions, imposed beforehand on the theory, about the behaviour of economic subjects, but that in first instance it is studied how those subjects have apparently behaved in reality, and subsequently it is contemplated whether a theory can be formulated on such observations.

This subtle difference in approach has far-reaching consequences: The most important being that evolutionary economics relegated one of the fundamentals of the neoclassical model, the central assumption as to the behaviour of entrepreneurs in a market economy, to the realm of fantasy. Neoclassical theory supposes that producers strive after profit maximization by expanding their production up to the point where marginal costs and marginal revenues are equal. A massive literature, based on empirical research into how companies tried to survive in reality, solidly showed that this simply could not have been the case and even .... *could* not have been, simply because companies usually disposed of insufficient information to make even a slightly reliable estimate of their marginal costs and revenues curves. In practice, companies only know their *total* costs and their strategy generally is that starting from an estimate of their sales, they fix a cost-covering price for their product and subsequently increase this by a specific percentage. The resulting profits are used in part for investments in product and process innovation (*research & development*), in part for expansion investments and finally, is partly paid to entitled parties.[24]

A second point in which evolutionary economics differs from the neoclassical approach is the manner in which technological change is considered to influence the economic system. In the standard neoclassical model, new technological possibilities are like manna from heaven: Everyone who wants, can dispose of them for free. In later versions of the neoclassical growth theory this highly unrealistic assumption is amended: Technological knowledge is then considered a scarce item that is traded on a market and is at the disposal of everyone who is willing to pay the market price. The evolutionary economy sets against this that also the latter approach is far from realistic and, worse even, passes over the essence of the technology phenomenon. As regards technology two things immediately catch the eye: Firstly, that it is a phenomenon that is highly concentrated (for instance: In research laboratories of large companies, in institutes and universities of technology, and there, in addition, divided over very specific and highly specialized departments) and moreover, that technological innovations pre-eminently happen where there already is a strong concentration of high-quality knowledge. Secondly, it is clear that technology only exerts influence in economic sense when it is actually applied in everyday life, and the actual application does not happen without any resistance, but is the result of endless, strenuous experiments in which 'knowledge' (numerous highly specialized disciplines) and 'know-how'(a multitude of likewise specialized engineering disciplines) are smoothly interwoven.[25] The result of this is, that the so-called *spill-over effect* (the designation used in neoclassical theory for the phenomenon that an organization that develops new technology is not able to avoid that new technology will be 'leaking away' to other parties, and thus in the long run becomes available 'free of charge', or at a fraction of the total development costs to outsiders) in reality plays a much smaller role than neoclassical theory tends to think.[26]

The consequence of this line of thought is, that the development of technological progress in fact becomes unpredictable. On the one hand, success achieved in the past in a specialized field, forms a knowledge bank that undeniably augments the chance of future successes in the same field, resulting in slighter survival chances for 'newcomers' than for organizations that in the past have managed to secure a dominant position.[27] On the other hand, the fact that the knowledge bank is specialized in a highly specialized domain, renders historically successful organizations extremely vulnerable to ambient changes which have the nature of a trend break: If the surroundings change in such a manner that the domain in which the organization is specialized for one reason or other, suddenly drops on the social priorities list, then precisely because of the specialized nature of its knowledge, it becomes more difficult for it rather than for the 'newcomers' to survive in the changed surroundings.[28] Technological change, evolutionary economics argues, is characterized by *limited path dependence*: Success achieved in the past in a specific domain and the (at least in part: Exclusive) specialist knowledge obtained in the process augments under 'normal' circumstances the chance for future success, but sudden, intermittent changes (for example: An unexpected scientific breakthrough which turns the existing technology completely upside down) present 'newcomers' with an enlarged chance of success and reduces the chance of survival of established organizations.

Let me try to capture in few words the essential difference between the neoclassical view on economic development and an evolutionary perspective. The central point is in the fundamental supposition of how economic subjects behave. Evolutionary economics rejects the 'maximization hypothesis' of neoclassical theory, and also the idea that economic subjects dispose of complete and free information. Against this, it argues that the uncertainty about the future is a fundamental fact in the reality of everyday, and based on that, economic subjects lack the opportunities to behave 'in a maximizing fashion': They never know in advance which behaviour will have 'maximizing' effects and which will not. Instead, evolutionary economics argues that subjects (individuals and organizations) behave *routinely*: They observe in principal rules of conduct that have proven successful in the past, and so their behaviour (and the results of that behaviour) becomes path dependent in principle.

The routine behaviour leads to a process of economic change that in many respects shows similarities to a process of biological evolution. Routine behaviour shows in principle the same invariability as the genetic material passed on in biological reproduction. The change in the environment in which such acts are performed, continuously selects certain individuals and organizations that act in accordance with 'routines that are adjusted' to the specific environment of that moment, and also sees to it that individuals and organizations that act in accordance with 'unadjusted' routines, make their exit. The change in the environment is, just as with biological evolution, in part exogenous (the extinction of dinosaurs as a result of the impact of a meteorite shows similarities to the disappearance of wine production in England at the end of the Middle Ages as a result of a change in climate) and is in part the result of earlier evolutionary developments. At the same time not *all* behaviour is strictly routine, no more than biological evolution is *exclusively* determined by natural selection within an unchanging gene pool. Just as there are mutations in biological evolutions, in the behaviour of individuals and organizations there are likewise 'behavioral experiments'. Some of such behavioral experiments lead to superior 'routines', resulting in earlier routines (whether or not in full) being ousted by selection. Other behavioral experiments may not have resulted in adjusted routines, and so disappeared from the scene through the selection mechanism before they had managed to nestle into society.

For economic theory the consequences of the evolutionary view on processes of economic change are drastic. The most important point probably is, that in the evolutionary view on economic development, the selection mechanism may indeed be constantly operative, but the selection is incomplete, in the sense that it is possible — not to say: Probable — that more than one series of routine acts survives. Just as in biology different animal species coexist (and in part in a symbiotic relation), in the economic reality different organizations and individuals following different 'routines' coexist, in spite of the fact that some of the routines under the given circumstances are economically more efficient than others. This is a result of the fact that in reality it is not 'full competition' that is the prevailing market form, as is assumed by neoclassical theory, but 'limited competition'.

7.8 A new reintegration: History and economics

For the relation between economic theory and economic history the evolutionary view is, if possible, even more important. If neoclassical theory is pre-eminently a-historical, for evolutionary economics the reverse applies. The central idea of limited path dependence implies that there is no such thing as a general theory for economic development. In that sense, evolutionary economics is a clear answer to the big problem of the *École des Annales*, which I earlier characterized as the problematic quest for the 'primal structure' in the thinking of the *Annales* historians. This one, unique 'primal structure' does not exist, because every process of economic development, in any case in part, is determined by its own prehistory. And the implication of this is, that its specific historical development shall always be an integral part of the explanation for every individual process of economic development.

7.9 Economic development: The difference between why and how

The ultimate consequence of the facts that there is no unique 'primal structure', and that every process of economic development is partly determined by its own history, is that the question *why* economic development emerges, cannot be answered in general and certainly not from an economic perspective. Unless you hide in that perspective a number of assumptions about human behaviour that in their interrelationship lead to the unavoidable conclusion that it is human nature that causes economic development to *always* emerge. That is precisely what neoclassical theory did and that is also the reason why neoclassical theory is unfit as a universal theory for economic development.

Neoclassical theory, however, is indeed fit to explain *how* in their specific historic instances successful economic development has occurred and *how* — again in specific instances — an initially successful process of economic development in the long run degenerated into stagnation and decline.

7.10 Epilogue: Cultural context is decisive for economic development

In the history of thinking about economic development (as practised in pure economics) and in the empirical study of processes of economic development in the past (as practised in economic history) three lines may be clearly distinguished.

In the first place, there is the conclusion that both disciplines constantly have mutually influenced each other, although the measure in which one discipline dominated over the other, strongly varied over the course of time. In the heydays of classical economics, empirical studies had a great impact on the development of theories, whereas in the age of the supremacy of neoclassical economics, precisely the reverse was going on.

Second, it is striking that the factor considered dominant, which in last instance would have been decisive, was strongly influenced by the environment in which theoretical economics and economic history operated. In pre-modern times (when the creation of capital and technological development were occurring excruciatingly slow) great emphasis was placed on the importance of geographic factors (climate, soil conditions, location at a 'junction' of economic activities), while the creation of capital and technological development (in the nineteenth and twentieth centuries) emerged as dominant factors, precisely when an historically unprecedented growth occurred of the stock of capital goods and an acceleration in technological innovation.

Thirdly, the line indicating that with the shift over time of the factors that were considered dominant, there was no question of the earlier factors being completely relegated to the background yet of a change in priority. Still few economists and economic historians would want to insist that geographic c.q. geological factors are *completely* negligible for the height of the real income per head of the population (and those who do, will be promptly punished with the example of Saudi Arabia), but at the same time most authors will agree with the position that geographical factors only very rarely play a decisive role.

With this, the question what *finally* is decisive to initiate a process of continuous economic growth, which is the most striking feature of economic modernization, gets the nature of a story full of comments.
No one denies that an increase in the stock of capital goods is an absolute condition for modern economic growth, but ...no one denies that when the formation of capital exclusively consists of 'more of the same' the growth will finally be smothered in diminishing marginal returns. No one denies that only technological innovation, embodied in new capital goods, forms the solution to get out of the law of diminishing returns and no one denies that investments in human capital are an absolute condition for technological innovation, but ...why are there such extreme differences in the extent to which different societies are prepared to invest in R&D and human capital?
The last phase of this game full of contradictions, is that economic growth *has a chance* to develop only in those societies where the prevailing ideology awards a high political priority to promoting economic development. This means that economic development is determined decisively by cultural context.

267

Notes

1   A special issue of the *Journal of Economic History*, entitled 'The Tasks of Economic History', was devoted to what — in the thoughts of the editors — apparently was to be considered as the authoritative 'schools' within the economic history at that moment. In addition, for the first time an important place was made available for the École des Annales (Forster, 1978). Mind you, that was the end of the seventies of the past century!

2   The most famous (in the view of the followers of neoclassical theory of course: Infamous) example is the debate that is known under the name 'Cambridge controversy'. The name is derived from the fact that the two camps were rather properly divided between the University of Cambridge in England and the University of Harvard and the MIT, both situated in the American Cambridge in Massachusetts. The point of departure was a study of the English economist Piero Sraffa (1960) *Production of Commodities by Means of Commodities*, in which he proves that it is impossible to measure the size of the stock of capital goods without making use of relative prices and the division of the production over the production factors labor and capital. This seems like an innocent conclusion, but nothing is farther from the truth: It is in fact

a devastating criticism on the neoclassical equilibrium model. In neoclassical theory of equilibrium the size of the stock of capital goods is, among other things, used to explain the relative prices and the division of production. The implication of Sraffa's position is that the entire neoclassical theory of equilibrium is a circular argument. It may be clear that Sraffa's book launched a fierce debate: The so-called *battle between the Cambridges*. The odd thing is now, that the result of that debate is generally interpreted as a victory for the critics of neoclassical theory (see, for instance: Harcourt, 1972; Hodgson, 1999: pp. 46-59) but that nevertheless, the neoclassical equilibrium model continued to dominate theoretical economics to the present day. In part this emanated from the fact that the champions of neoclassical theory indeed admitted that the criticism was indeed to the point (see for instance: Samuelson, 1966; Levhari & Samuelson, 1966), but that the critics could not offer a sound alternative. In part this was also a result of what I would like to call 'paradigmatic path dependence': A so generally accepted paradigm within a certain discipline becomes immune to criticism to an extreme measure, *precisely because* it is so generally accepted. The contours of a second attack on the neoclassical stronghold became first visible at the beginning of the seventies with the emergence of what later would be called evolutionary economics, precisely when the worst smoke of the *battle between the Cambridges* had cleared. It took ten years for the second attack to result in a standard work that in any case had the pretension to offer an alternative to the general theory of equilibrium as a foundation for economic theory. That was the publication of *An Evolutionary Theory of Economic Change* (Nelson & Winter, 1982). And it took still another ten years for evolutionary economics to get its own international scientific discussion platform: The founding in 1991 of *The Journal of Evolutionary Economics*. Since then evolutionary economics has developed into a flourishing independent specialty within economic sciences with a rapidly growing number of followers. To say that they have meanwhile taken over the hegemony from neoclassical theory would go much too far: In the standard textbooks for economics, evolutionary ideas are too few and far between and the neoclassical approach still prevails, albeit that you get the impression that gradually ever more attention is given to the meanwhile abundant studies which analyse the deviations from the general equilibrium model, the so-called disequilibrium theory, in the literature. See, for instance: (Colander & Gamber, 2002).

3 To illustrate: there is no country in the world that has produced as many Nobel laureates in economics as the United States. In the United States itself, the University of Chicago has produced the most Noble laureates in economics by far, and it is hardly an exaggeration to state that what the faculty of economics of the University of Chicago is to neoclassical theory, is very similar to what the Vatican is to the Roman Catholic church.

4 Mokyr's dissertation *Industrialization in the Low Countries* (Mokyr, 1976) is the first cliometric study about the economic history of the Netherlands.

5 See for instance: (North, 1961; 1963; 1965; 1966; 1966a; 1968; 1968a).

6 In view of the fundamental role North awards to population pressure in processes of structural economic change, he has sometimes been reproached that his theory would in effect be 'Malthusian' (see, for instance: Coelho, 2001: p.4), and that was not exactly meant as a compliment. The point is that a Malthusian theory is doomed to fail as explanation for the western economic development process, because in the Malthusian population theory there is no room at all for the role of technological change in economic development, while technological change in reality has played a decisive role in the economic development of the western world. This criticism of North, I think, is neither here nor there: The population pressure functions in North's development model as the pre-eminent factor leading to the realization of more efficient economic organizational forms and in that sense, North's theory is rather 'Boserupian' than 'Malthusian' (by 'Boserupian' I mean development theories in which population pressures do not inevitably result in an existence crisis, such as with Malthus, but is precisely the ultimate factor which 'forces' societies to look for more efficient forms of production and thus promotes technological progress and in this way in the long run leads to a higher standard of living instead of a lower one. The term 'Boserupian' is named for Ester Boserup (1965), a Danish anthropologist and economist whose life's work was to show, on the basis of empirical evidence, derived from pre-modern agrarian cultures, that the relationship between population pressure and standard of living in reality is the exact opposite of what the Malthusian theory suggests).

7 *Free-riding* is the situation in which economic subjects attempt to appropriate goods and services without proportionally contributing to the production costs for such goods and services (the classic example is 'fare dodging' in public transportation) or in which economic subjects attempt to shift the costs emanating from their own activities on to third parties (classic example: The illegal discharge of contaminants on surface water). By *rent-seeking* is meant: All activities undertaken by economic subjects for the purpose of securing an income without offering any results of their own economic actvities in return, and/or attempts to secure higher revenue from economic activities than is justified by the market value of such activities (classic example: Enforce government subsidies by pressure groups).

8 A very important and explanatory study in this connection is *Trust: The Social Virtues and the Creation of Prosperity* by Francis Fukuyama (1996), in which he argues that the extent to which 'trust' plays a role in the set of standards and values of any society is the decisive factor in answering the question whether such society will attain prosperity or not. Fukuyama is a political scientist

269

and no economist or economic historian, which explains why his work in the literature on economic development has always remained slightly underexposed. This does not alter the fact that his view, from a totally different angle, smoothly coincides with that of Douglass North.

9   The *voting paradox* by Kenneth Arrow (1951) is a stainless steel brainteaser from economic theory, with which is proven, among other things, that democratic decision-making leads to logically inconsistent results if there are more than two parties involved and more than two preferred options. For the devotee: Three brothers, Alex, Ben and Clint are planning to go on vacation together and must choose between Xanadu, Yellowstone and Zanzibar. Alex prefers Xanadu to Yellowstone and Yellowstone to Zanzibar (in mathematical stenography: X>Y>Z); for Ben it is Y>Z>X and for Clint: Z>X>Y. They are in quite a jam now, because a majority (Alex and Clint) has the opinion that Xanadu is to be preferred to Yellowstone, while there is also a majority (Alex and Ben) that favours Yellowstone rather than Zanzibar. That would logically imply that there would also be a majority giving preference to Xanadu instead of Zanzibar, but odd enough, that is not correct; rather, there is a majority (Ben and Clint) which holds the exact opposite view.

10 The neoclassical theory talks of 'economic subjects' as the units taking the decisions in the economic process and distinguishes economic subjects further solely according to the nature of the decisions they take in the context of their economic function (producers, consumers, etc.). With this, the concept of 'economic subjects' in neoclassical theory is reduced more or less in the same manner as for example happens to the concept of 'point' in mathematics: A body without measurements.

11 With this conclusion, it may even be justified that neoclassical theory does not distinguish between individuals and organizations. If that conclusion is correct, it does not matter any longer whether an economic subject is an individual or an organization, indeed: The economic subject is by definition the most efficient 'decisive' entity under the given circumstances!

12 Vries (2001) has written an admirably lucid analysis of North's view on the matter, of which I gratefully have made use.

13 See: Chapter 5, par. 5.6, p. 150 ff., above.

14 See: chapter 6, par. 6.7, p. 212 ff., above.

15 See: Chapter 6, par. 6.8, p. 216 ff., above.

16 Most distinct, this finds expression in (David, 2001), in which he even explains the contumacious popularity of neoclassical theory and the concomitant aversion in economic theory to integrating specifically historical phenomena into the theory, from that which he calls *sunken cost hysteresis*, which implies phenomena which are dominated by ...path dependence.

17 See: (Hodgson, 1999; p. 157 ff.).

18 (Winter, 1964). For an extensive analysis of Winter's criticism, see: (Hodgson, 1994; 1999: p. 158 ff.).

19 Confusion may arise here: Of course there are indeed dynamic models on neoclassical foundation (all models from the neoclassical theory of growth, for instance, describe time schedules of the various variables and hence are dynamic by definition). The point in question is, that the manner in which the static model is made dynamic abstracts precisely from the essence of the dynamics that characterizes the economic process. The dynamics is in fact considered as exogenously determined: The analysis in those models concentrates on the question of how an exogenous shock (a change in the speed of growth of the population, for instance) produces a new equilibrium. The criticism of evolutionary economics is that this question is not relevant, since this equilibrium will never be obtained in fact, and that by reasoning towards that new equilibrium, you pass over all other possible time schedules the system could have followed.

20 Compare: Chapter 2, especially par. 2.2, p. 40 ff., above.

21 In his *Evolution and Institutions: On Evolutionary Economics and the Evolution of Economics*, Geoffrey Hodgson (1999) has convincingly proven that in the development of theoretical economics a clear relation may be found between the attention for dynamic processes gradually fading into the background, and the emergence of the formalization of the theory. Conspicuous in this is that in such early attention for economic dynamics, several authors at that time already thought to seek alliance with ideas based on the theory of evolutions.

22 (Nelson & Winter, 1973; 1974; 1975; 1976; 1977; 1978; 1980; 1982).

23 See: (Hodgson, 1999: p. 167 ff.).

24 Evolutionary Economics in this point links up with a specialty within economic history, namely 'business history', which was flourishing since the 1970s, especially because of the works of Alfred D. Chandler (1962; 1977; 1990). The description Chandler and his followers had given of the manner in which large multinationals had managed to maintain their ground in the course of time, smoothly connected with the results of the empirical research, and that description is at odds with the relevant assumptions of neoclassical theory. It is telling that in new economic history, which reasoned from neoclassical principles, the development of the history of industrial enterprise has been neglected systematically.

25 It is at this point that the recent work of Paul David and of Joel Mokyr forms an essential support for the body of thought of evolutionary economics.

26 A good example is the supreme position of the company *Microsoft* in the development of computer software. The lion's share in the software innovation for years has originated with *Microsoft* and no other company, which suggests that the earlier acquired know-how in a particular specialist domain gives a great advantage in creating successful new developments. And still, the source

271

code of the commercially highly successful *Windows* program for decades remained a well-kept secret within the organization, despite intense pressure
from the outside to disclose the source code.

27 The implication of this is that another foundation of neoclassical theory (free
market access) is undermined as a result.

28 A prime example is glass-fibre technology. The development of fibre-optic
cables was based on the expectation that in the near future through the rapid
development in communications technology such an increase in the quantity
of data per time unit would arise that existing (metal) cable networks would
not be able to handle such growth. That was the reason for installing new
networks of fibre-optic cable, which indeed happened in The Netherlands
and elsewhere to some extent, demanding heavy infrastructure investments.
Unexpected developments in the software area, more in particular the dou-
ble-quick development of all kinds of relatively inexpensive techniques to
'compress' during transmission, implied that the expected capacity problems
of 'metal' cable networks took longer to manifest than originally expected.
The result was that companies which had specialized in the construction and
maintenance of fibre-optic cable networks went bankrupt en masse.

References

Abramovitz, M. (1956), "Resource and output trends in the United States since 1870", *American Economic Review*, 46 (No.2), pp. 5-23.

Abramovitz, M. (1986), "Catching Up, Forging Ahead and Falling Behind", *Journal of Economic History*, 46, pp. 385-406.

Abramovitz, M. (1989), *Thinking about Growth, and Other Essays on Economic Growth and Welfare* (New York, etc.).

Abramovitz, M. (1991), "The Postwar Productivity Spurt and Slowdown: Factors of Potential and Realisation", in: (Bell (Ed.) 1991: pp. 19-37).

Abramovitz, M. (1993), "The Search for the Sources of Growth: Areas of Ignorance, Old and New", *Journal of Economic History*, 53 (No. 2), pp. 217-243.

Abramovitz, M (1994), "The Origins of the Postwar Catch-up and Convergence Boom", in: (Fagerberg, Verspagen & Von Tunzelmann (Eds.) 1994: pp. 21-51).

Abramovitz, M. & Eliasberg, V. (1957), *The Growth of Public Employment in Great Britain* (Princeton).

Abramovitz, M. & David, P.A. (1973), "Economic Growth in America", *De Economist*, 121 (No. 3), pp. 251-273.

Abramovitz, M. & David, P. A. (2001), "Two Centuries of American Macro-economic Growth: From Exploitation of Resource Abundance to Knowledge-Driven Development", *Discussion Paper No. 01-05 from the Stanford Institute for Economic Policy Research (revised version)* (Stanford CA).

Aerts, E. et. al. (Eds.) (1993), *Studia Historia Oeconomica. Liber Alumnorum Herman van der Wee* (Leuven).

Aerts, E. et. al. (Eds.) (1993a), *Studia Historia Oeconomica. Liber Amicorum Herman van der Wee* (Leuven).

Albers, R.M. (1997), "Human Capital and Economic Growth: Operationalising Growth Theory with Special Reference to The Netherlands in the 19th Century", *Research Memorandum No. GD-34 from the Groningen Growth and Development Centre of the University of Groningen* (Groningen).

Albers, R.M. (1998), *Machinery Investment and Economic Growth: The Dynamics of Dutch Development, 1800-1913* (Ph.D.-thesis) (Groningen).

Albers, R.M. (1999), "The Role of Human Capital in the Very Long Run: An Application to The Netherlands, 1800-1996", *Paper, Presented to a Seminar at the European University Institute of Economic History at Florence* (Groningen).

Albers, R.M. & Groote, P.D. (1994), "Kapitaalvorming in Spoor- en Tramwegen, 1838-1913", *NEHA-Jaarboek voor Economische, Bedrijfs- en Techniekgeschiedenis*, 57, pp. 353-375.

Albers, R.M. & Groote, P.D. (1996), "The Empirics of Growth", *De Economist*, 144, pp. 429-444.

Alexandre, P. (1987), *Le climat au Moyen Age: Contribution à l'histoire des variations climatiques de 1000 à 1425, d'après les sources narratives de l'Europe occidentale* (Paris).

Allen, R.C. (1979), "International Competition in Iron and Steel", *Journal of Economic History*, 29, pp. 911-937.

Allen, R.C. (1982), "The Efficiency and Distributional Consequences of Eighteenth-Century Enclosures", *Economic Journal*, 92, pp. 937-953.

Ames, E. & Rosenberg, N. (1968), "The Enfield Arsenal in Theory and History", *Economic Journal*, 78, pp. 827-842.

Anderson, J.L. (1991), *Explaining Long-term Economic Change* (Series: New Studies in Economic and Social History) (Cambridge, etc.).

Andreano, R.L. (Ed.) (1970), *The New Economic History: Recent Papers on Methodology* (New York).

Ark, B. van (2001), "Productiviteit, Technologie en Groei: een Zaak van Investeren?", *Rede, uitgesproken op 10 april 2001 bij de aanvaarding van het ambt van bijzonder hoogleraar in de Economie van Productiviteit en Technologiebeleid aan de Rijsuniversiteit te Groningen* (Groningen).

Ark, B. van, Barrington, L. & McGuckin, R.H. (2000), "Are Poor Nations Closing the Gap In Living Standards?", *Perspectives on a Global Economy Research Report* 1263-00-RR, edited by the Conference Board (New York).

Ark, B. van & Smits, J.P. (2001), "Technology Regimes and Growth in The Netherlands, An Empirical Record of Two Centuries", *Unpublished Paper, Groningen Growth & Development Centre* (Groningen).

Ark, B. van, Kuipers, S.K. & Kuper, G.H. (Eds.) (2000), *Productivity, Technology and Economic Growth* (Boston, etc.).

Arrow, K.J. (1951), *Social Choice and Individual Values* (Oxford, etc.).

Atack, J. & Passell, P. (1994), *A New Economic View of American History* (2nd ed.) (New York, etc.).

Bakker, G.P. den, Huitker, Th. A. & Bochove, C.A. van (1987), *Macro-economische Ontwikkelingen 1921-1939 en 1969-1985 (Centraal Bureau voor de Statistiek)* (Den Haag).

Barnard, A., Butlin, N.G. & Pincus, J.J. (1982), *Government and Capitalism: Public and Private Choice in Twentieth-Century Australia* (London).

Barro, R.J. (1996), "Determinants of Economic Growth: A Cross-Country Empirical Study", Working Paper 5698, *National Bureau of Economic Research Working Paper Series* (Cambridge Mass.).

Barro, R.J. (1997), *Determinants of Economic Growth: A Cross-Country Emprical Study* (Cambridge Mass.).

Baudet, H. & Meulen, H. v.d. (Eds.) (1978), *Kernproblemen der Economische Geschiedenis* (Groningen).

Baudet, H. & Drukker, J.W. (1977), "De afschuw van het getal, Een nabeschouwing over de Jaarrede van de Voorzitter van het Historisch Genootschap", *Bijdragen en Mededelingen betreffende de Geschiedenis der Nederlanden*, 92 (Afl. 1), pp. 1 - 15.

Baumol, W.J., Nelson, R.R. & Wolff, E.N. (Eds.) (1994), *Convergence of Productivity: Cross-National Studies and Historical Evidence* (Oxford, etc.).

Bell , G. (Ed.) (1991), *Technology and Productivity: The Challenge for Economic Policy* (Paris).

Berg, M. & Bruland, Kristine (Eds.) (1998), *Technological Revolutions in Europe* (Cheltenham).

Berkel, K. van (1990), *Denken over Cultuur: een Beschouwing over de Samenhang in de Geschiedenis tussen Idee en Mentaliteit* (Groningen).

Bie, R. van der & Dehing, P. (Eds.), *Nationaal Goed: Feiten en Cijfers over Onze Samenleving (ca.) 1800-1999* (Voorburg, Heerlen, Amsterdam).

Bläsing, J.F.E (Eds.) (1992), *Van Amsterdam naar Tilburg en toch weer terug: Liber Amicorum Joh. de Vries* (Leiden).

Blitz, R.C. (1968), "Review of Simon Kuznets' *Modern Economic Growth: Rate, Structure, and Spread*", *Journal of Economic History*, 38, pp. 140-142.

Bolles, A.S.B. (1881), *Industrial History of the United States* (3rd ed.) (New York), reprinted as: *Reprints of Economic Classics* by August M. Kelly Publishers (1966), (New York).

Bordo, M.D., Choudri, S.V. & Schwartz, A.J. (1995), "Could Stable Money Have Averted the Great Contraction?", *Economic Inquiry*, 33, pp. 484-505.

Bos, R.W.J.M. (1976). "Van periferie naar centrum: enige kanttekeningen bij de Nederlandse industriële ontwikkeling in de negentiende eeuw", *Maandschrift Economie, tijdschrift voor algemeen-economische, bedrijfseconomische en sociale vraagstukken*, 40, pp. 181-205.

Brands, M.C. (1970), *Historisme als Ideologie: Het 'Anti-normatieve' en 'Onpolitieke' Element in de Duitse Geschiedwetenschap* (Assen).

Brandt, L. (1985), "Chinese Agriculture and the International Economy, 1870-1930s: A Reassessment", *Explorations in Economic History*, 22, pp. 168-193.

Braudel, F. (1949), *La Méditerranée et le monde méditerranéen sous l'époque de Philips II* (Paris).

Braudel, F. (1969), *Écrits sur l'histoire ; 1. Science de l'histoire ; 2. Champs* (Paris).

Braudel, F. (1986), *l'Identité de la France* (Paris).

Braudel, F. & Labrousse, E. (Eds.) (1979-1982), *Histoire économique et sociale de la France* (3 Vols.) (Paris).

Brinkman, H.J., Drukker, J.W. & Slot, B.S. (1988), "Lichaamslengte en Reëel Inkomen: een Nieuwe Schattingsmethode voor Historische Inkomensreeksen", *Economisch- en Sociaal-Historisch Jaarboek*, 51, pp. 35-79.

Brinkman, H.J., Drukker, J.W. & Stuurop, H.J. (1989), "The Representativeness of Dutch Military Registers as a Source for Quantitative History", *Economic and Social History in The Netherlands*, 1, pp. 149-170.

Brito, D.L. & Williamson, J. (1973), "Skilled Labor and 19th Century Anglo-American Behavior", *Explorations in Economic History*, 10, pp. 235-251.

Broeze, F. (1973), "The New Economic History, the Navigation Acts, and the Continental Tobacco Market, 1770-1790", *Economic History Review*, 26 (November), pp. 668-678.

Brookfield, H. (1975), *Interdependent Development* (London).

Bücher, K. (1893), *Die Entstehung der Volkswirtschaft: Vorträge und Aufsätze* (Tübingen).

Burger, A. (1994), "A Five-Country Comparison of Industrial Labour Productivity 1850-1990", *Paper, Presented to the Seminar on Comparative Historical National Accounts in European Perspective* (Amsterdam).

Burger, A. (1996), "Dutch Patterns of Development: Economic Growth and Structural Change in The Netherlands, 1800-1910", *Economic and Social History in The Netherlands*, 7, pp. 161-180.

Butlin, N.G. (1962), *Australian Domestic Product, Investment and Foreign Borrowing, 1861-1938/39* (Cambridge).

Butlin, N.G. (1964), *Investment in Australian Economic Development, 1861-1938/39* (Cambridge).

Butlin, N.G. (1984), *Our Original Agression: Aboriginal Populations of Southeastern Australia, 1788-1850* (London).

Callewaert, A. (1992), "Estimating Dutch Industrial Growth, 1850-1914", *Paper, Presented to the Workshop on National Accounts* (Utrecht).

Cannarella, G. & Tomaske, J. (1975), The Optimum Utilization of Slaves", *Journal of Economic History*, 35, pp. 621-629.

Carlson, L.A. (1978), "The Dawes Act and the Decline of Indian Farming", *Journal of Economic History*, 38, pp. 274-276.

Castaneda, C. (1968), *The teachings of Don Juan: A Yaqui-way of knowledge* (New York).

Castaneda, C. (1972), *A Journey to Ixtlan: The lessons of Don Juan* (New York).

Chandler, A.D. (1962), *Strategy and Structure: Chapters in the History of the Industrial Enterprise* (Cambridge, Mass.).

Chandler, A.D. (1977), *The Visible Hand: The Managerial Revolution in American Business* (Cambridge, Mass.).

Chandler, A.D. (1990), *Scale and Scope: The Dynamics of Industrial Capitalism* (Cambridge, Mass.).

Clemens, A.H.P., Groote, P.D. & Albers, R.M. (1996), "The Contribution of Physical and Human Capital to Economic Growth in The Netherlands, 1850-1913", *Economic and Social History in The Netherlands*, 7, pp. 181-197.

Clough, S.B. (1968), *European Economic History: The Economic Development of Western Civilization* (2nd revised edition) (New York, etc.).

Coase, R. (1960), "The Problem of Social Cost", *Journal of Law and Economics*, 3, pp. 1-44.

Coatsworth, J. (1981), *Growth Against Development: The Economic Impact of Railroads in Porfirian Mexico* (De Kalb Ill.).

Cobb, C.W. & Douglas, P.H. (1928), "A Theory of Production", *American Economic Review*, 18 (no.1, Supplement), pp. 139-165.

Cochran, T. C. (1969), "Economic History, Old and New", *American Historical Review*, 74, pp. 1561-1572.

Coelho, P.R.P. (1973), "The Profitability of Imperialism: The British Experience in the West-Indies", *Explorations in Economic History*, 10, pp. 253-280.

Coelho, P.R.P. (2001), "Review of Douglass C. North and Robert Paul Thomas *The Rise of the Western World: A New Economic History*", *Economic History Services* (December 21, 2001); URL: http://www.eh.net/bookreviews/library/coelho.shtml

Cohen, J.S. (1979), "Fascism and Agriculture in Italy: Policies and Consequences", *Economic History Review*, 32, pp. 70-87.

Colander, D.C. & Gamber, E.N. (2002), *Macroeconomics* (Upper Saddle River).

Coleman, D.C. & Mathias, P. (Eds.) (1984), *Enterprise and History: Essays in Honour of Charles Wilson* (Cambridge).

Collingwood, R.G. (1946), *The Idea of History* (Oxford).

Conrad, A.H. & Meyer, J.R. (1957), "Economic Theory, Statistical Inference and Economic History", *Paper, presented to the NBER-EHA Conference on Income and Wealth*, herdrukt in: (Conrad & Meyer 1964, pp. 3-30).

Conrad, A.H. & Meyer, J.R. (1958), "The Economics of Slavery in the Antebellum South", *Journal of Political Economy*, herdrukt in: (Conrad & Meyer 1964, pp. 43-114).

Conrad, J.H. & Meyer, J.R. (1964), *The Economics of Slavery and Other Studies in Econometric History* (Chicago).

Crafts, N.F.R. (1983), "Gross National Product in Europe 1870-1910: Some New Estimates", *Explorations in Economic History*, 20, pp. 387-401.

Crafts, N.F.R. (1985), *British Economic Growth during the Industrial Revolution* (New York, etc.).

Crafts, N.F.R (1997), "Endogeneous Growth: Lessons for and from Economic History", in: (Krebs & Wallis (Eds.) 1997, Vol. 2, pp. 38-78).

Crafts, N.F.R. & Harley, C.K. (2000), "Simulating the Two Views of the Industrial Revolution", *Journal of Economic History*, 60, pp. 819-841.

Cramer, J.S. (1991), "Lichaamslengte en Economische Omstandigheden tijdens de Groei", *Economisch- en Sociaal-Historisch Jaarboek*, 54, pp. 17-21.

David, P.A. (1964), "Economic History through the Looking Glass", *Econometrica*, 32, pp. 694-696.

David, P.A. (1966), "The Mechanization of Reaping in the Ante-Bellum Midwest", in: (Rosovsky (Ed.) 1966, pp. 3-39).

David, P.A. (1967), "The Growth of Real Product in the United States Before 1840: New Evidence; Controlled Conjectures", *Journal of Economic History*, 27, pp. 151-197.

David, P. A. (1969), "Transport innovation and economic growth: Professor Fogel on and off the rails", *Economic History Review*, 22, pp. 506-525.

David, P.A. (1970), "Learning by Doing and Tariff Protection: A Reconsideration of the Case of the United States Cotton Textile Industry", *Journal of Economic History*, 30, pp. 521-601.

David, P.A. (1971), "Econometric Studies of History: Comments", in: (Intriligator M. (Ed.) 1971, pp. 459-467).

David, P.A. (1971a), "The Landscape and the Machine: Technical Interrelatedness, Land Tenure and the Mechanization of the Corn Harvest in Victorian Britain", in: (McCloskey (Ed.) 1971, pp. 145-205).

David, P.A. (1975), *Technical Choice, Innovation and Economic Growth: Essays on American and British Experience in the Nineteenth Century* (Cambridge, etc.).

David, P.A. (1975a), "Labor Scarcity and the Problem of Technical Practice and Progress in 19th Century America", in: (David 1975: pp. 19-91).

David, P.A. (1986), "Understanding the Economics of QWERTY: The Necessity of History", in: (Parker (Ed.) 1986: pp. 30-49).

David, P. A., Gutman, H., Sutch, R. & Wright, G. (1976), *Reckoning with Slavery* (Oxford).

David, P.A. (1990), "The Dynamo and the Computer: A Historical Perspective on the Modern Productivity Paradox", *American Economic Review (Papers and Proceedings)*, 80, pp. 335-361.

David, P.A. (2001), "Path dependence, its critics and the quest for 'historical economics'", in: (Garrouste, P. & Ioannides, S. (Eds.) 2001.

David, P.A. & Temin, P. (1974), "Slavery: The Progressive Institution?", *Journal of Economic History*, 34, pp. 739-783.

David, P.A. & Temin, P. (1979), "Explaining the Relative Efficiency of Slave Agriculture in The Antebellum South: A Comment", *American Economic Review*, 69, pp. 213-218.

Davis, L.E (1966), "Professor Fogel and the New Economic History", *Economic History Review*, 19, pp. 657-663.

Davis, L. E. (1968), "'And it never will be literature': The New Economic History: A Critique", *Explorations in Entrepreneurial History* (2nd ser.), 6, pp. 75-92.

Davis, L.E. (1971), "Specification, Quantification and Analysis in Economic History", in: (Taylor & Ellsworth (Eds.) 1971, pp. 106-120).

Davis, L.E., Easterlin, R.A., Parker, W.N, *et. al.* (1972), *American Economic Growth: An Economist's History of the United States* (New York).

Davis, L. E., Hughes, J.R., & Reiter, S., "Aspects of Quantitative Research in Economic History" (1960), *Journal of Economic History*, 20, pp. 539-547.

Davis, L.E. & Huttenback, R. (1982), "The Political Economy of British Imperialism: Measures of Benefit and Support", *Journal of Economic History*, 42, pp. 119-130.

Davis, L.E. & Huttenback, R. (1986), "Imperialism and Social Class (Apologies to Marx and Schumpeter): Imperial Investors in the Age of High Imperialism", in: (Wagener & Drukker (Eds.) 1986: pp. 156-185).

Davis, L.E. & North, D.C. (1971), *Institutional Change and American Economic Growth* (Cambridge, etc.).

Davis, L.E. & Stettler, L. (1966), "The New England Textile Industry, 1825-1860", in: (National Bureau for Economic Research (Ed.) 1966: pp. 213-233).

Deane, Phyllis & Cole, W.A. (1964), *British Economic Growth, 1688-1959* (Cambridge).

Deane, Phyllis & Cole, W.A. (1967), *British Economic Growth, 1688-1959* (2nd ed.) (Cambridge).

Denison, E.F. (1979), *Accounting for Slower Economic Growth: The United States in the 1970s* (Washington).

Denison, E.F. (1985), *Trends in American Economic Growth, 1929-1982* (Washington).

Denison, E.F. & Chung, W.K. (1976), *How Japan's Economy Grew So Fast* (Washington).

Desai, M. (1968), "Some issues in Econometric History", *Economic History Review*, 21, pp. 1-16.

Dickerson, O. (1963), *The Navigation Acts and the American Revolution* (New York).

Dorpema, B.S. (Ed.) (1987), *Ontwerpen voor Kleine en Middelgrote Series: Vormgeving* (Enschede).

Drukker, J.W. (1973), "De Wijze en de Rekenmeester, of enkele methodologische aspekten van de toepassing van ekonomische theorie en kwantitatieve technieken op de ekonomische geschiedenis", *Maandschrift Ekonomie*, 37 (1973), pp. 242-266 (deel 1); 291-315 (deel 2) (herdrukt in: (Noordegraaf (Ed.) 1991, pp. 327-368).

Drukker, J.W. (1980), "The New Economic History: een aanloop naar het werk van Robert Fogel", *Intermediair*, 16, Nr. 23 (6 juni 1980), pp. 49-59 (reprinted in: Huussen, Kossmann & Renner (Eds.) 1981).

Drukker, J.W. (1980a), "Robert William Fogel: Primus inter pares van 'The New Economic History", Intermediair, 16, Nr. 25 (20 juni 1980), pp. 74-83, reprinted in: (Huussen, Kossmann & Renner (Eds.) 1981).

Drukker, J.W. (1987), "Tussen Machine en Fetisj: Geschiedenis en Innovatie", in: (Dorpema (Ed.) 1987: pp. I-1 — I-13).

Drukker, J.W. (1999), "Klassiekers: Robert William Fogel & Stanley L. Engerman, Time on the Cross: The Economics of American Negro Slavery (1974)", *Groniek, Historisch Tijdschrift*, 33, pp. 85-101.

Drukker, J.W. & Harbers, E. (1979a), "NINIANN2, Een model van de Nederlandse volkshuishouding 1922 - 1938", *Z.W.O.-rapport* (Groningen).

Drukker, J.W. & Harbers, E. (1979b), "Het nieuw vermakelijk begrootingspel: een educatief simulatie-model van de Nederlandse volkshuishouding 1922-1938", in: (Klein & Borger (Eds.) 1997, pp. 38-46).

Drukker, J.W., Brinkman, H.J. & Meerten, M.A. van (1991), "Economische Ontwikkeling en de Lengte van Lotelingen: Afgekeurd voor Alle Diensten?", *Economisch- en Sociaal-Historisch Jaarboek*, 54, pp. 1 —16.

Domar, E.D. (1947), "Expansion and Employment", *American Economic Review*, 37, pp. 34-55.

Drummond, I. (1967), "Labor Scarcity: A Comment", *Journal of Economic History*, 27, pp. 383-390.

Dümke, R.H. (1977), " Intra-German Trade in 1837 and Regional Economic Development", *Vierteljahrschrift für Sozial- und Wirtschaftsgeschichte*, 64, pp. 469-496.

Easterlin, R.A. (2001), "Review of Simon Kuznets *Modern Economic Growth: Rate, Structure and Spread*", *Economic History Services*, October 29, 2001, URL: http://www.eh.net/bookreviews/library/easterlin.shtml

Edelstein, M. (1976), "Realized Rates of Return on U.K. Home and Overseas Investment in the Age of High Imperialism", *Explorations in Economic History*, 13, pp. 283-329.

Edelstein, M. (1982), *Overseas Investment in the Age of High Imperialism* (New York).

Eddie, S.M. (1977), "The Terms and Patterns of Hungarian Foreign Trade, 1882-1913", *Journal of Economic History*, 37, pp. 329-358.

Eichengreen, B. (1982), "Did Speculation Destabilize the French Franc in the 1920s?", *Explorations in Economic History*, 19, pp. 71-100.

Einstein, A. (1916), *Die Grundlage der allgemeine Relativitätstheorie* (Leipzig).

Engels, F. [1845] (1932), *Die Lage der Arbeitende Klasse in England. Im Auftrage des Marx-Engels-Lenin-Institut in Moskau* (Vienna).

Engerman, S.L. (1984), "Economic Change and Contract Labor in the British

Carribean: The End of Slavery and the Adjustment to Emancipation", *Explorations in Economic History*, 21, pp. 133-151.

Engerman, S.L. & Klein, H.S. (1979), "A Note on the Mortality in the French Slave Trade in the Eighteenth Century", in: (Gemery & Hogendorn (Eds.) 1979).

Fagerberg, J. (1994), "Technology and International Difference in Growth Rates", *Journal of Economic Literature*, 32, pp. 1147-1175.

Fagerberg, J., Verspagen, B. & Tunzelmann, N. von (1994), "The Economics of Convergence and Divergence: An Overview", in: (Fagerberg, Verspagen & Von Tunzelmann (Eds.) 1994: pp. 1-20).

Fagerberg, J., Verspagen, B. & Tunzelmann, N. von (Eds.) (1994), *The Dynamics of Technology, Trade and Growth* (Brookfield, Verm.).

Febvre, L.P.V. (1942), *Le problème de l'incroyance au XVIe siècle : la religion de Rabelais* (Paris).

Feeny, D.H. (1979), "Paddy, Princes, and Productivity: Irrigation and Thai Economic Development, 1900-1940", *Explorations in Economic History*, 16, pp. 132-150.

Feinstein, C. H. (1972), *National Income, Expenditure and Output of the United Kingdom 1855-1965* (Cambridge).

Feinstein, C.H. (1978), "Capital Formation in Great Britain", in: (Mathias & Postan (Eds.) 1978, Vol. VII, Part 1, pp. 28-96).

Fenoaltea, S. (1969), "Public Policy and Italian Industrial Development, 1861-1913", *Journal of Economic History*, 29, pp. 176-179.

Fenoaltea, S. (1984a), *The Industrialization of Italy: A Progress Report* (Williamstown Ma.).

Fenoaltea, S. (1984b), *Public Works Construction in Italy 1861-1913: New Evidence on the International Kuznets Cycle* (Williamstown Ma.).

Fishlow, A. (1965), *Railroads and the Transformation of the Ante-Bellum Economy* (Harvard).

Fishlow, A. (1966), "Productivity and Technical Change in the Railroad Sector 1840-1910", in: (National Bureau of Economic Research (Ed.) 1966).

Fleury, M. & Henry, L. (1965), *Nouveau manuel de dépouillement et d'exploitation de l'état civile sous l'ancien regime* (Paris).

Floud, R. (1976), *The British Machine Tools Industry 1850-1914* (Cambridge).

Floud, R. & McCloskey, D.N. (Eds.) (1981), *The Economic History of Britain since 1700*, Vol. 1 : 1700-1860 ; Vol 2. : 1860 to the 1970s (Cambridge, etc.).

Floud, R. & McCloskey, D.N. (Eds.) (1994), *The Economic History of Britain since 1700* (2nd Rev. Ed.), Vol.1: 1700-1860; Vol. 2: 1860-1939; Vol. 3: 1939-1992 (Cambridge, etc.).

Flynn, D.O. (1978), "A New Perspective on the Spanish Price Revolution: The

Monetary Approach to the Balance of Payments", *Explorations in Economic History*, 15, pp. 388-406.

Fogel, R.W. (1960), *The Union Pacific Railroad: A Case in Premature Enterprise* (Baltimore).

Fogel, R.W. (1964), *Railroads and American Economic Growth: Essays in Econometric History* (Baltimore).

Fogel, R.W. (1964a), "Reappraisals in American Economic History-Discussion", *American Economic Review*, 54, pp. 377-389.

Fogel, R.W. (1965), "The Reunification of Economic History with Economic Theory", *American Economic Review*, 55, pp. 92-99.

Fogel, R.W. (1966), "The New Economic History: Its Findings and Methods", *Economic History Review*, 19, pp. 642-656.

Fogel, R.W. (1967), The Specification Problem in Economic History", *Journal of Economic History*, 27, pp. 283-308.

Fogel, R.W. (1970), "Historiography and Retrospective Econometrics", *History and Theory*, 9 pp. 245-264.

Fogel, R.W. (1979), "'Scientific' History and Traditional History", *Unpublished Manuscript* (Harvard University).

Fogel, R.W. (1989), *Without Consent or Contract: The Rise and Fall of American Slavery* (New York).

Fogel, R.W. & Engerman, S.L. (1971), "A Model for the Explanation of Industrial Expansion during the Nineteenth Century: With an Application to the American Iron Industry", in: (Fogel & Engerman (Eds.) 1971: pp. 148-162).

Fogel, R.W. & Engerman, S.L. (1971a), "The Economics of Slavery", in (Fogel & Engerman (Eds.) 1971: pp. 311-341).

Fogel, R.W. & Engerman, S.L. (Eds.) (1971), *The Reinterpretation of American Economic History* (New York, etc.).

Fogel, R.W. & Engerman, S.L. (1974), *Time on the Cross, The Economics of American Negro Slavery* (2 vols.) (London).

Fogel, R.W. & Engerman, S.L. (1977), "Explaining the Relative Efficiency of Slave Agriculture in the Antebellum South", *American Economic Review*, 67, pp. 672-690.

Fogel, R.W. & Engerman, S.L. (1980), "Explaining the Relative Efficiency of Slave Agriculture in the Antebellum South: A Reply", *American Economic Review*, 70, pp. 672-690.

Fogel, R.W. & Engerman, S.L. (1992), *Without Consent or Contract: Technical Papers* (New York).

Fogel, R.W., Engerman, S.L. & Trussell, J. (1982), "Exploring the Uses of Data on Height: The Analysis of Long-Term Trends in Nutrition, Labor Welfare, and Labor Productivity", *Social Science History*, 6, pp. 401-422.

Fogel, R.W., Galantine, R.A., Manning, R.L. & Cardell, N. (1992), *Without Consent or Contract: Evidence and Methods* (New York).

Forrester, J.W. (1971), *World Dynamics* (Cambridge Mass., enz.).

Forster, C. (Ed.) (1970), *Australian Economic Development in the Twentieth Century* (London).

Franses, P.H. & Hobijn, B., "Convergence of Living Standards: An International Analysis", *Report 9534/A from the Econometric Institute of the Erasmus University* (Rotterdam).

Fremdling, R. (1977), "Railroads and German Economic Growth: A Leading Sector Analysis with A Comparison to the United States", *Journal of Economic History*, 37, pp. 419-443.

Friedman, M. (1953), "The Methodology of Positive Economics", in: *Essays in Positive Economics* (Chicago, etc.), pp. 3-43.

Friedman, M. & Jacobson Schwartz, A. (1963), *A Monetary History of the United States, 1867-1960* (Princeton).

Frijhoff, W.Th.M. (1981), *La Société Néerlandaise et ses Gradués 1575-1814 : une Recherche Serielle sur le Statut des Intellectuels* (Amsterdam).

Frijhoff, W.Th.M. (1984), *Cultuur, Mentaliteit: Illusie van Elites?* (Nijmegen).

Frijhoff, W.Th.M. (1996), *Autodidaxies XVIᵉ -XIXᵉ Siècles* (Paris).

Frijhoff, W. (2001), "Uneasy history : Some reflections on ego, culture and social institutions", *NEHA-Jaarboek voor economische, bedrijfs- en techniekgeschiedenis*, 64, pp. 86-107.

Fukuyama, F. (1992), *The End of History and the Last Man* (London, etc.).

Fukuyama, F. (1996), *Trust : The Social Virtues and the Creation of Prosperity* (New York, etc.).

Galtung, J. (1971), "A Structural Theory of Imperialism", *Journal of Peace Research*, 8, pp. 81-117.

Garrouste, P. & Ioannides, S. (Eds.) (2001), *Evolution and Path Dependence in Economic Ideas : Past and Present* (Cheltenham).

Gemery, H.A. (1980), "Emigration from the British Isles to the New World, 1630-1700: Inferences from Colonial Populations", *Research in Economic History*, 5, pp. 179-231.

Gemery, H.A. & Hogendorn, J.S. (1974), "The Atlantic Slave Trade: A Tentative Economic Model", *Journal of African History*, 15, pp. 223-246.

Gemery, H.A. & Hogendorn, J.S. (Eds.) (1979), *The Uncommon Market: Essays in the Economic History of the Atlantic Slave Trade* (New York).

Gerschenkron, A. (1962), "Description of an Index of Italian Industrial Development, 1881-1913", in: (Gerschenkron 1962a, pp. 367-421).

Gerschenkron, A. (1962a), *Economic Backwardness in Historical Perspective* (Cambridge Mass., etc.).

Gobel, E. (1983), "Danish Trade to the West-Indies and Guinea, 1671-1754", *Scandinavian Economic History Review*, 31, pp. 21-49.

Goldin, C. (1976), *Urban Slavery in the American South, 1820-1860* (Chicago).

Goldin, C. (1995), "Cliometrics and the Nobel", *Journal of Economic Perspectives*, 9 (No.2), pp. 191-209.

Good, D.F. (1984), *The Economic Rise of the Habsburg Empire, 1750-1914* (Berkeley).

Goody, J.R. (2001), "Culture and the economy: Landes and the Wealth of Nations", *NEHA-Jaarboek voor economische, bedrijfs- en techniekgeschiedenis*, 64, pp. 61-74.

Gordon, R.J. & Bresnahan (Eds.) (1997), *The Economics of New Goods* (Chicago).

Goubert, P.M.J. (1959), *Familles marchandes sous l'Ancien Regime: les danse et les motte de Beauvais* (Paris).

Goubert, P.J.M. (1960), *Beauvais et les Beauvaisis de 1600 à 1730: Contribution à l'histoire sociale de la France du XVII siècle;1. Texte; 2. Cartes et graphiques* (Paris).

Goubert, P.J.M. (1982), *La vie quotidienne des paysans français de XVIIe siècle* (Paris).

Goubert, P.M.J. (1987), *La prostitution et la police des mœurs au XVIIIe siècle* (Paris).

Grantham, G. (1975), 'Scale and Organization in French Farming, 1840-1880', in: (Parker & Jones (Eds.) 1975: pp. 293-326).

Grantham, G. (1980), "The Persistence of Open Field Farming in Nineteenth-Century France", *Journal of Economic History*, 40, pp. 515-531.

Green, G. (1968), "Comment on 'Potentialities and Pitfalls in Economic History'", *Explorations in Entrepreneurial History* (2nd Ser.), 5, pp. 109-115.

Gregory, P. (1974), "Somre Empirical Comments on the Theory of Relative Backwardness: The Russian Case", *Economic Development and Cultural Change*, 22, pp. 654-665.

Gregory, P. (1984), *Russian National Income, 1855-1913* (Cambridge).

Griffiths, R.T. & De Meere, J.M.M. (1983), "The Growth of the Dutch Economy in the Nineteenth Century: Back to Basics?", *Tijdschrift voor Geschiedenis*, 96, pp. 563-572.

Groote, P.D. (1991), "Work in Progress. Capital Formation in Dutch Railways, 1839-1913", *Paper, Presented to the Workshop on National Accounts at Leuven University* (Groningen).

Groote, P.D. (1995), *Kapitaalvorming in Infrastructuur in Nederland, 1800-1913* (Dissertatie) (Groningen).

Groote, P.D. & Albers, R.M. (1996), "Dutch Rail and Tram Ways in Comparative Perspective", *Economic and Social History in The Netherlands*, 7, pp. 41-55.

Gutman, H. (1975), *Slavery and the Numbers Game: A Critique of Time on the Cross* (Urbana).

Gutman, H. (1975a), "The World Two Cliometricians Made: A Review Essay", *Journal of Negro History*, 60, pp. 53-57.

Habakkuk, H.J. (1962), *American and British Technology in the Nineteenth Century: The Search for Labour-Saving Inventions* (Cambridge, etc.).

Haig, B.D. & Cain, N.G. (1983), "Industrialization and Productivity: Australian Manufacturing on the 1920s and 1930s", *Explorations in Economic History*, 20, pp. 183-198.

Hamilton, E.J. (1934), *American Treasure and the Price Revolution in Spain, 1501-1650* (Cambridge Mass.).

Hamilton, E.J. (1936), *Money, Prices and Wages in Valencia, Arragon, and Navarre, 1351-1500* (Cambridge Mass.).

Hamilton, E.J. (1947), *War and Prices in Spain, 1651-1800* (Cambridge Mass.).

Hansen, S.A. (1974), *Økonomisk Vaekst i Danmark* (Copenhagen).

Harcourt, G.C. (1972), *Some Cambridge Controversies in the Theory of Capital* (Cambridge, etc.).

Harley, C.K. (1971), "The Shift from Sailing Ships to Steam Ships, 1850-1890", in: (McCloskey (Ed.) 1971, pp. 215-231).

Harley, C.K. (1974), "Skilled Labour and the Choice of Technique in Edwardian Industry", *Explorations in Economic History*, 11, pp. 391-414.

Harley, C.K. (1982), "British Industrialization Before 1841: Evidence of Slower Growth During the Industrial Revolution", *Journal of Economic History*, 42, pp. 267-290.

Harley, C. K. (1998), "Cotton Textile Prices and the Industrial Revolution", *Economic History Review*, 51, pp. 49-83.

Harley, C.K. (2002), "Review of Phyllis Deane & W.A. Cole *British Economic Growth, 1688-1959: Trends and Structure*", *Economic History Services*, September 18, 2001, URL: http://www.eh.net/bookreviews/library/harley.shtml

Harley, C.K. (2002), "Computational General Equilibrium Models in Economic History and an Analysis of British Capitalist Agriculture", *European Review of Economic History*, 6, pp. 165-191.

Harper, L. (1943), "Mercantilism and the American Revolution", *Canadian Historical Review*, 23, pp. 1-15.

Harper, L. (1964), "The Effect of the Navigation Acts on the Thirteen Colonies" (Reprint), in: (Scheiber (Ed.) 1964).

Harrod, R. F. (1939), "An Essay in Dynamic Theory", *Economic Journal*, 49, pp. 14-33.

Harrod, R.F. (1948), *Towards a Dynamic Economics* (London).

Hartwell, R.M. & Engerman, S.L. (1975), "Models of Immiseration: The Theoretical Basis of Pessimism", in: (Taylor (Ed.) 1975, pp. 189-213).

Haskell, T. (1975), "The True and Tragical History of 'Time on the Cross'", *The New York Review of Books* (October), pp. 33-39.

Hawke, G. (1970). *Railroads and Economic Growth in England and Wales, 1840-1870* (Oxford, etc.).

Herwaarden (Ed.), J. van (1973), *Lof der Historie* (Rotterdam).

Heston, A. & Kumar, D. (1983), "The Persistence of Land Fragmentation in Peasant Agriculture: An Analysis of South Asian Cases", *Explorations in Economic History*, 20, pp. 199-220.

Heston, A.W. & Lipsey, R.E. (Eds.) (1999), *International and Interarea Comparisons of Income, Output, and Prices* (Chicago).

Hjerppe, R. (1989), *The Finnish Economy, 1860-1985: Growth and Structural Change* (Helsinki).

Hodgson, G.M. (1994), "Optimisation and Evolution: Winter's Cririque of Friedman Revisited", *Cambridge Journal of Economics*, 18, pp. 413-430.

Hodgson, G.M. (1999), *Evolution and Institutions, On Evolutionary Economics and the Evolution of Economics* (Cheltenham, etc.).

Hoffmann, W.G. (1965), *Das Wachstum der deutschen Wirtschaft seit der Mitte des 19. Jahrhunderts* (Berlin).

Hohenberg, P. (1972), "Change in Rural France in the Period of Industrialization, 1830-1914", *Journal of Economic History*, 32, pp. 219-240.

Horlings, E. (1993), "De Ontwikkeling van de Nederlandse Bevolking in de 19ᵉ Eeuw, 1795-1913", *Research Memorandum, University of Amsterdam* (Amsterdam).

Horlings, E. (1995), *The Economic Development of the Dutch Service Sector, 1800-1850. Trade and Transport in a Premodern Economy* (Ph.D.-Thesis) (Amsterdam).

Horlings, E. & Smits, J.P. (1996), "Private Consumer Expenditure in The Netherlands, 1800-1913", *Economic and Social History in The Netherlands*, 7, pp. 15-40.

Horlings, E. & Smits, J.P. (2000), "De Welzijnseffecten van Economische Groei in Nederland 1800-2000" (*Unpublished Paper*), Amsterdam & Groningen.

Horlings, E., Smits, J.P. & Zanden, J.L. van (1994), "Structural Change in the Dutch Economy 1800-1913", in: (Maddsion & Van der Wee (Eds.) 1994).

Horlings, E. & Zanden, J.L. van (1996), "Exploitatie en Afscheiding. De Financiën van de Rijksoverheid in Nederland en België, 1815-1850", *Paper, Presented at The Conference 'Vergelijkende Historische Nationale Rekeningen in Nederland en België'*, Leuven, 28 november 1996 (Utrecht).

Hughes, J.R.T. & Reiter, S. (1958), "The First 1945 British Steamships", *American Statistical Journal*, III (No. 282), pp. 360-391.

Huussen, A.H., Kossmann, E.H. & Renner, H. (Eds.) (1981), *Historici van de twintigste eeuw* (Utrecht, etc.).

Hyde, C.K. (1977), *Technological Change in the British Iron Industry 1700-1870* (Princeton, etc.).

Iggers, G.G. (1983), *The German Conception of History: The National Tradition of Historical Thought from Herder to the Present* (rev. ed.) (Middletown CT).

Intriligator, M. (Ed.) (1971), *Frontiers of Quantitative Economics* (Amsterdam).

James, J. & Thomas, M. (Eds.) (1994), *Capitalism in Context: Essays in honour of R.M. Hartwell* (Chicago).

Jansen, M. (2000), *De Industriële Productie in Nederland, 1800-1850* (Dissertatie) (Amsterdam).

Jonge, J.A. de (1969), "Van geval tot getal", *Rede, uitgesproken bij de aanvaarding van het ambt van hoogleraar in de economisch-sociale geschiedenis aan de Vrije Universiteit te Amsterdam op 17 oktober 1969* (Amsterdam) (herdrukt in: Noordegraaf (Ed.) 1991, pp. 310-326).

Jonung, L. (1983), "Monetization and the Behavior of Velocity in Sweden, 1871-1913", *Explorations in Economic History*, 20, pp. 418-439.

Joskow, P. & McKelvey, E. (1973), "The Fogel-Engerman Iron Model: A Clarifying Note", *Journal of Political Economy*, 81, pp. 1236-1240.

Jorberg, L. & Bengtsson, T. (1975), "Market Integration in Sweden during the 18th and 19th Centuries: Spectral Analysis of Grain Prices", *Economy and History*, 18, pp. 93-106.

Kelley, A.C. & Williamson, J.G. (1974), *Lessons from Japanese Development: An Analytic Economic History* (Chicago).

Kendrick, J.W. (1956), *Productivity Trends: Capital and Labor* (National Bureau of Economic Research Occasional Paper No. 53) (Ann Arbour, Mich.: University Microfilms).

Kendrick, J.W. (1961), *Productivity Trends in the United States* (National Bureau of Economic Research) (Princeton).

Kendrick, J.W. (1973), *Postwar Productivity Trends in the United States, 1948-1969* (National Bureau of Economic Research) (New York).

Kennedy, W.P. (1974), "Foreign Investment, Trade and Growth in the United Kingdom, 1870-1913", *Explorations in Economic History*, 11, pp. 415-444.

Keynes, J.M. (1936), *The General Theory of Employment, Interest and Money* (London).

Klapwijk, J. (1970), *Tussen Historisme en Relativisme: Een Studie over de Dynamiek van het Historisme en de Wijsgerige Ontwikkelingsgang van Ernst Troeltsch* (Assen).

Klein, W. I. (1915), *The Wealth and Income of the People of the United States* (London).

Klein. P.W. & Borger, G.J. (Ed.) (1997), *De Jaren Dertig: Aspecten van Crisis en Werkloosheid* (Amsterdam).

Klep, P.M.M. (2001), "'Reculturalisation'in economic and social history ?", *NEHA-Jaarboek voor economische-, bedrijfs- en techniekgeschiedenis*, 64, pp. 6-27.

Knibbe, M. (1993), *Agriculture in The Netherlands. Production and Institutional Change* (Ph.D.-Thesis) (Amsterdam).

Kolchin, P. (1992), "More Time on the Cross? An Evaluation of Robert William Fogel's *Without Consent or Contract*", *Journal of Southern History*, 58 (No. 3), pp. 491-502.

Komlos, J. (1983), *The Habsburg Monarchy as a Customs Union: Economic Development in Austria-Hungary in the Nineteenth Century* (Princeton, etc.).

Komlos, J. (1996), "Modern Economic Growth and the Biological Standard of Living", *Paper, presented to the European Social Science History Conference (Economics-session 23: Biological Standards of Living in Rural Regions during the Early Nineteenth Century)* (Noordwijkerhout 1996).

Komlos, J. (1996a), "Anomalies in Economic History: Toward a Resolution of the Antebellum Puzzle, *Journal of Economic History*, 56, pp. 202-214).

Komlos, J. (Ed.) (1983), *Economic Development in the Habsburg Monarchy in the Nineteenth Century: Essays* (New York).

Komlos, J. (Ed.) (1994), *Stature, Living Standards, and Economic Development: Essays in Anthropometric History* (Chicago, etc.).

Komlos, J. (Ed.) (1995), *The Biological Standard of Living on Three Continents: Further Explorations in Anthropometric History* (Boulder, etc.).

Komlos, J. & Baten J. (Eds.) (1998), *The Biological Standard of Living in Comparative Perspective: Contributions to the Conference, Held in Munich January 18-22, 1997, for the XIIth Congress of the International Economic History Association* (Stuttgart).

Komlos, J. & Cuff, T. (Eds.) (1998), *Classics in Anthropometric History* (St. Katharinen).

Kooij, P. (1978), "De industriële revolutie", in: (Baudet & Van der Meulen (Eds.) 1978: pp. 204-214).

Krantz, O. (1988), "New Estimates of Swedish GDP since the Beginning of the Nineteenth Century", *Review of Income and Wealth*, 34, pp. 165-182.

Kravis, I.B., Heston, A.W. & Summers, R. (1982), *World Product and Income: International Comparisons of Real Gross Product, Produced by the Statistical Offices of The United Nations and the World Bank* (Baltimore).

Krebs, D.M. & Wallis, K.F. (Eds.) (1997), *Advances in Economics and Econometrics: Theory and Applications* (Cambridge, etc.).

Krugman, P. (1997), "How Fast Can the U.S. Economy Grow? Not as fast as "new economy" pundits would like to think", *Harvard Business Review*, pp. 123-129.

Kuhn, T.S. (1962) *The Structure of Scientific Revolutions* (Chicago).

Kuznets, S. S. (1953), *Economic Change: Selected Essays in Business Cycles, National Income and Economic Growth* (New York).

Kuznets, S. S. (1961), *Capital in the American Economy: Its Formation and Financing* (Princeton NJ).

Kuznets, S.S. (1966), *Modern Economic Growth: Rate, Structure and Spread* (New Haven, etc.).

Kuznets, S. S. (1971), *Economic Growth of Nations, Total Output and Prodcution Structure* (Cambridge Mass.).

Kuznets, S. S., Moore, W. E. & Spengler, J. J. (Eds.) (1955), *Economic Growth: Brazil, India, Japan* (Durham NC).

Landes, D.S. (1998), The Wealth and Poverty of Nations: Why Some Are So Rich and Some So Poor (New York, etc.).

Laslett, P. (1965), *The World We Have Lost* (London).

Laslett, P. (Ed.) (1972), *Household and Family in Past Time, Comparative Studies in the Size and Structure of the Domestic Group over the Last Three Centuries in England, France, Serbia, Japan and Colonial North-America, with Further Materials from Western-Europe* (Cambridge, etc.).

Latham, A.J.H. (1978), "Merchandise Trade Imbalances and Uneven Development in India and China", *Journal of Economic History*, 7, pp. 33-60.

Lazonick, W. (1981a), "Factor Costs and the Diffusion of Ring Spinning in Britain Prior to World War 1", *Quarterly Journal of Economics*, 96, pp. 89-109.

Lazonick, W. (1981b), "Prodcution Relations, Labor Productivity, and Choice of Technique: British and U.S. Coton Spinning", *Journal of Economic History*, 41, pp. 491-516.

Lee, C.H. (1977), *The Quantitative Approach to Economic History* (London).

Leff, N. (1968), *The Brazilian Capital-Goods Industry, 1929-1964* (Cambridge Mass.).

Le Goff, J.L. (1957), *Les intellectuels au Moyen Âge* (Paris).

Le Goff, J.L. (1974), "Les mentalités: une histoire ambiguë", in : (Le Goff & Nora 1974, vol. 3 : pp. 76-94).

Le Goff, J.L. (1981), *La naissance du purgatoire* (Paris).

Le Goff, J.L. & Nora, P. (Eds.) (1974), *Faire de l'histoire: Nouveaux Objets (3 Vols.); 1. Nouveaux Problèmes ; 2. Nouvelles Approches ; 3. Nouveaux Objets* (Paris).

Le Roy Ladurie, E.B. (1966), *Les Paysans de Languedoc; 1. Texte ; 2. Annexes, Sources, Graphiques* (Paris).

Le Roy Ladurie, E.B. (1967), *l'Histoire du climat depuis l'an mil* (Paris)

Le Roy Ladurie, E.B. (1977), *Montaillou, village occitan de 1294 à 1324* (Paris).

Le Roy Ladurie, E.B. (1979), *Le Carnaval de Romans, De la Chandeleur au mercredi de Cendrey 1579-1580* (Paris).

Le Roy Ladurie, E.B., Bernageau, N. & Pasquet, Y. (1969), "Le Conscrit et l'Ordinateur. Perspectives de Recherches sur les Archives Militaires du XIX$_j^e$ Siècle Français", *Studi Storici*, 10, pp. 260-308.

Le Roy Ladurie, E.B. & Bernageau, N. (1970), "Étude sur un Contingent Militaire (1868). Mobilité Géographique, Délinquance et Stature, mise en Rapport avec d'autres Aspects de la Situation des Conscrits", *Annales de Démographie Historique*, 7, pp. 311-336.

Levhari, D. & Samuelson, P. A. (1966), "The Nonswitching Theorem is False", *Quarterly Journal of Economics*, 80, pp. 503-517.

289

Lévy-Leboyer, M. (1968), "La croissance économique en France au XIXe siècle", *Annales. Économies, Sociétés, Civilizations*, 23, pp. 788-807.

Lévy-Leboyer, M. & Bourguignon, F. (1985), *l'Économie française au XIXe siècle* (Paris).

Lindert, P.H. & Trace, K. (1971), "Yardsticks for Victorian Entrepreneurs", in : (McCloskey (Ed.) 1971, pp. 239-274).

Lindert, P.H. & Williamson, J.G. (1982),"Revising England's Social Tables, 1688-1812", *Explorations in Economic History*, 19, pp. 385-408.

Loschky, D. (1973), "Studies of the Navigation Acts: New Economic Non-History", *Economic History Review*, 26, pp. 689-691.

Lyons, J.S. (1977), *The Lancashire Cotton Industry and the Introduction of the Power Loom, 1815-1850* (Ph.D. dissertation) (Berkeley).

Maddison, A. (1982), *Phases of Capitalist Development* (Oxford, etc.).

Maddison, A. (1986), "Marx and Bismarck: Capitalism and Government 1883-1983", in: (Wagener & Drukker (Eds.)1986, pp. 197-213).

Maddison, A. (1989), *The World Economy in the 20th Century* (OECD Development Centre Studies) (Paris).

Maddison, A. (1991), *Dynamic Forces in Capitalist Development, A long-run Comparative View* (Oxford, etc.).

Maddison, A. (1995), *Monitoring the World Economy* (Paris).

Maddison, A. (1998), *Chinese Economic Performance in the Long Run* (Paris).

Maddison, A. (1999), "Poor Until 1820", *The Wallstreet Journal Europe*, January 11, p. 8.

Maddison, A. (2001), *The World Economy: A Millenium Perspective* (Paris).

Maddison, A. & Wee, H. van der (Eds.) (1994), *Economic Growth and Structural Change. Comparative Approaches over the Long Run on the Basis of Reconstructed National Accounts (11th International Economic History Congress at Milan 1994)* (Milan).

Malthus, T.R. (1798), *Essay on the principles of population as its effects the future improvement of society* (London).

Mandemakers, C. & Zanden, J.L. van (1990), "Lengte van Lotelingen en het Nationaal Inkomen: Schijnresultaten en Misvattingen", *Economisch- en Sociaal-Historisch Jaarboek*, 53, pp. 1-23.

Mantoux, P. [1906] (1959), *La Révolution Industrielle du XVIIième siècle : Essai sur les Commencements de la Grande Industrie en Angleterre* (Paris).

Marczewski, J. & Markovitch, T.J. (1965), *Le produit fysique de l'économie française de 1789 à 1913: comparaisson avec la Grande Bretagne; l'Industrie française de 1789 à 1964 : Sources et méthodes* (Paris).

Margo, R. A. & Steckel, R. H. (1982), "The Heights of American Slaves: New Evidence on Slave Nutrition and Health", *Social Science History*, 6, pp. 516-538.

Markovitch, T.J. (1966), *l'Industrie française de 1789 à 1964 (3 Vols.); 1. Analyse des faits; 2. Analyse des faits (suite) ; 3. Conclusions génerales* (Paris).

Marr, W.L. & Patterson, D.G. (1980), *Canada : An Economic History* (Toronto).

Mathias, P. & Postan, M.M. (Eds.) (1978), *The Cambridge Economic History of Europe, Vol. VII, The Industrial Economies: Capital, Labour and Enterprise* (Cambridge).

Matthews, R.C.O. (1954), *A Study in Trade Cycle History; Economic Fluctuations in Great Britain, 1833-1842* (Cambridge).

Matthews, R.C.O., Feinstein, F.H. & Odling-Smee, J.C. (1982), *British Ecnomic Growth, 1856-1973* (Oxford).

McClelland, P. D. (1968), "Railroads, American economic growth and the New Economic History: A Critique", *Journal of Economic History*, 28, pp. 102-123.

McClelland, P.D. (1969), "The Cost to America of British Imperial Policy", *American Economic Review*, 59, pp. 370-381.

McClelland, P.D. (1972), "Social Rates of Return on American Railroads in the 19th Century", *Economic History Review*, 25, pp. 471-488.

McClelland, P.D. (1973), "The New Economic History and the Burdens of the Navigation Acts: A Comment", *Economic History Review*, 26, pp. 679-686.

McClelland, P. D. (1975), *Causal Explanation and Model Building in History, Economics, and The New Economic History* (Ithaca, etc.).

McCloskey, D.N. (1970), "Did Victorian Britain Fail?", *Economic History Review*, 23, pp. 446-459 (herdrukt in: (McCloskey 1981).

McCloskey, D.N. (Ed.) (1971), *Essays on a Mature Economy: Britain after 1840* (London).

McCloskey, D.N. (1973), *Economic Maturity and Entrepreneurial Decline: British Iron and Steel , 1870-1913* (Cambridge, Mass., etc.).

McCloskey, D.N. (1981), *Enterprise and Trade in Victorian Britain: Essays in Historical Economics* (London).

McCloskey, D.N. (1987), *Econometric History* (Series: Studies in economic and social history) (Houndmills, etc.).

Meadows, D.L. *et al.* (Eds.) (1972), *The Limits to Growth: A Report for the Club of Rome's Project on the Predicament of Mankind* (London).

Meere, J.M.M. de (1982), *Economische groei en levensstandaard in Nederland gedurende de eerste helft van de negentiende eeuw. Aspecten en trends* (Den Haag).

Meerten, M.A. van (1996), *Gross Private Fixed Asset Formation in Belgium, 1910-1954* (Ph.D.-dissertation, University of Groningen) (Groningen).

Menger, K. (1883), *Untersuchungen über die Methode der Sozialwissenschaften und der Politischen Ökonomie insbesondere* (Wien).

Metzer, J. (1974), "Railroad Development and Market Integration: The Case of Tsarist Russia", *Journal of Economic History*, 34, pp. 529-550.

Mitchell, B.R. (1962), *Abstract of British Historical Statistics* (Cambridge).

Mitchell, B.R. (1988), *British Historical Statistics* (Cambridge).

Mitchell, B.R. & Jones, H.G. (1971), *Second Abstract of British Historical Statistics* (Cambridge).

Mokyr, J. (1975), "Capital, Labour and the Delay of the Industrial Revolution in The Netherlands", *Economisch- en Sociaal Historisch Jaarboek*, 38, pp. 288-299.

Mokyr, J. (1976), *Industrialization in the Low Countries* (New Haven, Conn., etc.).

Mokyr, J. (1977), "Demand vs. Supply during the Industrial Revolution", *Journal of Economic History*, 37, pp. 981-1008

Mokyr, J. (1980a), "Industrialization and poverty in Ireland and The Netherlands", *Journal of Interdisciplinary History*, 9 (No. 3), pp. 429-458.

Mokyr, J. (1980b), "The deadly fungus: an econometric investigation into the short-term demographic impact of the Irish famine", *Research in Population Economics*, 2, pp. 237-277.

Mokyr, J. (1980c), "Malthusian models and Irish history", *Journal of Economic History*, 40, pp. 159-16.

Mokyr, J. (1985), *Why Ireland Starved: A Quantitative and Analytical History of the Irish Economy 1800-1850* (London, etc.).

Mokyr, J. (Ed.) (1985), *The Economics of the Industrial Revolution* (Totowa NJ).

Mokyr, J. (1990), *The Lever of Riches: Technological Creativity and Economic Progress* (New York).

Mokyr, J. (1994), "Progress and Inertia in Technological Change", in: (James & Thomas (Eds.) 1994: pp. 230-254).

Mokyr, J. (1994a), "Cardwell's Law and the Political Economy of Technological Progress", *Research Policy*, 23, pp. 561-574.

Mokyr, J. (1994b), "That Which We Call an Industrial Revolution", *Contention*, 4, pp. 189-206.

Mokyr, J. (1997), "Why Was There More Work for Mother? Technological Change and the Household, 1880-1930", *Paper, Presented at The Economic History Association Annual Conference in Brunswick, September 1997* (Chicago).

Mokyr, J. (1998), "Science, Technology, and Knowledge: What Historians Can Learn from an Evolutionary Approach", *Unpublished paper, Max Planck Institute for Research in Economic Systems, Papers on Economics and Evolution*, pp. 89-103.

Mokyr, J. (1998a), "Editor's Introduction: The New Economic History and the Industrial Revolution", in: (Mokyr (Ed.) 1998.

Mokyr, J. (1998b), "Induced Technical Innovation and Medical History: An Evolutionary Aproach", *Journal of Evolutionary Economics*, 8, pp. 119-137.

Mokyr, J. (1998c), "The Political Economy of Technological Change: Resistance and Innovation in Economic History", in: (Berg & Bruland (Eds.) 1998: pp. 39-64).

Mokyr, J. (2000), "Evolutionary Phenomena in Technological Change", in: (Ziman (Ed.) 2000: pp. 52-65).

Mokyr, J. (2000a), "Knowledge, Technology, and Economic Growth during the Industrial Revolution", in: (Van Ark, Kuipers & Kuper (Eds.) 2000: pp. 253-292).

Mokyr, J. (2002), *The Gifts of Athena: Historical Origins of the Knowledge Economy* (Princeton NJ).

Mokyr, J. (Ed.) (1998), *The British Industrial Revolution: An Economic Perspective* (2nd Edition) (Boulder).

Mokyr, J. (Ed.), (1991) *The Vital One: Essays in Honor of Jonathan R.T. Hughes (Research in Economic History: A Research Annual, Supplement 6)* (Greenwich, Conn., etc.).

Mokyr, J. & Stein, R. (1997), "Science, Health and Household Technology: The Effect of the Pasteur Technology on Consumer Demand", in: (Gordon & Bresnahan (Eds.) 1997: pp. 143-205).

Molinas, C. & Prados de la Escosura, L. (1989), "Was Spain Different ? Spanish Economic Backwardness Revisited", *Explorations in Economic History*, 26, pp. 385-402.

Morris, M.D. (1965), *The Emergence of an Industrial Labor Force in Bombay: A Study of the Bombay Cotton Mills* (Berkeley).

Morris, M.D. (1983), "Industrialization in South Asia", in: (Kumar & Desai (Eds.) 1983).

Mosk, C.A. (1978), "Fecundity, Infanticide and Food Consumption in Japan", *Explorations in Economic History*, 15, pp. 269-289.

Murphy, G.G.S. (1965), "The 'New' History", *Explorations in Entrepreneurial History* (2nd Ser.), 2, pp. 132-146.

Murphy, G.G.S. (1969), "On Counterfactual Propositions", *History and Theory (Beiheft 9)*, pp. 14-38.

Murphy, G.G.S. & Mueller, M.G. (1967), "On Making Historical Techniques More Specific: 'Real Types' Constructed with a Computer", *History and Theory*, 6 (No. 1), pp. 14-32.

National Bureau of Economic Research (Ed.) (1966), *Output, employment and productivity in the United States after 1800: Studies in Income and Wealth* (Vol. 30) (New York, etc.).

Nauta, L.W. (Eds.) (1975), *Het Neopositivisme in de Sociale Wetenschappen : Analyse, Kritiek, Alternatieven* (Amsterdam).

Nelson, R.R. (1995), "Recent Evolutionary Theorizing About Economic Change" , *Journal of Economic Literature*, 33, pp. 48-90.

Nelson, R.R. (1997), "How New is New Growth Theory", *Challenge*, 40 (No. 5), pp. 29-58.

Nelson, R.R. & Winter, S.G. (1973), "Towards an Evolutionary Theory of Economic Capabilities", *American Economic Review*, 63, pp. 440-449.

Nelson, R.R. & Winter, S.G. (1974), "Neoclassical vs. Evolutionary Theories of Economic Growth: Critique and Prospects", *Economic Journal*, 84, pp. 886-905.

Nelson, R.R. & Winter, S.G. (1975), "Growth form an Evolutionary Perspective: The Differential Productivity Puzzle", *American Economic Review*, 65, pp. 338-344.

Nelson, R.R. & Winter, S.G. (1976), "Technical Change in an Evolutionary Model", *Quarterly Journal of Economics*, 90, pp. 90-118.

Nelson, R.R. & Winter, S.G. (1977), "Simulation of Schumpeterian Competition", *American Economic Review*, 67, pp. 271-276.

Nelson, R.R. & Winter, S.G. (1978), "Forces Generating and Limiting Concentration under Schumpeterian Competition", *Bell Journal of Economics*, 9, pp. 524-548.

Nelson, R.R. & Winter, S.G. (1980), "Firm and Industry Response to Changing Market Conditions: An Evolutionary Approach", *Economic Inquiry*, 18, pp. 179-202.

Nelson, R.R. & Winter, S.G. (1982), "The Schumpeterian Tradeoff Revisited", *American Economic Review*, 73, pp. 114-132.

Nelson, R.R. & Winter, S.G. (1982a), *An Evolutionary Theory of Economic Change* (Cambridge (Mass.), etc.).

Nelson, R.R. & Winter, S.G. (2002), "Evolutionary Theorizing in Economics", *Journal of Economic Perspectives*, 16 (No. 2), pp. 23-46.

Neuhaus (Ed.), P. (1979), *A Economia Brasileira: Una Visao Historica* (Rio de Janeiro).

Noordegraaf, L. (Eds.) (1991), *Ideeën en ideologieën, Studies over economische en sociale geschiedschrijving in Nederland 1894-1991* (2 delen) (Amsterdam).

North, D.C. (1961), *The Economic Growth of the United States, 1790-1860* (New York).

North, D.C. (1963), "Quantitative Research in American Economic History", *American Economic Review*, 53, pp. 128-130.

North, D.C. (1965), "The State of Economic History", *American Economic Review*, 55, pp.86-91.

North, D.C. (1966), "Early National Income Estimates of the United States", *Economic Development and Cultural Change*, 9.

North, D.C. (1966a), *Growth and Welfare in the American Past: A New Economic History* (Englewood Cliffs).

North, D.C. (1968), "Sources of Productivity Change in Ocean Shipping 1600-1850", *The Journal of Political Economy*, 76, pp. 953-970 (reprinted in: Fogel & Engerman (Eds.) 1971: pp. 163-174)

North, D.C. (1968a), "HISTORY: Economic History", in: (Sills (Ed.) 1968, vol. 6, pp. 468-474).

North, D.C. (1971), "Institutional Change and Economic Growth", *Journal of Economic History*, 31, pp. 118-125.

North, D.C. (1977), "Markets an Other Allocation Systems in History: The Challenge of Karl Polanyi", *Journal of European Economic History*, 6, pp. 703-716.

North, D.C. (1978), "Structure and Performance: The Task of Economic History", *Journal of Economic Literature*, 16, pp. 963-978.

North, D.C. (1981), *Structure and Change in Economic History* (New York, etc.).

North, D.C. (1984), "Government and the Cost of Exchange in History", *Journal of Economic History*, 44, pp. 255.264.

North, D.C. (1990), *Institutions, Institutional Change and Economic Performance* (Cambridge, etc.).

North, D.C. & Thomas, R.P. (1971), "The Rise and Fall of the Manorial System: A Theoretical Model", *Journal of Economic History*, 31, pp. 777-803.

North, D.C. & Thomas, R.P. (1973), *The Rise of the Western World: A New Economic History* (Cambridge, etc.).

North, D.C. & Thomas, R.P. (1977), "The First Economic Revolution", *Economic History Review*, 30, pp. 229-241.

North, D.C. & Weingast, B.R. (1989), "Constitutions and Commitment. The Evolution of Institutions Governing Public Choice in 17th Century England", *Journal of Economic History*, 49, pp. 803-832.

Ó Gráda, C. (1975), "Supply Responsiveness in Irish Agriculture During the Ninetheenth Century", *Economic History Review*, 28, pp. 312-317.

Ó Gráda, C. (1981), "Agricultural Decline 1860-1914", in: (Floud & McCloskey (Eds.) 1981, Vol. 2, pp. 175-197).

Parker, W.N. (1963), "Review of *American and British Technology in the 19th Century* by H.J.Habakkuk", *Business History Review*, 37.

Palmer, R.R. & Colton, J.G. (1995), *A History of the Modern World* (8th Rev. Ed.) (New York).

Parker, W.N. (1971), "Productivity Growth in American Grain Farming: An Analysis of its 19th-Century Sources", in: (Fogel & Engerman (Eds.) 1971; pp. 175-186).

Parker, W.N. (1971a), "Productivity Growth in American Grain Farming: An Analysis of its 19th Century Sources", in: (Fogel & Engerman (Eds.) 1971: pp.175-186).

Parker, W.N. (Ed.) (1986), *Economic History and the Modern Economist* (Oxford, etc.).

Parker, W. & Jones, E. (Eds.) (1975), *European Peasants and Their Markets: Essays in Agrarian Economic History* (Princeton).

Passell, P. (1974), "An Economic Analysis of the Peculiar Economic Institution", *New York Times Book Review* (April 28), p.4.

Passmore, J.A. (1966), *A Hundred Years of Philosophy* (2nd ed.) (London).

295

Patrick, H.T. (Ed.) (1976), *Industrial Growth and Consequences in Japanese Economic Development* (Berkeley).

Peeters, S. et .al. (1986), "Reconstruction of the Belgian National Income, 1920-1939. Methodology and Results", *Workshop on Quantitative Economic History Discussion Paper 86.01* (Leuven).

Polanyi, K. (1957), *The Great Transformation* (New York).

Polanyi, K. (1977), *The Livelyhood of Man* (New York).

Pope, D.H. (1976), "Australian Immigration: A Critique of the Push-Pull Model", *Australian Economic History Review*, 16, pp. 144-152.

Popper, K.R. (1961), *The Poverty of Historicism* (*rev. ed.*) (London, etc.).

Previant Lee, S., & Passell, P. (1979) *A New Economic View of American History* (New York, etc.).

Pritchett, L. (1996), "Forget Convergence: Divergence, Past, Present, Future", *Finance and Development*, 33 (No. 2), pp. 40-43.

Pritchett, L. (1997), "Divergence, Big Time", *Journal of Economic Perspectives*, 11 (No. 3), pp. 3-17.

Purdue University (Ed.) (1967), *Purdue Faculty Papers in Economic History 1956-1966* (*Hermann C. Krannert Graduate School of Industrial Administration Monograph Series, No. 4*) (Homewood, Ill.).

Ransom, R. (1968), "British Policy and Colonial Growth: Some Implications of the Burdens of the Navigation Acts", *Journal of Economic History*, 28, pp. 427-435.

Rapp, R.T. (1976), *Industry and Economic Decline in Seventeenth Century Venice* (Cambridge, Mass., etc.).

Rawski, T.G. (1980), *China's Transition to Industrialism: Producer Goods and Economic Development in the Twentieth Century* (Ann Arbor).

Redlich, F. (1965), " 'New' and traditional approaches to economic history and their interdependence", *Journal of Economic History*, 25 (December 1965), pp. 480-495.

Redlich, F. (1968), "Potentialities and Pitfalls in Economic History", *Explorations in Entrepreneurial History* (2nd Ser.), 6, pp. 93-108.

Ricardo, D. (1817) (3rd ed.: 1821), *The Principles of Political Economy and Taxation* (London).

Reid, J. (1970), "On Navigating the Navigation Acts with Peter McClelland", *American Economic Review*, 60, pp. 949-958.

Reid, J. (1978), "Economic Burden: Spark to the Revolution?", *Journal of Economic History*, 38, pp. 81-100.

Riel, A. van & Zanden, J.L. van (2000), *Nederland 1780-1914. Staat, Instituties en Economische Ontwikkeling* (Amsterdam).

Ritschl, A. & Woitek, U. (2000), "Did Monetary Forces Cause the Great Depression? A Bayesian VAR Analysis for the U.S. Economy" (Working Paper

No. 50), *Working Paper Series of the Institute for Empirical Economics of the University of Zurich* (Zurich).

Rockoff, H. (1971), "Money, Prices and Banks in the Jacksonian Era", in: (Fogel & Engerman (Eds.) 1971: pp. 448-458).

Roehl, R. (1976), "French Industrialization: A Reconsideration", *Explorations in Economic History*, 13, pp. 233-281.

Romer, P.M. (1994), "The Origins of Endogeneous Growth", *Journal of Economic Perspectives*, 8 (No. 1), pp. 3-22.

Rompuy, V,. van (Eds.) (1986), *Actuele Economische Problemen: Theorie en Politiek* (Leuven).

Rosovsky, H. (Ed.) (1966), *Industrialization in Two Systems, Essays in honor of Alexander Gerschenkron* (New York).

Rostow, W.W. (1953), *The Process of Economic Growth* (Oxford).

Rostow, W.W. (1957), "The Interrelation of Theory and Economic History", *Paper, presented to the NBER-AEHA Conference on Income and Wealth*, herdrukt in: (*Journal of Economic History*, 17, pp. 509-523.

Rostow, W.W. (1960), *The Stages of Economic Growth: A Non-communist Manifesto* (Cambridge).

Rothbarth, E. (1946), "Causes of the Superior Efficiency of USA Industry as Compared to British Industry", *Economic Journal*, 56, pp. 383-390.

Rousseau, P.L. (2002), "Jacksonian Monetary Policy, Specie Flows, and the Panic of 1837", *Journal of Economic History*, 62 (No. 2), pp. 457-488.

Rudolph, R.L. (1983), "Economic Revolution in Austria?", in: (Komlos (Ed.) 1983).

Samuelson, P.A. (1966), "A Summing Up", *Quarterly Journal of Economics*, 80, pp. 193-206.

Sandberg, L. G. (1974), *Lancashire in Decline: A Study in Entrepreneurship, Technology and International Trade* (Columbus, Ohio).

Sandberg, L.G. (1979), "The Case of the Impoverished Sophistocate: Human Capital and Swedish Economic Growth Before World War I", *Journal of Economic History*, 39, pp. 225-242.

Saxonhouse, G.R. (1978), "The Supply of Quality Workers and the Demand for Quality Jobs in Japan's Early Industrialization", *Explorations in Economic History*, 15, pp. 40-68.

Saxonhouse, G.R. & Wright, G. (Eds.) (1984), *Forms and Methods in Economic History: Essays in Honor of William N. Parker* (Greenwich, Conn.).

Schama, S. (1987), *The Embarrassment of Riches: An Interpretation of Dutch Culture in the Golden Age* (New York).

Schama, S. (1995), *Landscape and Memory* (London).

Schama, S. (1999), *Rembrandt's Eyes* (New York).

Scheiber, H. (Ed.) (1964), *United States Economic History* (New York).

Schöffer, I. (1965), "Het dode cijfer en het levende getal: Een en ander over

297

kwantificeren in het historisch onderzoek", *Tijdschrift voor Geschiedenis*, 78, pp. 257-272 (reprinted in: Noordegraaf (Ed.) 1991).

Scholliers, P. & Zamagni, V. (Eds.) (1995), *Labour's Reward* (Aldershot).

Schumpeter, J.A. (1954), *A History of Economic Analysis* (*Edited from manuscript by Elizabeth Boody Schumpeter*) (London).

Sheperd, J. & Walton, G. (1976), "Economic Change after the American Revolution: Pre- and Post-War Comparisons of Maritime Shipping and Trade", *Explorations in Economic History*, 13, pp. 397-422.

Shlomowitz, R. (1979), "The Search for Institutional Equilibrium in Queenland's Sugar Industry, 1884-1913", *Australian Economic History Review*, 19, pp. 91-122.

Sills, D.L. (Ed.) (1968), *International Encyclopedia of the Social Sciences* (New York, etc.).

Simon, W.M. (1963), *European Positivism in the Nineteenth Century: An Essay in Intellectual History* (Ithaca, NY).

Slicher van Bath, B.H. (1957), *Een Samenleving onder Spanning: Geschiedenis van het Platteland in Overijssel* (Assen).

Slicher van Bath, B.H. (1969), "Nieuwe wegen in de Amerikaanse economische en sociale geschiedenis", *Tijdschrift voor Geschiedenis, themanummer: Nieuwe wegen in de economische geschiedenis*, 82, pp. 206-232.

Smits, J.P. (1990), "The Size and Structure of the Dutch Service Sector in International Perspective", *Economic and Social History in The Netherlands*, 2, pp. 81-98.

Smits, J.P. (1995), *Economische Groei en Structurele Veranderingen in de Nederlandse Dienstensector 1850-1913. De Bijdrage van Handel en Transport aan het Proces van 'Moderne Economische Groei'* (Dissertatie) (Amsterdam).

Smits, J.P. (1998), "Paradise Lost and Regained: Technological Change and Industrial Growth in The Netherlands During the Nineteenth Century", *Research Memorandum University of Groningen* (Groningen).

Smits, J.P. (1999), "Economische Ontwikkeling, 1800-1999", in: (Van der Bie & Dehing (Eds.) 1999: pp. 15-33).

Smits, J.P. (2000), "The Determinants of Productivity Growth in Dutch Manufacturing, 1815-1913", *European Review of Economic History*, 4, pp. 219-242.

Smits. J.P., Horlings, E., & Zanden, J.L. van (2000), *Dutch GDP and its Components, 1800-1913* (Groningen Growth and Development Centre Monograph Series, No. 5) (Groningen).

Smits, J.P., Jong, H.J. de & Ark, B. van (1999), "Three Phases of Dutch Economic Growth and Technological Change, 1815-1997", *Research Memorandum of the Groningen Growth and Development Centre*, No. GD42 (Groningen).

Soete, A. (1989), *De Belgische Metaalnijverheid 1937-1960. Een structuuranalyse* (Unpublished Masterthesis, University of Leuven) (Leuven).

Soete, A. (1991), "Value added in the Coalmining Industry, 1847-1951. Preliminary Results", *Paper, presented at the European Postgraduate Seminar on the Reconstruction of National Accounts, Organised by the Posthumus Centre* (Zeist).

Solar, P.M. & Cassiers, I. (1990), "Wages and Productivity in Belgium, 1910-1960", *Oxford Bulletin of Economics and Statistics*, 52, pp. 437-499.

Solow, R.M. (1956), "A Contribution to the Theory of Economic Growth", *Quarterly Journal of Economics*, 70, pp. 65-94.

Solow, R.M. (1962), "Technical Progress, Capital Formation, and Economic Growth", *American Economic Review* (May 1962), pp. 76-86.

Solow, R.M (1987), "We'd Better Watch Out", *New York Times (Book Review Section)* (July 12), pp. 35-38.

Sombart, W. (1928), *Der Moderne Kapitalismus* (3 Vols.) (München).

Sraffa, P. (1960), *Production of Commodities by Means of Commodities: Prelude to a Critique of Economic Theory* (Cambridge, etc.).

Steckel, R.H. (1986), " A Peculiar Population: The Nutrition, Health, and Mortality of American Slaves from Childhood to Maturity", *Journal of Economic History*, 46, pp. 721-741.

Steckel, R.H. (1986a), "Birth Weights and Infant Mortality among American Slaves", *Explorations in Economic History*, 23, pp. 172-198.

Steckel, R.H. & Floud, R. (Eds.) (1997), *Health and Welfare during Industrialization (A National Bureau of Economic Research Project Report)* (Chicago, etc.).

Stoianovich, (T.) (1976), *French Historical Method. The Annales Paradigm* (Ithaca, NY).

Studenski, P. (1958), *The income of nations: Theory, measurement and analysis: Past and present* (New York).

Stuijvenberg, J.H. van (1977), "Traditionele en moderne economische geschiedenis", *Economisch- en Sociaal-Historisch Jaarboek*, 44, pp. 1-25 (reprinted in: Noordegraaf (Ed.) 1991, pp. 448-472).

Stuijvenberg, J.H. & De Vrijer, E.J.E. (1980), "Prices, Population and National Income in The Netherlands", *Research Memorandum of the Department of Economics of the University of Amsterdam*, No. 8101 (Amsterdam).

Summers, R. & Heston, A.W. (1991), "The Penn World Table (Mark 5): An Expanded Set of International Comparisons, 1950-1988", *Quarterly Journal of Economics*, 106 (no. 2), pp. 327-368 (also published as electronic database at: http://pwt.econ.upenn.edu).

Sutch, R. (1975), "The Treatment Received by American Slaves", *Explorations in Economic History*, 12, pp. 335-438.

Swan, T.W. (1956), "Economic Growth and Capital Accumulation", *Economic Record*, 32, pp. 334-361.

Sylla, R. (2001), "Review of Peter Temin *The Jacksonian Economy*", *Economic*

299

History Services, Aug. 17, 2001, URL: http://www.eh.net/bookreviews/library/sylla.shtml

Szirmai, A., Ark, B. van & Pilat, D. (Eds.) (1993), *Explaining Economic Growth. Essays in Honour of Angus Maddison* (Amsterdam).

Taylor, A.J. (Ed.) (1975), *The Standard of Living in Britain in the Industrial Revolution* (London).

Taylor, G.R. & Ellsworth, L.F. (Eds.) (1971), *Approaches to American Economic History* (Charlottesville).

Teijl, J. (1971), "Nationaal inkomen in Nederland in de Periode 1850-1900", *Economisch- en Sociaal-Historisch Jaarboek*, 34, pp. 232-262.

Teijl, J. (1973), "Brandstofaccijns en Nijverheid in Nederland gedurende de periode 1834-1864", in: (Van Herwaarden (Ed.) 1973: pp. 153-184).

Temin, P. (1964), *Iron and Steel in 19th Century America: An Economic Inquiry* (Cambridge, Mass.).

Temin, P. (1966), "Steam and Waterpower in the Early 19th Century", *Journal of Economic History*, 26, pp. 187-205.

Temin, P. (1966a), "Labor Scarcity and the Problem of American Industrial Efficiency in the 1850's", *Journal of Economic History*, 26, pp. 277-298.

Temin, P. (1968), "Labor Scarcity: A Reply", *Journal of Economic History*, 28, pp. 124-125.

Temin, P. (1969), *The Jacksonian Economy* (New York).

Temin, P. (1971), "Labor Scarcity in America", *Journal of Interdisciplinary History*, 1, pp. 251-264.

Temin, P. (1976), *Did Monetary Forces Cause the Great Depression?* (Cambridge).

Temin, P. (1997), "Is it Kosher to Talk about Culture?", *Journal of Economic History*, 57, pp. 267-287.

Temin, P. (Ed.) (1973), *New Economic History* (Harmondsworth).

Thomas, R.P. (1965), "A Quantitative Approach to the Study of the Effects of British Imperial Policy on Colonial Welfare", *Journal of Economic History*, 25, pp. 615-638.

Thomas, R.P. (1968), "The Sugar Colonies of the Old Empire: Profit or Loss for Great Britain?", *Economic History Review*, 21, pp. 30-35.

Tilly, R.H. (1982), "Mergers, External Growth, and Finance in the Development of Large-Scale Enterprise in Germany, 1880-1913", *Journal of Economic History*, 42, pp. 629-658.

Toniolo, G. (1977), "Effective Protection and Industrial Growth: The Case of Italian Engineering (1880-1913)", *Journal of European Economic History*, 42, pp. 659-673.

Tortella-Casares, G. (1975), *Los origines del capitalismo en España* (Madrid).

Toutain, J.C. (1987), *Le produit intérieur brut de la France de 1789 à 1982. Économies et Sociétés* (Grenoble).

Toynbee, A. [1884] (1956), *Lectures on the Industrial Revolution* (reprinted in 1959 as : *The Industrial Revolution*) (Boston).

Uselding, P. (1974), "Technical Progress in the Springfield Armoury", *Explorations in Economic History*, 11, pp. 291-316.

Uselding, P. & Juba, B. (1974), "Biased Technical Progres in American Manufacturing, 1839-1899", *Explorations in Economic History*, 11, pp. 55-72.

Vedder, R. (1975), "The Slave Exploitation (Expropriation) Rate", *Explorations in Economic History*, 12, pp. 453-458.

Vermaas, A. (1993), "Real Wages in The Netherlands, 1850-1913", *Paper, Presented to the 11ᵗʰ International Economic History Congress at Milan, 1994* (Amsterdam).

Verbeke, (Ed.), G. (1981), *Belgium and Europe: Proceedings of the International Francqui-colloquium, Brussels-Ghent, 12-14 November 1980* (Brussels).

Vermaas, A. (1995), "Real Industrial Wages in The Netherlands, 1850-1913", in: (Scholliers & Zamagni (Eds.) 1995: pp. 138-150).

Verstegen, W. (1996), "National Wealth and Income from Capital in The Netherlands, c. 1850-1913", *Economic and Social History in The Netherlands*, 7, pp. 73-108.

Voort, R. van der (1994), *Overheidsbeleid en Overheidsfinanciën in Nederland, 1850-1913* (Ph.D. dissertation) (Amsterdam).

Vries, P.H.H. (2001), "The role of culture and institutions in economic history: can economics be of any help?", *NEHA-Jaarboek voor economische, bedrijfs- en techniekgeschiedenis*, 64, pp. 28-60.

Vries, J. de (1981), *Barges and Capitalism: Passenger Transportation in the Dutch Economy, 1632-1839* (Utrecht).

Vries, J. de (1984), "The Decline and the Rise of the Dutch Economy", in: (Saxonhouse & Wright (Eds.) 1984: pp. 149-189).

Vries, J. de & Van der Woude, A. (1995), *Nederland 1500-1815: De Eerste Ronde van Moderne Economische Groei* (Amsterdam).

Wagener, H.J. & Drukker, J.W. (Eds.) (1986), *The Economic Law of Motion of Modern Society: a Marx-Keynes-Schumpeter Centennial* (Cambridge, etc.).

Wallerstein, I. (1974),*The Modern World-System (I): Capitalist Agriculture and the Origins of the European World_Economy in the Sixteenth Century* (New York).

Wallerstein, I. (1980), *The Modern World-System (II): Mercantilism and the Consolidation of the European World-Economy, 1600-1750* (New York).

Wallerstein, I. (1983), *Historical Capitalism* (New York).

Walton, G. (1971), "The New Economic History and the Burdens of the Navigation Acts", *Economic History Review*, 24, pp. 533-542.

Walton, G. (1975), "A Symposium on 'Time on the Cross'", *Explorations in Economic History*, 12, pp. 333-334.

Webb, S.B. (1980), "Tariffs, Cartels, Technology and Growth in the German Steel Industry, 1879-1914", *Journal of Economic History*, 40, pp. 309-330.

Webb, S.B. (1984), "The Supply of Money and Reichsbank Financing of Government and Corporate Debt in Germany, 1919-1923", *Journal of Economic History*, 44, pp. 499-508.

Weber, M. (1905; herdruk 1992), *Die Protestantische Ethik und der "Geist" des Kapitalismus* (Düsseldorf).

Wee, H. van der (1981), "Investment Strategy of Belgian Industrial Enterprise between 1830 and 1980 and its Influence on the Economic Development of Europe", in: (Verbeke (Ed.) 1981: pp. 75-91).

Wee, H. van der (1984), "Large Firms in Belgium, 1872-1974: An Analysis of their Structure and Growth", in: (Coleman & Mathias (Eds.) 1984: pp. 199-211).

Wee, H. van der & Dancet, G. (1986), "De Belgische Nationale Boekhouding, 1920-1985: Geschiedenis van haar Berekening en Reconstructiemethodologie", in: (Van Rompuy (Ed.) 1986: pp. 145-168).

Wee. H. van der & Meerten, M.A. van (1992), "Een Vergelijking van de Private Investeringen en de Conjunctuur in België en Nederland in het Interbellum", in: (Bläsing, J.F.E (Ed.) 1992: pp. 225-234; 267-271).

Weir, D. (1984), "Life Under Pressure: France and England, 1670-1870", *Journal of Economic History*, 44, pp. 27-48.

Weiss, T. (2001), "Review of Robert William Fogel and Stanley L. Engerman *Time on the Cross: The Economics of American Negro Slavery*", *Economic History Services*, November 16, 2001, URL: http://www.eh.net/bookreviews/library/weiss.shtml

Wentzel, B. (1999), *Der Methodenstreit: ökonomische Forschungsprogramme aus der Sicht des kritischen Rationalismus* (*Europäische Hochschulschrifte, Reihe 5, Volks- und Betriebswirtschaft, Band 2425*) (Frankfurt am Main, etc.).

West, E.G. (1975a), "Educational Slowdown and Public Intervention in 19th Century Engeland: A Study in the Economics of Bureaucracy", *Explorations in Economic History*, 12, pp. 61-88.

West, E.G. (1975b), *Education and the Industrial Revolution* (London).

Whaples, R. (1991), "A Quantitative History of the Journal of Economic History and the Cliometric Revolution", *Journal of Economic History*, 51, pp. 289-301.

Whaples, R. (1995), "Where is there Consensus among American Economic Historians?", *Journal of Economic History*, 55, pp. 139-147.

Whaples, R. (1997), "The Great Depression: Consensus Among American Economic Historians", *EH.R: Forum: The Great Depression*, URL: http://www.eh.net/lists/archives/eh.res/feb-1997/0010.php

Williamson, J.G. (1968), "Review of Simon Kuznets' *Modern Economic Growth:*

Rate, Structure, and Spread", *Economic Development and Cultural Change*, 16, pp. 470-474.

Williamson, J.G. (1972), "Embodiment, Disembodiment, Learning by Doing and Returns to Scale in 19th Century Cotton Textiles", *Journal of Economic History*, 32, pp. 691-705.

Williamson, J.G. (1981), "Urban Disamenities, Dark Satanic Mills and the British Standard of Living Debate", *Journal of Economic History*, 41, pp. 75-84.

Williamson, S.H. (1991), "The History of Cliometrics", in: (Mokyr (Ed.) 1991, pp. 15-31).

Wilson, J.F. (2001), "Business Cultures and Business Performance: A British Perspective", *NEHA-Jaarboek voor economische, bedrijfs- en techniekgeschiedenis*, 64, pp. 108-123.

Winter, S.J. (1964), "Economic 'Natural Selection' and the Theory of the Firm", *Yale Economic Essays*, 4, pp. 225-272.

Wintle, M. (2000), *An Economic and Social History of The Netherlands: Demographic, Economic and Social Transition* (Cambridge, etc.).

Wolf, A.P. (2001), "Culture, culture, culture", *NEHA-Jaarboek voor economische, bedrijfs- en techniekgeschiedenis*, 64, pp. 75-85.

Woude, A. M. van der (1973), "Het gebruik van begrippen ontleend aan de sociale wetenschappen bij het analyseren van economische en sociale verschijnselen in het verleden", *A.A.G. Bijdragen*, 18, pp. 3-22 (herdrukt in: Noordegraaf (Ed.) 1991, pp. 399-416).

Wright, G. (1975), "Slavery and the Cotton Boom", *Explorations in Economic History*, 12, pp. 439-452.

Wrigley, E.A. (1969), *Population and history* (New York).

Wrigley, E.A. (1973), *Identifying people in the past* (London).

Wrigley, E.A. & Schofield, R.S. (1981), *The population history of England, 1541-1871: A reconstruction (Studies in Social and Demographic History)* (London).

Wrigley, E.A. (et. al) (1997), *English population history from family reconstruction 1580-1937 (Cambridge Studies in Population, Economy and Society in Past Time)* (Cambridge, etc.).

Yamamura, K. (1974), *A Study on Samurai Income and Entrepreneurship* (Cambridge Mass.).

Yamamura, K. (1976), "Introduction to Special Issues on Japanese Economic Hisory", in: (Patrick (Ed.) 1976).

Yamamura (Ed.), K. (1978), "Introduction to Special Issue on Japanese Economic History", *Explorations in Economic History*, 15, pp. 1-10.

Yamamura, K. & Hanley, S.B. (1978), *Economic and Demographic Change in Preindustrial Japan* (Princeton).

Zanden, J.L. van (1985), *De Economische Ontwikkeling van de Nederlandse Landbouw in de Negentiende Eeuw 1800-1914* (Wageningen).

303

Zanden, J.L. van (1987), "Economische Groei in Nederland in de Negentiende Eeuw: Enkele Nieuwe Resultaten", *Economisch- en Sociaal-Historisch Jaarboek*, 50, pp. 51-76.

Zanden, J.L. van (1987a), *De Industrialisatie van Amsterdam, 1825-1914* (Bergen).

Zanden, J.L. van (1993), "The Dutch Economy in the Very Long Run. Growth in Production, Energy Consumption and Capital in Holland (1500-1805 and The Netherlands (1805-1910)", in: (Szirmai, Van Ark & Pilat (Eds.) 1993: pp. 267-283).

Zanden, J.L. van (1994), "Regionale Verschillen in Landbouwproductiviteit en Loonpeil aan het Begin van de Negentiende Eeuw", *NEHA-Jaarboek voor Economische-, Bedrijfs- en Techniekgeschiedenis*, 57, pp. 271-286.

Zanden, J.L. van (1995), "The Development of Government Finances in a Chaotic Period", *Economic and Social History in The Netherlands*, 7, pp. 57-72.

Zanden, J.L. van (2000), "Surveying Two Centuries of Dutch Growth, 1807-1995: (Dis)equilibrium Growth Regimes in International Perspective", in: (Van Ark, Kuipers & Kuper (Eds.) 2000: pp. 67-89.

Zanden, J.L van & Riel, A. van (2000), *Nederland 1780-1914: Staat, Instituties en Economische Ontwikkeling* (Amsterdam).

Zevin, R.B. (1971), "The Growth of Cotton Textile Production After 1815", in: (Fogel & Engerman (Eds.) 1971: pp. 122-147.)

Ziman (Ed.), J. (2000), *Technological Innovation as an Evolutionary Process* (Cambridge, etc.).

Index of authors

8 50 1